VEGETARIAN CUISINE

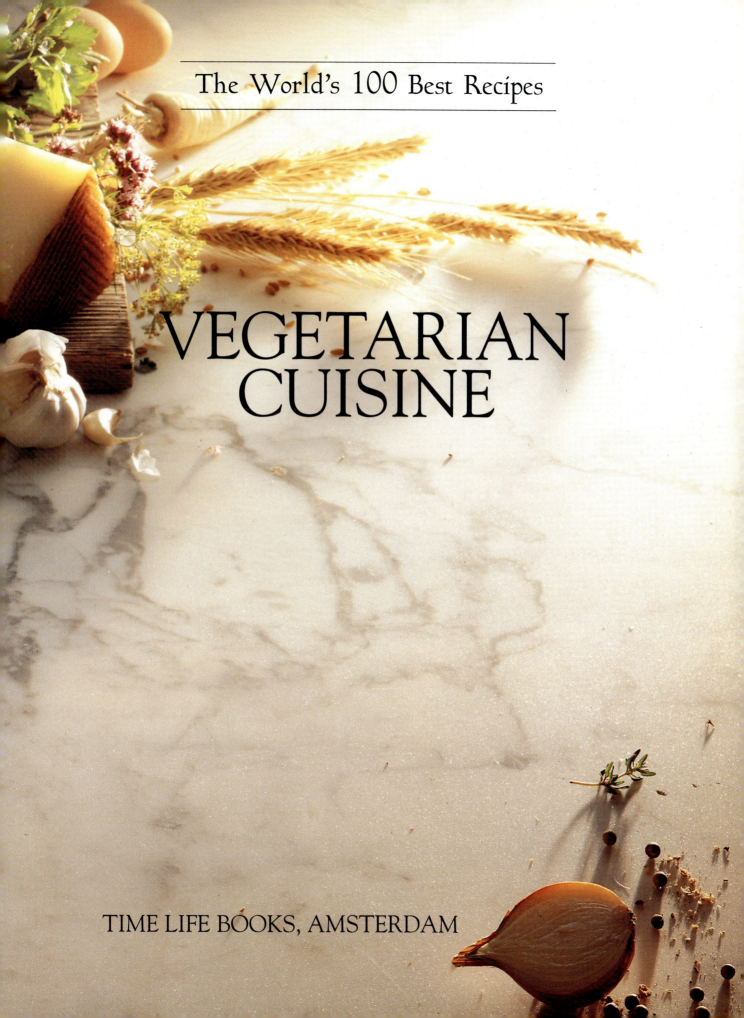

VEGETARIAN CUISINE

The World's 100 Best Recipes

TIME LIFE BOOKS, AMSTERDAM

Contents

INTRODUCTION	6
GENERAL TECHNIQUES	8
HERBS AND SPICES	10

PORTUGAL
Fried Aubergine with Tomato Sauce — 12

SPAIN
Vegetable and Egg Bake — 14
Mixed Vegetables — 16
Courgette Gratin — 18
Vegetarian Paella — 20
Garlic Mushrooms — 22

FRANCE
Hot Vegetable Quiche — 24
Artichokes with an Egg Vinaigrette — 26
Stuffed Kaiserling Mushrooms — 28
Tomato Pasty — 30
Mangold Stuffed Pancakes — 32
Red Rice with Provençal Vegetables — 34
Hot Potato Terrine with Cold Ratatouille — 36

BRITISH ISLES
Yorkshire Pudding with Vegetables — 38
Spinach Tartlets — 40
Asparagus with Poached Eggs — 42

BELGIUM
Vegetable 'Tagliatelle' with Millet Risotto — 44

HOLLAND
Millet Pancakes — 46

DENMARK
Rice and Cheese Balls — 48

POLAND
Blinis — 50

CHECHNYA
Ceps with Potato Noodles — 52

GERMANY
Jacket Potatoes with a Spicy Filling — 54
Vegetables in Riesling Sauce — 56
Herb Pancakes — 58
Asparagus Tart — 60
Pumpkin and Broccoli Terrine — 62
Corncakes with Cucumber Sauce — 64
Chanterelle Parcels — 66
Fried Sesame Bread with a Tomato and Pepper Salad — 68
Mushroom Maultaschen — 70

AUSTRIA
Potato 'Snails' — 72
Schwammerlknödel — 74
Kaiserschmarren with Plum Compôte — 76

SWITZERLAND
Cabbage and Chestnut Rolls — 78
Rösti with Scrambled Eggs and Mushrooms — 80

ITALY
Saffron Risotto with Summer Truffles — 82
Fennel Risotto — 84
Risotto with Red Peppers — 86
Risotto with Spinach and Gorgonzola — 88
Fried Polenta and Mushroom Sandwiches — 90
Vegetable Maccaroni Cheese — 92
Mushroom Cannelloni — 94
Wholewheat Tortelloni with Ricotta and Herbs — 96
Egg Flan with Herbs and Mushrooms — 98
Pizza Verdura — 100
Polenta-stuffed Courgette — 102
Fettuccine with White Truffles — 104
Gnocchi in Fresh Tomato Sauce — 106
Buckwheat Dumplings — 108

SLOVENIA
Pearl Barley with Pumpkin — 110

CROATIA
Pumpkin Flowers with Red Pepper Sauce — 112
Millet with Vegetables — 114

GREECE
Lahaniká Yahní, — 116
Moussaka with Tomatoes in Olive Oil — 118
Aubergine and Spicy Rice Rolls — 120

TURKEY
Stuffed Eggs with White Bean Salad — 122
Warm Aubergine Salad — 124
Cracked Wheat with Mushrooms — 126

MOROCCO
Spicy Vegetables	128
Briks	130

ISRAEL
Pan-fried Pepper Bread	132
Falafels	134

IRAN
Vegetable Patties with Lentils	136

PAKISTAN
Fried Cauliflower	138

INDIA
Okra and Mixed Vegetable Curry	140
Kath Katha	142
Mango and Banana Curry	144
Cauliflower Curry	146
Papaya and Sweet Potato Curry	148

THAILAND
Fried Rice in Pineapple	150
Fried Vegetables with Egg Noodles	152
Fried Tofu with Peanuts and Vegetables	154

INDONESIA
Vegetable Fried Rice with Eggs	156
Banana and Vegetable Stuffed Pancakes	158

MALAYSIA
Rice with Sweet Potato and Tofu	160
Biryani Rice with Aubergines	162

SINGAPORE
Rice-stuffed Pumpkin	164

CHINA
Tofu Envelopes	166
Fried Aubergine with Tofu	168
Mixed Vegetables with Quail's Eggs	170
Asparagus and Pak Choi	172
Rice Noodles with Mixed Vegetables	174
Choisum and Paprika with Rice Noodles	176

JAPAN
Tofu and Vegetable Nimono	178

AUSTRALIA
Spaghetti with a Shallot and Red Wine Sauce	180

USA
Risotto with Peas and Asparagus	182
Green Bean Stew	184
Bean Sprout Patties	186
Oatmeal Soufflé	188
Vegetable Gratin	190
Sweetcorn and Vegetable Hotpot	192
Sweetcorn Pasta with a Vegetable Sugo	194
Lentils with Radicchio	196
Pumpkin with Spicy Rice	198
Broccoli and Potato Gratin	200
Fried Artichokes in Batter	202

MEXICO
Salsa Verde	204
Stuffed Pancakes with Vegetables	206

PERU
Quinoa Seed Risotto with Beetroot	208

ARGENTINA
Ragout of Mushrooms with Polenta	210

UTENSILS	212
INDEX	213

ALL RECIPES ARE FOR 4 SERVINGS UNLESS OTHERWISE INDICATED

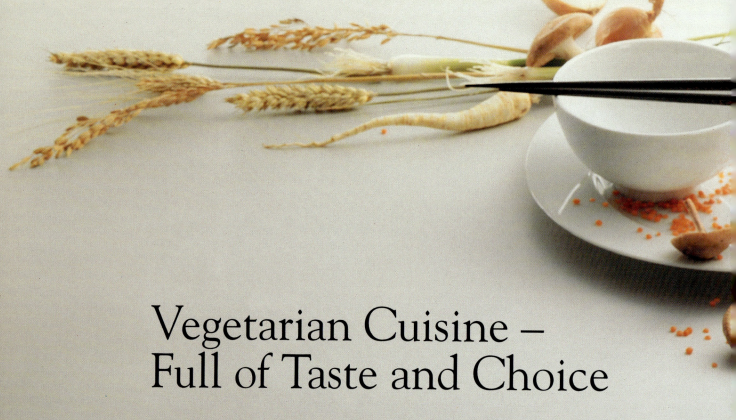

Vegetarian Cuisine – Full of Taste and Choice

While many people abstain from eating meat on purely philosophical grounds, vegetarian cuisine today has acquired a totally different set of values. Ever-increasing numbers of people from different social groups are switching over to vegetarian cuisine, not so much for religious or ethical reasons, but out of a concern for their own health, as well as for the culinary variations it offers. A lot of people have grown tired of the same old meat dishes and are showing a preference for decorative vegetable dishes and highly nutritious food. Chefs preparing *haute cuisine* have also latched onto this trend in recent years and have moved over to lighter, healthier food, putting more and more vegetable dishes from all over the world onto their menus.

This book is not dedicated to any particular world-view or ideology. With its collection of recipes from around the world, it aims to present the vegetarian gastronomy of other nations, and its chief concern is to show that vegetarian cuisine, far from being dull or bland diet food, can taste truly delicious. This positive attitude towards vegetarian food is underpinned by a new philosophy. Whereas previously people took great pains to replace the steak or chop on their plate with pseudo-products, modern vegetarian cuisine rejects them out of hand. No more soya burgers instead of hamburgers and no soya sausages instead of pork. The presumption that a meal could not be made solely with vegetables and that the missing meat had to be replaced with as close an imitation as possible no longer applies. The emphasis these days is on enjoyment – not sacrifice. It is not a question of finding a tasty ersatz meat: vegetarian cuisine is all about pushing the intrinsic flavours of individual ingredients to the fore.

For this reason, the best vegetarian cuisine only uses top quality ingredients. The fruit and vegetables should be fresh from the market and only highly nutritious pure vegetable oils should be used. Aromatic herbs, highly nutritious cereals, nuts and seeds, dairy products and eggs complete the vegetarian larder. Freshness is the touchstone of vegetarian cooking, as only really fresh vegetables pack in the flavour and contain the vitamins that are vital for a healthy diet. The old adage, 'You have to know how to shop if you want to be a good cook' is particularly applicable to vegetarian cuisine

INTRODUCTION

A HEALTHIER ALTERNATIVE

The word 'vegetarian' itself would seem to indicate that a vegetarian diet is healthy: the Latin word 'vegetus' translates as 'hale and hearty', 'vigorous' or 'full of vitality'. From a scientific point of view as well, there is no longer any doubt that vegetarians lead healthier lives than meat-eaters, especially ovo-lacto-vegetarians, who also eat eggs and dairy products. The benefits are also there even for those people who aren't strict vegetarians, but who have cut out most of the meat in their diet. A number of studies carried out in the last few years have confirmed that vegetarians are less prone to both coronary disease and cancer, as well as other major and minor illnesses They suffer less from obesity and enjoy a better physical constitution all round.

It would be erroneous, though, to assume that a meat-free diet is fundamentally healthy. It is much more important that the diet be balanced, delivering sufficient quantities of protein, vitamins and minerals. Unlike vegans, who will not eat any kind of animal protein, ovo-lacto-vegetarians should not have to worry about a lack of protein in their diet as eggs and dairy products can supply more than enough. However, completely replacing meat and fish protein by eating eggs and cheese is not ideal. Egg yolks are high in cholesterol and many cheeses are high in saturated fat. Instead, the best way to increase protein intake is to eat plenty of pulses, nuts, seeds and cereals. Furthermore, combined vegetable and animal protein is more nutritious than just animal protein on its own. A Vegetarian diet also contains an abundance of bio-active ingredients that can enhance physical and mental well-being. These include enzymes and micro-organisms that regulate blood pressure, fight bacteria and viruses, prevent blood clotting, help digestion, reduce inflammation and lower the level of cholesterol.

VEGETARIAN FOOD FROM AROUND THE WORLD

Culinary influences from all over the world have played a major role in the rising popularity of vegetarian cuisine. Many vegetable dishes, such as tasty, fluffy soufflés, light vegetable terrines or delicate stews originated in Mediterranean countries and Asian cooking boasts a great variety of delicious vegetarian dishes. The Chinese love their vitamin-rich wok stir-fries, where the short cooking time keeps vegetables nice and crispy and full of goodness. In India, on the other hand, they are expert at preparing exotic curry dishes that slowly simmer away in creamy sauces enriched with a whole host of herbs and spices. Even the USA , the home of the hamburger, can lay claim to a wide range of meat-free dishes and their are marvellous recipes that originate from northern Europe, South America and the Middle East.

With the explosion in popularity of vegetarian cookery, people have begun looking further and further afield for new recipes and ingredients. This has led to the rediscovery of certain types of cereal which, although popular in the past, had practically been consigned to the culinary history books. Now, however grains like quinoa, from South America, or millet are being served up with startling invention to be enjoyed by a whole new generation. The variety of vegetables, pulses and cereals from all over the world that are available in our shops has mushroomed in recent years and no-one should have any great difficulty finding even the most unusual ingredients they need. Similarly, the choice of spices has become ever greater and it really is worth seeking out the correct ones for the recipes concerned, as these are the ingredients that give many of the dishes their unmistakable flavour.

GENERAL TECHNIQUES

Vegetable Stock

THE FOUNDATION OF GOOD VEGETARIAN CUISINE

Vegetable stock is used in vegetarian dishes in much the same way that meat stock or broth is used in meat and poultry dishes. It is not as strongly flavoured as meat stock but a light, aromatic, vegetable stock can form the basis of many delicious sauces and stews, as well as being good for cooking rice and pasta. There are no hard and fast rules as to which vegetables should be used in the stock, in relation to those in the dish itself, and almost any mix of vegetables will make good stock. Carrots and tomatoes are almost always included, however, as these give a vegetable stock its attractive colouring. Too much cabbage is not a good idea and, similarly, celery should be used sparingly, as it has such a strong flavour. Mushroom and asparagus trimmings can be included but only in small amounts so as not to influence the flavour too much. The inclusion of a browned onion half adds a lot of colour and taste to the finished stock. To brown an onion half, lay it, cut side down, on a griddle or non-stick frying pan and dry fry. Salt should only be added extremely sparingly, as the process of reducing the stock may make it more salty than you might want it to be.

100 g broccoli stalks; 250 g leeks; 300 g carrots
200 g celery; 150 g courgettes; 20 g butter
2 medium onions, peeled and sliced into thick rings
250 ml white wine; 3 litres water
1/2 small onion, browned
1 sprig each thyme and rosemary
1 bay leaf; 1/2 clove garlic; 1 clove

Wash and finely chop all the vegetables, then follow the illustrated instructions, below.

Melt the butter in a large pan and lightly soften the onion rings.

Add the chopped vegetables and sweat these briefly. Slake with the white wine, then add the water.

Add the browned onion half, together with the herbs and spices and mix everything well. Bring to the boil over a moderate heat.

Leave the stock to cook for 30-40 minutes, skimming from time to time.

Strain the stock through a cloth lined sieve into a second pan, reheat and cook until reduced to about 1.5 litres of liquid.

GENERAL TECHNIQUES

Preparing Vegetables, Pulses and Bean Sprouts

CHOPPING, SOAKING AND FORCING

The most important tool when cutting vegetables is a really sharp knife. The general rule is that the shorter the time a vegetable takes to prepare, the shorter the time it takes to actually cook as well. Holding vegetables correctly, when cutting, is very important - only the fingertips should rest on the vegetable and these should be turned slightly under to avoid catching the blade. Pulses cook more quickly if they are soaked beforehand and some must be soaked overnight. During soaking, remove any odd pieces that float to the top. Various kinds of young bean sprouts are very good for you and the fresher they are the higher their vitamin content. Beans and other pulses can be forced in a glass jar (which is a simple but always amazing process), as shown in the illustrated instructions, right.

Chopping carrots

First peel the carrots. Chop them horizontally into 5 cm long sections, then cut them vertically into very thin slices.

Bundle a few slices together and slice them vertically again into strips.

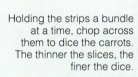

Holding the strips a bundle at a time, chop across them to dice the carrots. The thinner the slices, the finer the dice.

Forcing bean sprouts in a jar

Put chick peas, or other pulses, into a storage jar and cover with lukewarm water. Cover the jar with a muslin cloth, held in place by an elastic band and leave to stand for a few hours. Strain off the water through the cloth, then discard the cloth. Rinse the chick peas well and cover with fresh water and a fresh cloth. Leave to stand for 10 minutes then strain again. Leave the jar tipped up so all the water drains off through the cloth. Repeat this process, daily, for the next 3-5 days, until the beans sprout.

Chopping onions

Cut the onion in half, lengthways and lay the cut side down on the work surface. Make a series of short cuts through the onion, at right angles to the root.

Slice through the onion several times again, this time working parallel to the work surface.

Thinly slice the onion crossways, so that it breaks up into small pieces.

Soaking pulses

Put the beans into a bowl and cover generously with water. Any that float to the top should be discarded at this stage.

Leave to soak for 8-12 hours, then strain through a sieve. Discard the water.

Rinse the beans thoroughly under cold running water and pick them over. The beans are ready to cook when they have swollen to 2 or 3 times their original size.

From the Spicy to the Exotic

A great number of soya-based spicy sauces are used in Asian cooking. There are both light and dark soya sauces, the difference between them being more one of colour than of flavour. Light soya sauce, though, is slightly milder whilst the dark sauce has a spicier aroma. Shitake mushrooms add that special touch to vegetarian oyster sauce. In the foreground of the picture you can see mirin, a rice-wine product.

SPICES AND HERBS REALLY SHINE IN VEGETARIAN COOKING

As vegetarian cooking completely foregoes such varied providers of flavour as fish, meat and seafood, great emphasis is put on proper seasoning. Every country has its own tradition of seasoning, and Asian cooking, more than any other, never fails to surprise with its variety. In Indian cooking, for instance, there is no end of delicious curry dishes that have very little in common with the curry powders available in this country. The true meaning of curry is a dish cooked in a special spicy sauce, usually served with rice and many curries require their own specially concocted mixture of spices - known as *masalas* - in which the spices are first roasted or grilled until their full aroma is released. Chinese and Thai cookery are also renowned for the subtlety with which most of their recipes are spiced and the endless variety of tastes and flavours that they can achieve.

The following list provides a run-down of the most important spices in vegetarian cooking the world over. Anyone who has experimented with spices and their special aromas can use them creatively in his or her own cooking.

Spice mixtures play a particularly important role in regional Indian dishes. In the jar, ready-made curry mixture for vegetables. In the mortar, *garam masala*, one of the most commonly used basic mixtures for curry dishes, made of cinnamon, cloves, black pepper and a little star aniseed and coriander. In the foreground, *panch foron*, the Indian five spice mixture.

1) Juniper berries – spicy, bitter resinous taste, used in stews and herb dishes. 2) Pimiento – dried berries from the pimento tree, picked before they are ripe, they taste of cloves, cinnamon and nutmeg, used in curries and baking. 3) Ginger, dried or fresh – indispensable in Asian cooking. 4) Coriander leaves – a great favourite in Mexico and Asia, their characteristic aroma is not to everyone's taste. 5) Paprika powder – highly flavoured, sweetish, rich in colour and moderately spicy. 6) Chilli peppers – hot and spicy. 7) Nutmeg – the seeds of the crowfoot plant, pepper-like in taste and spicy. 8) Saffron – the strands are extracted from the stigma of the saffron crocus. 9) Galingale, dried – spicy, similar in taste to ginger. 10) Lemon grass – an important spice all over South-east Asia for sauces, vegetables and curries. 11) Fenugreek seeds – only release their flavour when cooked; raw, they have a rather curious smell.

HERBS AND SPICES

12) Coriander seeds - in contrast to the leaves, the ripe seeds are pleasantly mild. 13) Star aniseed – hot and smells of camphor. 14) Black star aniseed – spicier than light aniseed 15) Caraway seed – probably the oldest known spice in Europe. 16) Turmeric – extracted from the rhizome of the turmeric plant, gives curries their yellow colouring. 17) Turmeric, dried – belongs to the ginger family. 18) Cardamom – used for confectionery, bread and gingerbread, an important ingredient in curry mixes. 19) Cardamom pods, light – picked shortly before they ripen, dried and blanched. 20) Cardamom pods, dark – unblanched pods. 21) Mustard seeds, yellow – a hot taste, like radish. 22) Mustard seeds, black – smaller and hotter than the yellow ones. 23) Pepper, black – not the corns, but the berries of the pepper bush; green, yellow or red, depending on ripeness. 24) Pepper, white – produced from almost ripe watered red peppers from which the peel is removed, milder than black. 25) Szechuan pepper – very hot. 26) Pepper, red – ripe berries. 27) Pepper, green – green berries dried in a special process, very aromatic. 28) Cassia vera – the bark of the cassia tree, similar to cinnamon in aroma. 29) Ceylon cassia – the finest cassia bark in the world. 30) Mace – not the flowers but the dried seedcover of the nutmeg tree, pleasantly spicy. 31) Nutmeg apples – the seed grains from the same tree. 32) Sesame, peeled. – the oil seeds belong to the oldest cultivated plants in the world. 33) Onion seeds – used primarily in curries. 34) Fennel seeds – sweet and spicy, taste is reminiscent of anis. 35) Aniseed – a popular spice the world over. 36) Poppy seeds – only release their nutty flavour when roasted or grilled. 37) Ajwan seeds – very popular in the East, similar in taste to thyme.

PORTUGAL

Fried Aubergine with Fresh Tomato Sauce

AN INTERESTING COMBINATION OF FLAVOURS: THE SUBTLE TASTE OF AUBERGINE IN A CRISP, SPICY COATING

Recipes for cooking aubergine in different crispy coatings, adding both texture and taste, can be found all over southern Europe. This recipe uses a mixture of breadcrumbs and tangy cheese. If possible, the cheese should be the famous Portuguese Serra de Estrela but, failing this, any good ripe, strong goat's milk cheese will make a suitable substitute.

1 kg aubergines; 2 tsp salt; 150 g breadcrumbs
100 g cheese, freshly grated; 2 eggs; 80 g flour
For the tomato sauce
600 g tomatoes; 30 g onion; 2 cloves garlic
1 small red chilli pepper; 3 tbsp olive oil
2 tsp tomato purée; salt; freshly ground pepper
In addition
125 ml vegetable oil for frying
young basil leaves, to garnish

Portuguese cheeses range from mild to tangy. Top left: a Monte Verde from northern Portugal; top right: a Casteloan cheese; below left: an Alvorca and, in the immediate foreground, a ewe's milk Serra de Estrela.

1. Wash and trim the aubergines, then slice them lengthways into 1 cm thick slices. Sprinkle with the salt and leave them to stand for 10 minutes.

2. For the sauce, wash, deseed and roughly chop the tomatoes. Peel and finely chop the onion and the garlic. Halve and deseed the chilli pepper, remove the fibres and thinly slice the flesh.

3. Heat the olive oil in a saucepan, add the onion and the garlic and sweat until just transparent. Add the chopped tomato, chilli pepper and tomato purée, season with salt and pepper, cover and leave to simmer, over a very low heat, for about 30 minutes. Strain the sauce through a sieve and season again to taste.

4. Put the breadcrumbs and the grated cheese into a shallow bowl and mix well. Beat the eggs in a second bowl and put the flour into a third. Wipe the aubergine slices completely dry with kitchen paper. Dip them first into the flour, then into the egg and finally into the breadcrumbs and cheese, coating them evenly in all three.

5. Heat the vegetable oil in a pan and fry the aubergine slices over a moderate heat for 3 minutes on each side, or until golden brown. Take out and drain well on kitchen paper. Arrange the aubergine slices on individual dishes with the tomato sauce and garnish with basil leaves to serve.

The fresh tomato sauce is spicy and fruity and also makes a good visual contrast to the fried aubergine.

SPAIN

Vegetable and Egg Bake

A VEGETARIAN VARIATION ON THE FAMOUS *HUEVOS A LA FLAMENCA*

Preparing this dish takes time but the result is well worth the effort. With the exception of the potato and the peas, which need to be precooked, the ingredients are all slowly sautéed in olive oil before being baked in the oven.

500 g small firm potatoes
350 g each red and green peppers (small pointed variety)
450 g tomatoes
200 g carrots
100 g onions; 2 cloves garlic
1 small Spanish sweet pepper
150 g fresh peas, shelled
4 tbsp olive oil
salt; freshly ground pepper; 4 eggs
In addition
1 tbsp chopped parsley
coarsely ground black pepper

The eggs add a decorative note to this dish. To ensure that they do not break or spread during cooking, it is best to break them into a spoon and then slide them carefully into the pan.

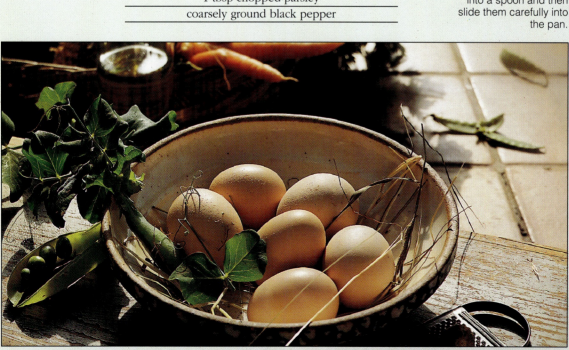

Fresh from the farm, free range eggs are richer in protein and flavour than battery eggs, making them particularly suitable for vegetarians.

SPAIN

1. Wash the potatoes and boil them for 20 minutes. Leave to cool a little, then peel and cut them into 5 mm thick slices.

2. Roast the peppers – except the Spanish sweet pepper – in a preheated oven at 220°C, until the skins blister. Take out, put into a plastic bag and leave to sweat. Skin the peppers, working from top to bottom and pulling off the skin in strips, then halve and deseed them, remove the fibres and dice the flesh into 5 mm cubes.

3. Scald, skin and deseed the tomatoes, then dice the flesh. Peel and finely dice the carrots. Peel and finely chop the onions and the garlic. Halve and deseed the Spanish pepper, remove the fibres and finely chop the flesh. Cook the peas in boiling, salted water for 3 minutes, then refresh.

4. Heat the oil in a large, flame- and ovenproof pan and lightly soften the onion and the garlic over a low heat. Add the carrot and, stirring continuously, cook for a further 5 minutes. Add all of the peppers and the diced tomato and simmer for a final 3 minutes. Mix in the sliced potato and the peas. Season with salt and pepper.

5. Make four small wells in the vegetable mixture and break an egg into each. Bake in a preheated oven at 200°C for about 15 minutes. Sprinkle with the chopped parsley and coarsely ground pepper and serve.

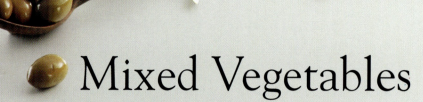

Mixed Vegetables

IN SPAIN, VEGETABLES COOKED *AL HORNO*, OR 'IN THE OVEN', ARE OFTEN SERVED AS A MEAL ON THEIR OWN, WITH JUST A CHUNK OF BREAD AS AN ACCOMPANIMENT

In Andalucia, the southernmost province of Spain, the local cuisine is strongly influenced by the Moorish cookery of North Africa. Both are based on natural, plain ingredients which are always deliciously fresh. Authentic local cuisine, in direct contrast to the usual tourist fare, benefits from the rich harvests of fresh fruit and vegetables and the wide range of herbs which flourish in the hot climate. This recipe is also influenced by the cuisine of northern Spain, which in turn has borrowed the tapenade from French Provence, where it was originally made with anchovies. This mix of influences has created a wonderfully flavourful dish.

450 g small firm potatoes
150 g shallots, peeled; 300 g red peppers
400 g courgettes; 400 g aubergines
3 red peperoni; 6 small fleshy tomatoes
4 cloves garlic, peeled; 2 sprigs thyme

For the green tapenade
150 g green olives, stoned
20 g capers preserved in salt; 2 cloves garlic, peeled

Mixed vegetable dishes need not always be served as mere accompaniments. One as good as this can easily be transformed into a main course simply by serving it with a spicy tapenade and a chunk of crusty bread.

1 tsp Dijon mustard; 3 tbsp olive oil
1 squeeze lemon juice
salt; freshly ground white pepper

For the vinaigrette sauce
juice of 1 lemon; 4 tbsp olive oil

In addition
4 tbsp olive oil; salt; freshly ground black pepper

Harvesting olives in the burning sun of Andalucia is hard work. Since meat has always been expensive, there is a long tradition of serving simple meatless meals.

1. Wash the potatoes thoroughly and halve them, without peeling. Cut the shallots in half. Deseed the peppers, remove the fibres and roughly chop the flesh. Wash and trim the courgettes and the aubergines, then halve both of these lengthways

SPAIN

and cut them into 1.5 cm long pieces. Trim the stalks from the peperoni, then leave them whole. Rinse and halve the tomatoes.

2. Add 4 tablespoons olive oil to a roasting tin, place the potato halves in this, cut side down, and roast in a preheated oven at 180°C for about 10 minutes. Spread the shallots and the garlic over the potatoes and roast for a further 20 minutes.

3. Add the peppers, courgettes, aubergines and peperoni to the tin, lay the sprigs of thyme on top and cook for a further 10 minutes. Carefully add the tomatoes to the tin and cook for a further 45 minutes.

4. To prepare the tapenade, cut the olives into small pieces. Using a sieve, rinse the salt from the capers. Purée the olives, capers, garlic and mustard together in a mixer, gradually adding the olive oil. Add the lemon juice and season with salt and pepper to taste.

5. To prepare the vinaigrette, gradually mix the lemon juice with the oil to a smooth consistency.

6. At the end of the 45 minutes cooking time, take the vegetables out of the oven. Arrange them on a serving dish, sprinkle with the vinaigrette and season with salt and pepper, then dot with the tapenade to serve.

SPAIN

Courgette Gratin

CALABACINES AL HORNO – A SPANISH VEGETABLE CASSEROLE TOPPED WITH CHEESE

In Spain, vegetable dishes usually include some sort of meat, such as diced ham or spicy sausage. However, the meatless version is equally delicious. If a spicier flavour is preferred, a finely chopped chilli pepper, with the seeds and fibres removed, may be added to the tomato mixture.

150 g onions
2 cloves garlic
100 g carrots
750 g tomatoes
6 tbsp olive oil
1 tsp dried thyme
2 tsp mild paprika powder
salt; freshly ground white pepper

900 g courgettes
30 g flour
100 g Manchego cheese, freshly grated
In addition
oil for the oven dish

1. Peel and finely chop the onions. Peel and very finely chop the garlic. Wash, peel and finely dice the carrots. Scald, skin and deseed the tomatoes, then dice the flesh.

2. Heat 3 tablespoons of the olive oil in a pan and soften the onion and the garlic over a low heat, until the onion is transparent. Add the carrot and sweat this too for 3-4 minutes, then add the tomato, dried thyme and paprika and season with salt and pepper to taste. Leave to simmer over a moderate heat for 10-12 minutes.

3. Wash and trim the courgettes, then chop them into 1.5 cm cubes, season with salt and turn them in the flour. Heat the remaining olive oil in a second pan and fry the diced courgette, turning continuously, until they are a light golden brown.

4. Brush a large ovenproof dish with oil and line with a layer of courgette, followed by a layer of tomato mixture, a second layer of courgette, then a final layer of tomato mixture. Top with the grated cheese and bake in a preheated oven at 200°C for 15-20 minutes.

5. Take the dish out of the oven and serve with a chunk of fresh bread.

Using the right cheese in this dish makes all the difference, and in Spain the choice ranges from a variety of mild cow's milk cheeses, to sharper ewe's milk cheeses such as Manchego. The latter, which is now available here in specialist cheese shops, adds a delicious tang to the vegetable gratin.

SPAIN

Paella tastes so much better when cooked over an open fire. However, be careful to cook the rice through without burning the paella.

Vegetarian Paella

A DELICIOUS VEGETARIAN VERSION OF THE SPANISH NATIONAL DISH

While the ingredients of a paella may vary according to the time of year, an all-vegetarian variation is very rare. Normally chicken, chorizo sausage, ham or, for a paella Valenciana, seafood would be included.

6 tbsp olive oil; 400 g Spanish paella rice
3/4 litre vegetable stock
1 bay leaf; 1 g saffron threads
250 g each red and green peppers
400 g tomatoes
100 g onions; 5 cloves garlic
200 g green beans; 150 g leeks; 150 g carrots
1 tbsp mild paprika
salt; freshly ground pepper
100 g black olives
In addition
vegetable stock as required

A truly authentic paella should be made with real Spanish rice, grown in the Ebro delta and the area around Valencia. However, Italian *vialone* rice makes a good substitute if this is not available.

Saffron reached Spain from north Africa via the Romans. Today, Spain is the largest producer of saffron in Europe. 80,000 saffron crocus flowers are needed to produce 1 kg of the fine flavouring and colourant, which is now used all over the world.

1. Heat 3 tablespoons of the olive oil in a pan, add the rice in a stream and, stirring continuously, fry for 3 minutes until transparent. Add the vegetable stock and the bay leaf and crumble in the saffron. Cover and leave to cook for about 10 minutes, when the rice will be part-cooked.

2. Roast the peppers in a preheated oven at 220°C until the skins blister. Take out, put into a plastic bag and leave to sweat. Skin the peppers, working from top to bottom and pulling off the skin in strips, then halve and deseed them, remove the fibres and cut the flesh into 1.5 cm long pieces.

3. Scald, skin and deseed the tomatoes, then dice the flesh. Peel and finely chop the onions and the garlic. Wash and trim the green beans and the leeks, then cut the beans into 3 cm long pieces and the leeks into 1.5 cm thick rings. Peel the carrots and cut them into 4 cm long matchsticks.

4. Heat the remaining oil in a paella pan and sweat the onion and the garlic for 5 minutes, over a low heat. Stir in the paprika and cook briefly. Add the beans, leek and carrots and fry over a low heat for a further 5 minutes, then season with salt and pepper.

5. Add the part-cooked rice to the pan mixture, mix everything well together and fry over a moderate heat for about 15 minutes until cooked through. Add the tomato and the peppers 10 minutes before the end of the cooking time. If the rice begins to dry out too soon, add a little more stock as required. Finally, stir in the olives and serve on preheated plates.

SPAIN

Mushrooms always taste best when freshly picked. They should, ideally, be cooked and eaten on the day of purchase. Cultivated white mushrooms, or the French pinkish-coloured variety of the same type, are best for this recipe.

Garlic Mushrooms

GARLIC MUSHROOMS FRIED IN OLIVE OIL ARE OFTEN SERVED IN SPANISH TAPAS BARS

Served with garlic bread or, as here, with one of the famous Spanish potato omelettes or tortillas, these mushrooms make a delicious main dish.

For the garlic mushrooms
40 g shallots
4 cloves garlic
50 g celery
800 g mushrooms
4 tbsp olive oil
2 tbsp lemon juice
2 tbsp Amontillado sherry
1 tsp salt; freshly ground pepper
1 bunch parsley, chopped
50 ml vegetable stock
25 g breadcrumbs
15 g butter, in small pieces
For the tortilla
750 g floury potatoes
100 g onions
7 tbsp olive oil
salt; freshly ground pepper
6 eggs

1. Peel and finely chop the shallots and the garlic. Wash and trim the celery, then slice it thinly. Wash the mushrooms thoroughly and cut them into halves.

2. Heat the oil in a flameproof casserole and lightly sweat the shallots, garlic and celery. Add the mushrooms and flavour with the lemon juice,

Spoon 1/4 of the tortilla mixture evenly over the pan and fry for 5 minutes over a moderate heat, shaking the pan continuously to prevent the mixture sticking. To turn the tortilla, lay a flat plate or lid over the top of the pan. Holding plate and pan firmly together, turn the pan quickly upside down, so the tortilla sits on the plate, then immediately slide it, carefully, back into the pan to cook the underside.

SPAIN

sherry, salt and pepper. Sprinkle in the parsley and mix everything well together. Pour in the vegetable stock, sprinkle with breadcrumbs and dot with butter, then bake in a preheated oven at 200°C for about 20 minutes. At the end of this time, turn off the oven but leave the dish inside to keep warm.

3. To prepare the tortilla, peel and slice the potatoes into roughly 2 mm thick pieces. Peel and finely chop the onions. Heat 3 tablespoons of the oil in a large pan and fry the onions and the potato slices over a moderate heat, without allowing them to discolour. Season with salt and pepper and leave to cool a little. Beat the eggs in a large bowl, season with salt and pepper, then thoroughly mix the onion and potato mixture with the beaten egg.

4. Using an omelette pan 15 cm in diameter, heat 1 tablespoon of olive oil and fry 4 tortillas following the illustrated instructions, opposite.

5. Arrange the tortillas on preheated plates and serve the mushrooms from the casserole dish.

In Spain, many dishes are cooked *al ajillo*, meaning with lots of garlic.

FRANCE

Hot Vegetable Quiche
A CLASSIC SAVOURY FRENCH FLAN: STRONG FLAVOURS IN A SUBTLE EGG CREAM

About 19 new Comté cheeses ripen every day in the Vacherin cheese makers at Mont D'Or, and in summer it may be as many as 24. The cows that provide the milk for the cheese are the famous Montbéliard herds. The Doubs and the Jura regions produce about 45 kg of Comté each per day. True connoisseurs drink a dry white Jura wine with this cheese.

For the pastry
150 g wholemeal flour; 50 g wheat flour
100 g butter, in small pieces; 1/4 tsp salt

For the filling
200 g each small courgettes and tomatoes
80 g each spring onions and white mushrooms
40 g butter; salt; freshly ground white pepper
1 tbsp mixed herbs (sage and thyme), chopped

For the egg mixture
100 ml cream; 100 g crème fraîche
1 clove garlic, crushed; 3 eggs; salt; white pepper

For the sauce
150 g crème fraîche
1 tbsp mixed chopped herbs (chives and parsley)
salt; freshly ground white pepper
1/2 clove garlic, crushed

In addition
greaseproof paper and dried beans for blind baking
80 g freshly grated Comté cheese

Sift both types of flour onto a work surface and make a well in the centre. Place the butter, 4 tablespoons water and the salt into the well and work to a smooth dough. Roll into a ball, wrap in cling film and place in the refrigerator for 1 hour. For the filling, trim and thinly slice the courgettes. Scald, skin and quarter the tomatoes. Peel the onions, wipe and trim the mushrooms and slice both thinly. Melt the butter in a pan and sweat the vegetables for 2-3 minutes. Season with salt and pepper and sprinkle in the herbs. Leave to cool. Roll out the pastry to an even 4 mm thickness and a little larger than a flan dish 26 cm in diameter. Blind bake the pastry case following the illustrated instructions below. Discard the beans and the greaseproof paper and leave the flan case to cool a little. Spread the vegetables evenly over the flan case and sprinkle with the cheese. To prepare the egg mixture, beat all the ingredients together with a fork, then pour the mixture over the vegetables. Bake in a preheated oven at 200°C for about 40 minutes. To prepare the sauce, mix the crème fraîche to a creamy consistency with the herbs, fold in the garlic, season with salt and pepper to taste and serve with the hot quiche.

Roll the dough around the rolling pin and use this to lift it onto the buttered flan dish. Unroll the dough and press it firmly, but without stretching it, into the flan dish. Trim off any excess dough.

Weigh down a circle of greaseproof paper (cut to the same size as the flan dish, allowing for the edge) with dried beans. Place on top of the pastry, and press and pinch up to cover the edge of the flan.

Evenly spread enough beans over the paper to cover it completely. Blind bake in a preheated oven at 200°C for 10 minutes.

Artichokes with an Egg Vinaigrette

IN FRANCE, THE SLIGHTLY BITTER ARTICHOKE, WHEN PREPARED IN THE RIGHT WAY, IS OFTEN CONSIDERED TO BE HAUTE CUISINE

'No pain, no gain' is an expression that might well be applied to the preparation of artichokes, particularly when a recipe asks for the small variety which is used here. Nothing tastes as good, though, as really fresh artichoke. Bottled or tinned artichokes could be used for this recipe if time is of the essence, but it is absolutely essential that the egg vinaigrette is freshly made.

These small artichokes, which are cooked whole in this recipe, come from Provence. Similarly sized Italian varieties of artichoke may be used instead if these are not available.

12 artichokes (about 150 g each), with stalks
juice of 1 lemon; salt

The best, cold pressed olive oil – in France it would come from the valley of Les Baux – is the foundation for the egg vinaigrette which perfectly complements the artichokes.

For the egg vinaigrette
4 hard-boiled eggs
2 tsp Dijon mustard
30 ml white wine vinegar
150 ml olive oil
1 pinch sugar
3 tbsp snipped chives
1 tsp chopped lemon balm
salt; freshly ground black pepper

In addition
lemon balm leaves, to garnish

1. Break the stalks off the artichokes close to the base by giving them a sharp twist and tug. This should also pull out the hard woody underparts at the same time. Brush the bottoms immediately

FRANCE

with some of the lemon juice to prevent the artichokes from discolouring. Pull off the tough, small leaves from around the bases and, using scissors, trim the sharp tips off the other leaves. Using a sharp knife, slice the top off each artichoke and scrape out the choke.

2. Bring a generous amount of water, together with the remaining lemon juice and some salt, to the boil in a large pan. Add the artichokes and boil for 10 minutes. The artichokes are cooked when a leaf can be easily pulled out.

3. Meanwhile, prepare the egg vinaigrette. Shell and finely chop the hard-boiled eggs. Using a balloon whisk, whisk the mustard, vinegar and oil together in a bowl. Stir in the chopped egg, sugar, snipped chives, lemon balm and add salt and pepper to taste.

4. Using a draining spoon, take the artichokes out of the water and place upside down, to drain. Arrange the artichokes on plates with a portion of vinaigrette, garnish with lemon balm leaves, and serve immediately.

FRANCE

The white skin of the young kaiserling is typical of this variety of mushroom. Undamaged pieces of this skin should not be thrown away but cleaned and added to the filling.

Stuffed Kaiserling Mushrooms

MUSHROOMS AS EXQUISITELY DELICATE AS THESE ARE HARD TO FIND

The kaiserling likes warm, dry earth and grows at the base of ancient chestnut trees in the southern French woodlands. These attractive, orange coloured mushrooms are sold in Europe via the Paris markets but are rarely found over here. If you cannot find large enough kaiserlings, then other mushrooms can be used as a container and small kaiserlings diced and added to the filling.

400 ml vegetable stock; 100 g celery
50 g shallots; 120 g carrots
60 g crustless white bread
800 g large kaiserling mushrooms
4 tbsp vegetable oil; 1 clove garlic, chopped
1 tbsp celery leaves, chopped
salt; freshly ground pepper
20 g butter, in small pieces

In addition
30 g butter for the oven dish
1 tbsp chives, snipped

1. Bring the vegetable stock to the boil in a pan and cook until reduced by half. Trim and string the celery, peel the shallots and the carrots and finely dice all three. Dice the bread.

2. Clean and wipe the mushrooms thoroughly, first removing and reserving the skin, known as the vellum. Twist out the stalks. Hollow out the caps and dice the trimmings together with the vellum and the stalks.

3. Heat 2 tbsp of oil in a pan. Press in the garlic, using a garlic press and fry the diced bread to a golden brown.

4. Heat the remaining oil in a second pan and sweat the diced celery, shallots and carrots for 3 minutes. Add the diced mushroom and sauté for 1 minute. Sprinkle in the celery leaves, stir in the fried bread and season with salt and pepper.

5. Fill the mushroom caps with the mixture. Butter an ovenproof dish, arrange the stuffed mushrooms inside and dot with pieces of butter. Add the reduced stock. If any filling mixture remains, sprinkle it around the stuffed mushrooms. Bake in a preheated oven at 200°C for about 15 minutes.

6. Arrange the stuffed mushrooms on preheated plates, sprinkle with chives, coat with a little of the sauce from the oven dish and serve. Sauté potatoes go well with this dish.

A mushroom lover's dream. Parisian fruit and vegetable wholesalers carry a wonderful range of mushrooms in the autumn.

Tomato Pasty

A SIMPLE, BUT DELIGHTFUL, IDEA. THIS RECIPE TAKES A WHILE TO PREPARE AND REQUIRES CAREFUL ATTENTION TO DETAIL

This is a party dish for tomato lovers which is both fruity and lightly tangy, thanks to the combination of fresh and dried tomatoes. Tomato is the dominant flavour while shallots, garlic and basil all add to the overall taste. Served with a salad this makes an elegant main course, while a slice on its own is delicious as a starter.

For the filling
120 g shallots
3 cloves garlic
800 g fleshy tomatoes
200 g dried tomatoes, in oil
3 tbsp olive oil
100 g roasted almonds, chopped
peel of 1 untreated lemon, finely chopped
1 tbsp finely chopped basil; 2 eggs
salt; freshly ground black pepper

In addition
300 g puff pastry
1 egg yolk beaten with 1 tbsp water
greaseproof paper and butter

1. Peel and finely chop the shallots and the garlic. Scald, skin, quarter and deseed the fresh tomatoes, then finely dice the flesh.

2. Remove the dried tomatoes from their oil, drain well on kitchen paper and then finely chop.

3. Heat the olive oil in a pan and sweat the shallots and the garlic until just soft. Add the fresh tomato and cook, uncovered, until all the juices run clear. Take off the heat. Mix in the dried tomato, almonds, finely chopped lemon peel and basil and leave to cool at room

Fold one side of the pastry over half of the filling and brush the edge with egg yolk. Fold the other side over the other half and press lightly to seal. Line a baking sheet with buttered greaseproof paper and lay the pasty, sealed side down, on this. Cut 3 equidistant holes in the top of the pasty and roll up 3 pieces of foil to act as pastry funnels. Brush the top and sides of the pasty with egg yolk then cut the leftover pastry into decorative shapes, coat them with yolk and press them on.

FRANCE

temperature. Beat the eggs and stir them into the mixture. Season with salt and pepper.

4. Butter a 1 litre oblong terrine dish and line the base with a piece of buttered greaseproof paper, cut to size. Spoon the tomato mixture evenly into the terrine dish and smooth the top. Bake in a preheated oven at 180°C for 50-60 minutes. Leave the mix to cool in the terrine dish. When it is cold, take it out and discard the greaseproof paper.

5. Roll out the puff pastry on a floured work surface and cut to a 20 x 30 cm oblong, reserving the trimmings for decoration. Place the cooked block of tomato filling in the centre, then proceed following the illustrated instructions opposite. Use the pastry trimmings to make flower petals and edging for the pastry "funnels".

6. Bake the tomato pasty in a preheated oven at 200°C for 15-20 minutes, until the pastry is cooked. Remove the foil "funnels", slice the pasty and serve immediately.

Crispy puff pastry is at its best served hot. When cut, the fresh baked aroma makes this pasty irresistible.

FRANCE

Mangold Stuffed Pancakes

THESE WAFER-THIN PANCAKES TASTE WONDERFUL WITH A MANGOLD FILLING

Recipes for spinach-filled pancakes can be found all over the world, but those with a mangold filling are much rarer. The savoury mangold adds texture while the cheese gives it a tangy flavour.

For the pancake batter
50 g flour; 150 ml milk; 2 eggs
20 g butter, melted; salt; freshly ground pepper
25 g Comté cheese, freshly grated

For the filling
1 kg fresh, young mangolds; 100 g shallots
50 g butter; 80 g walnuts, chopped
100 ml cream; salt; freshly ground pepper
freshly grated nutmeg
1 egg; 50 g Gruyère or Comté cheese, freshly grated

For the sauce
10 g butter; 15 g flour; 250 ml milk; salt
freshly ground pepper; freshly grated nutmeg
1 egg yolk; 50 ml cream
20 g Comté cheese, freshly grated

In addition
30 g butter; butter for the oven dish
1 tsp each chopped parsley and oregano

The finished pancakes can be sprinkled with grated cheese before being put into the oven, if desired. This can either be the same cheese as that in the sauce or, to give the dish a slightly different flavour, a blue cheese, such as Roquefort.

There is no difference in taste between the two kinds of mangold – red and green. Raw, the red looks more attractive than the green, but it loses its colour when cooked.

1. Smoothly mix the flour and the milk together, stir in the eggs and drizzle the melted butter in a thin stream. Strain the resulting batter through a fine sieve to stop any lumps forming. Season with salt and pepper and stir in the grated cheese, then leave to stand for 1 hour.

2. Meanwhile prepare the filling. Trim the mangold stalks a little, remove any strings and

FRANCE

wash the leaves and stalks thoroughly. Finely chop the stalks and cut the leaves into strips. Peel and finely chop the shallots. Melt the butter in a pan and sweat the shallots until just transparent. Add the chopped walnuts and cook briefly, then add the mangold, pour over the cream and season with salt, pepper and nutmeg. Cover and leave to simmer over a very low heat for 10 minutes. Take off the heat and leave to cool a little. Beat the egg and stir this and the grated cheese into the pan. Mix everything well.

3. Melt a little butter in a 15 cm diameter pan and pour in a very thin layer of pancake batter. Fry to a golden brown on each side and repeat until you have 8 pancakes. Leave to cool.

4. To prepare the sauce, melt the butter in a pan, smoothly stir in the flour and, stirring continuously, cook this roux for 1-2 minutes, without allowing it to discolour. Add the milk, stir to a smooth consistency and season with salt, pepper and nutmeg. Cook the sauce for about 20 minutes, stirring continuously. Beat the egg yolk and the cream together, add this mix to the sauce and, still stirring, bring briefly to the boil. Strain the sauce through a sieve, reheat it and add the grated cheese, stirring until this has melted.

5. Place some filling in the middle of each pancake, roll them all up and place them in a buttered ovenproof dish. Pour the sauce over and bake in a preheated oven at 220°C for 12 minutes. Sprinkle with parsley and oregano to serve.

FRANCE

Red Rice with Provençal Vegetables

THE SOUTH OF FRANCE IS AN ENDLESS SOURCE OF WONDERFUL CHEAP VEGETABLES

In Europe, red rice is only grown in the Camargue. However it is actually Indian in origin and is a medium grain rice with a naturally red colour.

This recipe is typical of the region and the rice, which grows in the Rhône delta, is unique to it. The rice's lightly aromatic flavour is a wonderful complement to the spicy vegetables.

200 g red Camargue rice
700 ml vegetable stock; salt
For the vegetables
100 g onions; 2 cloves garlic
300 g aubergines; 300 g courgettes
100 g yellow peppers
100 g red peppers
300 g tomatoes
4 tbsp olive oil
salt; freshly ground pepper
200 ml vegetable stock
2 tbsp mixed herbs (thyme, rosemary, oregano, basil and rosemary)
In addition
butter for the oven dish
30 g Tomme de Savoie cheese, freshly grated

Rinse the rice thoroughly in a sieve under cold running water, turn out into a bowl, cover with cold water and leave to stand overnight. Next day, strain the rice. Bring the vegetable stock to the boil in a pan with a little salt, then add the rice, turn down the heat and leave to cook for 20-25 minutes. Strain and drain well. Peel and finely chop the onions and the garlic. Trim the aubergines and the courgettes and dice both into 1.5 cm cubes. Quarter and deseed the both types of pepper, remove the fibres and cut the flesh into strips. Scald, skin and deseed the tomatoes, then roughly chop the flesh. Heat the olive oil in a pan and lightly soften the onion and garlic. Add the aubergine, courgette and peppers and sauté briefly. Slake with the vegetable stock and leave to simmer for 5 minutes over the lowest possible heat. Add the tomato and leave to simmer for a further 3 minutes, then sprinkle in the mixed herbs and season to taste. Finish preparing the dish, following the illustrated instructions, below. Bake in a preheated oven at 220°C for 20 minutes and serve in the oven dish.

Butter a large, shallow casserole dish and spoon the cooked and drained rice into this.

Spread the vegetable mixture evenly over the layer of rice and sprinkle with the grated cheese.

FRANCE

France produces a wide range of goat's milk cheeses. From the mild flavoured, creamy cheeses to the harder, mature varieties, they all share the distinctive flavour and aroma of goat's milk. For this potato terrine, a semi-ripe, soft goat's milk cheese, of the kind sold in a roll, is ideal.

Hot Potato Terrine with Cold Ratatouille

A DELICIOUS AND UNUSUAL WAY OF COOKING POTATO

So that the slices will fit the terrine dish, the potatoes need to be large and slightly oblong in shape. They should also be of a floury texture to combine well with the cheese.

1 clove garlic, peeled and lightly crushed
20 g butter, melted
1 kg large, floury potatoes
250 g goat's milk cheese in a roll
For the ratatouille
150 g courgettes; 150 g aubergines
100 g shallots; 1 clove garlic
150 g tomatoes; 5 tbsp olive oil
100 g black olives
1 tbsp white wine vinegar
1 tsp salt; freshly ground black pepper
1 tbsp fresh thyme leaves
In addition
greaseproof paper, buttered

1. Rub the lightly crushed garlic around a 1.2 litre terrine dish, then carefully brush the dish with the melted butter. Wash and peel the potatoes, then cut them lengthways into 2 mm thick slices. This is best done with the cutting blade of a food processor. Blanch the potato slices in boiling, salted water for 1 minute, then take out, lay on a cloth and leave to drain completely.

2. Line and fill the terrine dish with potato slices and the cheese roll, following the illustrated instructions, right.

3. So that the finished terrine is firm and holds its shape, lay a piece of wood, cut to the right size, on top of the greaseproof paper and weight this

The firm, creamy goat's milk cheese makes a delicious centre to the terrine and an excellent contrast to the potato – both in flavour and texture. If only rinded cheese, as distinct from the roll style, is available, a St. Maur from the Touraine region is a good substitute – it has a light rind and is sometimes also coated in ash. The flavour is not that different but the cut cheese is not as attractive to look at.

Line the bottom and sides of the terrine dish with the potato slices. Cut the rind off the cheese, lay it in the terrine and fold the potato slices over and around it. Fill the terrine with the remaining potato slices and cover with buttered greaseproof paper.

FRANCE

down with a stone. Place the terrine in a bain-marie of boiling water and cook in a preheated oven at 150°C for 1 hour.

4. Meanwhile, prepare the ratatouille. Wash and trim the courgettes and the aubergines and dice them into 5 mm cubes. Peel and thinly slice the shallots. Peel and finely chop the garlic. Scald, skin and deseed the tomatoes, then dice the flesh into 5 mm cubes. Heat the oil in a pan and fry the shallots and garlic, then add the aubergine slices and briefly fry them. Add the courgettes and fry for 1 minute. Add the tomato and the olives and fry for 1 minute further.

5. Mix the vinegar, salt, pepper to taste and the thyme together in a bowl, and stir in the fried vegetables. When the terrine is cooked, take it out of the oven and leave it to cool a little, then turn it out of the terrine dish. Slice the terrine, season with salt and pepper and serve with a portion of the ratatouille.

BRITISH ISLES

At the beginning of the century, English cuisine was as big a tourist attraction as a boat ride on the Thames. This recipe is a variation on an original dating from that period.

Yorkshire Pudding with Vegetables

A TRADITIONAL ENGLISH DISH GIVEN A VEGETARIAN TWIST

Traditionally, of course, Yorkshire pudding is served with roast beef, but there is no reason not to combine it with other things. This recipe, with a Cheddar and Stilton sauce, is particularly good.

For 6 servings
For the Yorkshire puddings
200 ml milk; 130 g flour; 4 eggs
salt; freshly ground pepper

For the vegetables
200 g cauliflower; 120 g green beans
200 g kohlrabi
80 g celery
80 g carrots; 300 g fresh peas, in the pod
80 g onion; 40 g butter; 100 ml vegetable stock
salt; freshly ground pepper
1 tbsp young celery and kohlrabi leaves, chopped

For the cheese sauce
25 g butter; 20 g flour; 1/2 litre milk; salt
freshly ground pepper; freshly grated nutmeg
1 egg yolk; 100 ml cream
50 g Cheddar cheese, grated; 2 tbsp cream, whipped

In addition
butter for the pudding tray; 50 g Stilton cheese

Yorkshire puddings, straight out of the oven, smell and taste wonderful. It is critical to cook them at a high enough temperature to allow them to rise.

1. Mix all the ingredients for the Yorkshire pudding to a smooth batter and leave to stand in a cool place for 1 hour.

2. Wash the cauliflower. Wash and trim the beans and slice them diagonally into 4 cm long pieces. Peel the kohlrabi and chop into 1 cm cubes. Wash and trim the celery, peel the carrots and cut both into matchsticks 4 cm long and 5 mm thick. Shell the peas. Peel and finely chop the onion.

3. Melt the butter in a large pan and sweat the vegetables, adding them in the order of the ingredients list. Pour in the stock and leave the vegetables to simmer for 10-12 minutes. Season with salt and pepper and sprinkle with the kohlrabi and celery leaves.

4. To prepare the cheese sauce, melt the butter in a second pan and sprinkle in the flour, then, stirring continuously, cook this roux for 1-2 minutes over a low heat, without allowing it to discolour. Pour in the milk and stir to a smooth consistency, then season with salt, pepper and nutmeg. Cook for 20 minutes, stirring continuously. Beat the egg yolk and the cream together, stir this mix into the sauce, bring briefly to the boil, then strain through a fine sieve. Reheat the sauce, sprinkle in the cheese and stir carefully until this has melted. Fold in the whipped cream.

5. Butter a 6 tin Yorkshire pudding tray and add the batter. Bake in a preheated oven at 200°C for 15-20 minutes, to a golden brown. Take out, place 1 yorkshire pudding on each plate, spoon the vegetables into and around it, coat with the sauce and crumble a little Stilton on the top. Briefly pop under the grill until the cheese melts and serve.

BRITISH ISLES

The best Cheddars are still sold in the rind in which they were matured, and wrapped in a cloth, as above left.

Spinach Tartlets

EATEN HOT OR COLD, THESE MAKE A DELICIOUS STARTER ON A VEGETARIAN MENU

The pastry gets its tangy flavour from the sharp Cheddar cheese. So that the tartlets retain their shape – flat based and firm edged – the pastry needs to be blind baked. The finished pastry cases freeze well and can be prepared well in advance, defrosted and filled as required.

For the pastry
125 g flour; 125 g butter, in small pieces
125 g Cheddar cheese, freshly grated
1 egg yolk; 1/2 tsp salt
1/2 tsp paprika

For the filling
1 kg spinach; 100 g onions
1 clove garlic; 20 g butter

For the egg mixture
125 ml cream; 1 egg; 1 egg yolk
salt; freshly ground white pepper
freshly grated nutmeg

In addition
greaseproof paper and dried beans for blind baking
20 g Macadamia nuts, roasted and chopped

1. Sift the flour onto a work surface, make a well in the centre. Put the butter, cheese, egg yolk, salt and paprika into the well and work quickly to a smooth dough. Roll the dough into a ball, wrap in cling film and place in the refrigerator for 1 hour.

2. Meanwhile, to prepare the filling, clean and blanch the spinach. Refresh in ice cold water and leave to drain well. Using a cloth, squeeze the remaining moisture out of the spinach. Peel and finely chop the onions and the garlic. Melt the butter in a pan and soften the onion and the garlic over a low heat, then stir in the spinach. Take off the heat and leave to cool.

3. To prepare the egg mixture, beat the cream with the egg and the egg yolk using a fork. Season with salt, pepper and nutmeg.

4. On a floured work surface roll out the dough to an even 5 mm thickness. Cut the dough into circles large enough to fit into fluted tartlet tins 12 cm in diameter. Press the circles firmly into the tins, trimming off the excess. Prick the base of each tartlet several times with a fork. Line each tartlet with greaseproof paper cut to size and fill with dried beans to weigh this down and keep the base flat and the edges upright. Bake in a preheated oven at 200°C for 15 minutes.

5. Take the tartlets out of the oven and discard the beans and the paper. Spoon the spinach filling evenly into the cases, then pour in the egg mixture. Put the tartlets back into the oven and bake at 200°C for 20 minutes. If the pastry looks like overcooking, cover the tartlets with foil. Take out, sprinkle with the Macadamia nuts and serve.

There is nothing more likely to lift the spirits than a walk through the English countryside on a hot summer's day.

Asparagus with Poached Eggs

AN UNUSUAL SUMMER DISH WHOSE MAIN INGREDIENTS ARE TYPICALLY BRITISH

This dish might be described as perfectly simple – and simply perfect. A creamy and luxurious sauce – a parsley sabayon – turns traditional poached eggs and plain cooked asparagus into a real delicacy. Served with new potatoes it makes a light and original main course.

900 g white asparagus
salt; 1 squeeze lemon juice

For the eggs
1/2 litre vegetable stock
2 tbsp tarragon vinegar
4 eggs

For the parsley sabayon
30 g parsley leaves, without stalks; salt
2 tbsp vegetable stock; 80 ml white wine
2 egg yolks; 4 eggs
freshly ground white pepper
60 ml cream, lukewarm; 1 squeeze lemon juice

1. Trim the ends off the asparagus spears, then, using an asparagus peeler, peel them, working from the top down. Start just below the head, peeling thinly at the top and more thickly at the bottom. Fill a large pan

Hold a ladle in the stock, which should be just bubbling, and slide the egg into it. Poaching an egg this way ensures that the white does not disperse in the liquid but retains a rounded shape. Poach the eggs, for 3-4 minutes each, one after the other. Lift the eggs carefully out with the ladle and put them into lukewarm water to keep them warm without going hard. Trim the whites.

BRITISH ISLES

with water and bring this to the boil with a pinch of salt and the lemon juice. Add the asparagus and cook for 10-12 minutes, then drain it well and keep warm.

2. In a separate pan, bring the vegetable stock and the vinegar to the boil and poach the eggs, following the illustrated instructions, opposite.

3. To prepare the parsley sabayon, wash the parsley. Bring a small amount of salted water to the boil, add the parsley and bring briefly to the boil again. Strain immediately, refresh the parsley in ice-cold water and leave to drain well. Roughly chop the drained parsley, then purée, together with the vegetable stock, in a food processor. Bring the white wine to the boil in a pan and reduce it to 2 tablespoons of liquid. Whisk the parsley purée, the egg yolks and the eggs together in a whisking bowl, then stand this in a bain-marie of boiling water and whisk until the mixture is foaming and has doubled in volume. Season with salt and pepper. Stir in the reduced white wine, the cream and the lemon juice.

4. Divide the asparagus between four preheated plates, add a poached egg, and coat with the parsley sabayon. Serve with new potatoes.

New potatoes cooked in vegetable stock, or a chunk of crusty bread, are all the accompaniment this dish needs.

BELGIUM

Vegetable 'Tagliatelle' with Millet Risotto

NOT PASTA AT ALL, BUT FLAT RIBBONS OF VEGETABLE, LIGHTLY COOKED

This is an extremely refined and original way of presenting carrots, courgettes and celery: sliced into long, razor thin ribbons and briefly sautéed. Attractive and colourful, they taste as good as they look, as this method retains all their natural crispy goodness and flavour. The vegetables are served with a small portion of fresh tomato sauce and a millet risotto. Mimolette cheese shavings add the perfect finishing touch.

Mature Mimolette passes through a number of expert hands before it reaches the shops. Dutch Edam cheese is sent to France where it is treated by specialist *affineurs* (cheese finishers). It is then left to mature for at least 12 months.

For the millet risotto
30 g onion; 40 g carrots
30 g root parsley; 30 g leek
2 tbsp vegetable oil; 200 g millet
1/2 litre vegetable stock
salt; freshly ground pepper

For the vegetable tagliatelle
450 g carrots; 450 g courgettes
450 g celery
3 tbsp vegetable oil; salt
coarsely ground black pepper
1 tsp chopped celery leaves

For the tomato sauce
700 g tomatoes
1 clove garlic; 50 g onion; 2 tbsp vegetable oil
salt; freshly ground pepper
1 tbsp snipped thyme leaves

In addition
40 g Mimolette cheese, freshly shaved

1. To prepare the millet risotto, peel and finely dice the onion, carrots, root parsley and leek. Heat the oil in a pan and sweat the vegetables over a low heat. Stir in the millet and cook briefly, still over a low heat. Pour in the stock, bring briefly to the boil, then season with salt and pepper. Turn down the heat and leave to gently simmer, covered, for 20-25 minutes.

2. To prepare the vegetable tagliatelle, peel the carrots, trim the courgettes and trim and string the celery. Using a food slicer, slice all three, lengthways, into long, 1 mm thick ribbons, then cut the carrot and the courgette ribbons again, still working lengthways, into narrow strips roughly 5 mm wide.

3. To prepare the tomato sauce, skin and deseed the tomatoes, then finely dice the flesh. Peel and finely chop the garlic and the onion. Heat the oil in a pan and sweat the garlic and the onion until just transparent. Add the tomato and simmer for 5 minutes. Season with salt and pepper, then sprinkle in the thyme.

4. Heat the oil for the tagliatelle in a pan and sauté the carrots over a high heat, for 1 minute. Add the courgette and the celery and fry for a further 1 minute. Season with salt and pepper and sprinkle with the chopped celery leaves. Arrange the tagliatelle on preheated plates with a portion of tomato sauce and sprinkle with the Mimolette cheese. Serve the millet risotto separately.

HOLLAND

A wide range of Gouda cheeses, varying from mild to strong in flavour, are available in Holland. These include garlic, onion, caraway seed and various herb Goudas. There is even a nettle Gouda.

Millet Pancakes

TOPPED WITH COLOURFUL RED, YELLOW AND GREEN PEPPERS AND A TANGY GOUDA CHEESE SAUCE

Though millet was fairly popular in various ancient societies – the Romans used it to make a type of porridge – since then, until fairly recently, it has been virtually ignored. Now, as an ingredient in vegetarian recipes, it has once again become popular. Made into thin, tasty pancakes and topped with peppers and gouda cheese, this recipe makes it hard to imagine why millet had all but disappeared from European menus in the first place.

For 8 servings
For the pancakes
300 g millet; 1/2 litre water; salt; 4 eggs
1 tbsp finely chopped chives; 2 tbsp chopped parsley
freshly ground white pepper
freshly grated nutmeg; 80 g wholemeal semolina

For the topping
200 g each, red, yellow and green peppers
80 g white onion
1 clove garlic; 2 tbsp extra fine vegetable oil
1 tbsp snipped thyme leaves
salt; freshly ground white pepper

Pancakes of every description are favourite lunchtime dishes in Holland.

In addition
100 g butter for frying the pancakes
250 g strong Gouda cheese

The millet must first be cooked in water, over a very low heat, until it swells and absorbs the liquid. It is then ready to be used as a pancake mixture.

1. Add the millet and the water to a pan with a pinch of salt and bring to the boil. Immediately turn the heat down as low as possible and leave to gently simmer for 30 minutes, then take the pan off the heat and leave the millet to cool at room temperature. In a bowl, beat the eggs with the chives and the parsley, season with nutmeg and pepper, then stir well into the cooled millet. Stir in the semolina and set aside.

2. To prepare the topping, skin the peppers. To do this, roast them in a preheated oven at 220°C until the skins blister. Take out, put into a plastic bag and leave to sweat. Skin the peppers, working carefully from top to bottom and pulling off the skin in strips. Halve and deseed the peppers, remove the fibres and dice the flesh into 1.5 cm cubes.

3. Peel and thinly slice the onion and the garlic. Heat the oil in a pan and fry the onion and the garlic over a low heat, until just softened. Add the peppers and sweat these for 1 minute. Sprinkle in the thyme leaves and season with salt and pepper.

4. In a clean pan and using 1/8 of the butter each time, fry 8 millet pancakes, one after the other. Arrange the pancakes on ovenproof dishes, cover with a portion of peppers, cut the gouda into 8 slices and lay 1 slice of cheese on top of each pancake. Pop into a preheated oven at 180°C until the cheese melts, then take out and serve immediately.

DENMARK

Rice and Cheese Balls

FILLED WITH TWO KINDS OF CHEESE AND SERVED WITH A DELICIOUS TOMATO AND PEPPER SAUCE

Deep-fried rice balls, without the two-cheese filling, are a Far Eastern speciality. This Danish variation uses two uniquely Danish cheeses: Esrom, an aromatic semi-hard cheese and Danish Blue, a creamy, crumbly blue veined cheese.

For the rice balls
30 g butter; 50 g shallots, very finely chopped
200 g arborio rice
50 ml white wine; 1 litre vegetable stock
salt; freshly ground white pepper
60 g Esrom cheese, freshly grated

For the tomato and red pepper sauce
200 g red peppers; 700 g tomatoes
80 g onion; 1 clove garlic; 3 tbsp olive oil
salt; freshly ground white pepper

For the coating
2 eggs; 150 g white breadcrumbs

In addition
60 g Danish Blue cheese
oil for frying; a few oregano leaves

The crisp outside and the soft melted cheese inside give these rice balls a wonderful contrast of both flavours and textures.

1. Melt the butter in a pan and lightly soften the shallots. Add the rice and, stirring continuously over a low heat, cook until it turns transparent. Add the wine and simmer to reduce a little. Gradually add the vegetable stock, then, stirring occasionally, cook for 15 minutes until the rice is cooked through. Season with salt and pepper. Take the pan off the heat, leave to cool a little, stir in the Esrom and leave to cool further.

2. Roast the peppers in a preheated oven at 220°C until the skins blister. Take out, place in a plastic bag and leave to sweat. Skin the peppers, working from top to bottom and pulling off the

The Danes are nature lovers, something that is reflected in their cuisine, which relies heavily on natural products.

Photograph: Lennard, Dänisches Fremdenverkehrsamt.

DENMARK

skin in strips. Halve and deseed the peppers, remove the fibres and finely dice the flesh. Scald, skin and deseed the tomatoes, then dice the flesh. Peel and finely chop the onion and the garlic. Heat the oil in a pan and soften the onion and the garlic until just transparent. Add the tomato and the peppers, season with salt and pepper and simmer over a very low heat for 15 minutes.

3. Cut the Danish Blue cheese into 12 equally sized cubes. Divide the rice mixture into 12 portions of about 50 g each. Divide each portion in half, then flatten these with the ball of the hand. Place a cube of Danish Blue on the centre of one half portion of rice, lay the other half on top and roll into a small ball. Repeat for the remaining 11 rice balls.

4. Beat the eggs in a shallow dish and turn the breadcrumbs out into a second dish. Dip the rice balls first in the egg mixture, then into the breadcrumbs, coating evenly. Fry the balls in a deep-fat-fryer at 160°C for 5 minutes, then take them out and leave to drain on kitchen paper.

5. Divide the rice balls between four plates, add some of the tomato and red pepper sauce and sprinkle with oregano leaves to serve.

Blinis

EXQUISITE LITTLE PANCAKES, MADE WITH YEAST AND FILLED WITH A DELICIOUS MIXTURE OF SAUERKRAUT AND MUSHROOMS

Traditionally, *blinis* were made in Poland and Russia on Shrove Tuesday but today these little buckwheat and wheat flour pancakes are popular all year round. They are best made in a cast iron pan with freshly mixed batter.

For the blini batter
200 g wheatmeal; 200 g wheat flour; 20 g yeast
200 g buckwheat flour; 100 g butter, melted; 1 tsp salt

For the filling
500 g sauerkraut; 130 g onions; 80 g butter; 1 bay leaf
salt; freshly ground pepper; 400 g mushrooms

In addition
butter for frying
80 g soured cream; 1 tsp chopped parsley

Bring the wheatmeal to the boil with 700 ml water, then turn down the heat and leave for 15 minutes to swell and set. Turn the wheatmeal out into a bowl and leave to cool. Sift the wheat flour over the cooled wheatmeal, make a well in the centre of the flour. Finish mixing the batter following the illustrated instructions, right. While the batter is standing, chop the sauerkraut into small pieces and peel and finely chop the onions. Melt 40 g of butter in a pan and soften 2/3 of the chopped onion. Add the sauerkraut and the bay leaf, season with salt and pepper and then add 250 ml of water. Turn down the heat and leave to simmer, covered, for 30-40 minutes. Meanwhile, wipe, trim and slice the mushrooms. Melt the remaining butter in a pan and soften the remaining chopped onion. Add the mushrooms and sweat these for 2-3 minutes. Season with salt and pepper and stir into the sauerkraut mixture. Using a pan 18 cm in diameter, melt a knob of butter and fry 8 *blinis,* one at a time, to a golden brown on each side. Use a fresh knob of butter each time. Lay one *blini* on each plate, spread with a generous helping of sauerkraut and mushrooms and top with a second *blini*. Garnish with a spoonful of soured cream and sprinkle with parsley to serve.

Place the yeast in the well, add 3 tablespoons lukewarm water and mix everything together well. Cover and leave the mix to stand for 15 minutes.

Add the buckwheat flour and mix thoroughly, then add the melted butter and the salt and stir everything together once more.

Gradually stir in 350 ml of lukewarm water and, using a wooden spoon, stir to a smooth batter.

Cover the batter and leave to stand for a further 35 minutes, by which time it will have risen and doubled in volume.

Ceps with Potato Noodles

A RECIPE STRAIGHT FROM THE HEART OF THE BOHEMIAN WOODS

This recipe combines the freshest of Bohemian vegetables to create an unusual and delicate mixture of textures and flavours. The Chechen countryside is rich in mushrooms, including ceps, and potatoes in particular. The potato noodles – variations on which are found throughout Europe, from Austrian *spätzle* to Italian *gnocchi* – are characteristic of the local cuisine and come in a number of different shapes and sizes. In this recipe, mini potato noodles go perfectly with both the onions and the mushrooms.

For the potato noodles
400 g floury potatoes
150 g flour; 50 g Emmental cheese, freshly grated
3/4 tsp salt; freshly ground pepper; 2 eggs

For the onions
250 g small onions; 30 g butter
150 ml cream
salt; freshly ground pepper
1 sprig thyme

For the mushrooms
500 g ceps; 50 g butter
salt; freshly ground pepper
1 tbsp chopped parsley

In addition
1 tsp thyme leaves
1 tsp chopped parsley

1. Wash the potatoes and wrap them in foil. Bake them in a preheated oven at 200°C for 1 hour, then take out and peel. Heap the flour onto a work surface and make a well in the centre. Place the grated cheese, salt and pepper to taste in the well and, using a potato press, press the hot potato in a circle, over the top of the flour. Break

Roll out the potato dough into a 2 cm thick roll and sprinkle with flour. Using a large knife, slice the roll into 1 cm thick slices. Roll these, by hand, into noodle shapes with a point at each end.

CHECHNYA

This dish is a typically luxurious example of Bohemian cuisine. The generously creamy sauce does not mask the flavour of the onions but rounds off the dish perfectly.

the eggs into the well and then work everything to a smooth dough. Leave to stand for a few minutes, then proceed following the illustrated instructions opposite.

2. Peel the onions and halve them lengthways. Melt the butter in a saucepan and, stirring continuously, sweat the onions over a low heat for 10 minutes. Pour in the cream and season with salt and pepper. Add the sprig of thyme, cover and leave to cook for 10 minutes.

3. Carefully wipe the ceps clean (only wash them if absolutely necessary), then slice them thinly, lengthways. Melt the butter in a pan and sauté the ceps briefly, then season with salt and pepper and sprinkle with parsley.

4. Cook the potato noodles in lightly salted, boiling water for about 6 minutes. They are ready when they float to the surface. Take the noodles out with a draining spoon and drain well. Arrange on preheated plates, with a portion of ceps and a spoonful of onions, and sprinkle with thyme and parsley to serve.

Jacket Potatoes with a Spicy Filling

RED AND GREEN PEPPERS AND A GARLIC MAYONNAISE ARE THE MAIN INGREDIENTS FOR THIS DELICIOUS WAY OF SERVING BAKED POTATOES

Freshly dug potatoes should be used for this recipe if at all possible. If you are not able to get them direct from the garden or from a farm, it is important to buy the right kind of potatoes: they must only be slightly floury but also firmish when cooked.

Stuffed jacket potatoes are not a new idea but these are a little different, with their unusual filling of peppers, tomatoes, herbs and spices, together with a delicious garlic mayonnaise as an accompaniment.

4 large baking potatoes (about 250 g each)
For the filling
100 g onions
2 cloves garlic
200 g each green and red peppers
300 g tomatoes; 2 tbsp vegetable oil
4 tsp mild paprika
1/2 tsp ground caraway seed
1 tsp chopped marjoram
salt; freshly ground white pepper
For the garlic mayonnaise
1 egg; 1/2 tsp salt
1/4 tsp freshly ground white pepper
1/2 tsp lemon juice; 1 clove garlic, peeled
175 ml vegetable oil; 1 tbsp snipped chives

Served as a main dish, each potato should weigh about 250 g. Smaller ones may be used, in which case the cooking time should be reduced by about 15 minutes. A green salad, with a sharp vinaigrette sauce, makes a good accompaniment.

When the potatoes are cooked (they can be tested by inserting the point of a sharp knife) the foil is discarded and the top 1/3 of the potato sliced off.

1. Scrub the potatoes thoroughly, pat them dry and wrap them in foil. Bake in a preheated oven at 200°C for 1 hour.

2. Peel and finely chop the onions and the garlic. Wash, halve and deseed both types of peppers, remove the fibres and dice the flesh into 1 cm cubes. Scald, skin and deseed the tomatoes, then chop the flesh.

3. When preparing the mayonnaise it is essential that all the ingredients are at room temperature in order to make a smooth mayonnaise that does not separate. Break the egg into a blender jug, then add the salt, pepper and the lemon juice. Using a garlic press, crush the garlic into the jug. Switch the blender on to the slowest possible setting and,

GERMANY

as it is running, add the oil in a thin stream, through the opening in the blender lid. Blend until the mayonnaise is completely smooth and the same consistency throughout; this should only take a short time. Turn the mayonnaise out into a bowl and stir in the chives.

4. Heat the oil in a pan and soften the chopped onion and the garlic. Add the diced peppers and cook for 5 minutes over the lowest possible heat. Add the chopped tomato and simmer for a further 2 minutes. Stir in the paprika, caraway seed and fresh marjoram (1/2 teaspoon dried marjoram may be used if the latter is unavailable). Season with salt and pepper.

5. Take the potatoes out of the oven and remove the foil. Horizontally slice the top 1/3 off the potatoes. Make a hollow in the centre of the bottom 2/3, leaving a 4 mm edge all round. Scoop the potato out of the top of the potato, add it to that scooped out of the bottom and finely chop. Mix this with the pepper and tomato mixture. Season the mix with salt and pepper and spoon it generously into the potatoes. Top with a spoonful of the garlic mayonnaise and serve.

Vegetables in Riesling Sauce

CRUNCHY SUNFLOWER CRISPS MAKE A DELICIOUS CONTRAST TO THE DELICATE BABY VEGETABLES

This recipe, which is typical of German nouvelle cuisine, is easy to prepare and uses little in the way of flavouring. Instead, the quality of the ingredients is critical – the vegetables must be fresh baby vegetables and the Riesling must be a good one, preferably a Rheingau or an Alsace.

250 g new potatoes
4 small artichokes (about 100 g each)
juice of 1 lemon; salt; 200 g small onions
120 g mangetout; 150 g baby carrots
200 g small white turnips; 50 g butter; 1 tbsp sugar
freshly ground white pepper
200 ml Riesling; 300 ml cream
1 squeeze lemon juice
For the sunflower crisps
100 g sunflower tubers; oil for frying; salt

Sunflower crisps are made from the tuber of the sunflower plant. Peel the tubers and then shave them into 1 mm thick slices. Deep fry them at 180°C to a crispy golden brown, remove, drain well and lightly salt to serve.

1. Scrub the potatoes, boil them for 15 minutes in their skins, then strain them. Leave to cool a little, then peel and cut into 1 cm thick slices.

2. Break the stalk off each artichoke close to the base and immediately brush the base with lemon juice. Pull off the small, tough leaves from around the base and trim the tips from the other leaves, then slice the tops off the artichokes. Bring a pan of water to the boil with a pinch of salt and the remaining lemon juice and cook the artichokes for 10 minutes. Take them out, cut into quarters and scrape out the choke.

3. Peel the onions, clean and trim the mangetout. Scrape the carrots, leaving a little topknot of greenery attached. Peel the turnips and cut them into quarters, then into wedges. Cook all four vegetables in lightly salted, boiling water for 8 minutes, using just enough water to cover them. Strain the vegetables, reserving 400 ml of the cooking liquid, then leave to drain well.

4. Melt the butter in a pan. Add the artichokes, potatoes, onions and all the remaining vegetables, season with salt and sprinkle add the sugar. Sweat the vegetables, stirring constantly, for 2-3 minutes until they are glazed. Season with salt and pepper.

5. Take the vegetables out of the pan and set aside. Pour the wine into the pan and cook to reduce to 1/2 its original volume. Add the reserved cooking liquid from the vegetables and reduce again to 2/3 the volume. Stir in the cream. Cook the sauce to a creamy consistency, season with salt and pepper and add a squeeze of lemon juice. Whisk the sauce with a hand held mixer, then add the glazed vegetables, heat through, garnish with sunflower crisps and serve.

Herb Pancakes

COURGETTES ADD AN INTERNATIONAL FLAVOUR TO A CLASSIC GERMAN RECIPE

German cooks use eggs as frequently and in the same ways as they are used in Britain. Baked, poached, scrambled, fried or cooked in omelettes and pancakes, they are one of the mainstays of German cuisine.

For the pancake batter
6 eggs
20 g flour
salt
freshly ground pepper
4 tbsp chopped mixed herbs (red basil, parsley, nasturtium leaves, lovage, oregano and chives)
40 g butter

For the filling
300 g courgettes
50 g onion
20 g butter
salt; freshly ground pepper
1 tbsp thyme leaves

Fresh eggs can be used in so many different ways, but when prepared with mixed herbs and courgettes they taste even better than usual.

Pancakes are best fried in a non-stick pan. This requires less fat, making the pancakes less greasy. These pancakes, when made without the flour, become light omelettes which can be filled in the same way.

GERMANY

1. Beat the eggs in a bowl with the flour, mixed herbs and salt and pepper to taste. Wash and trim the courgettes and slice them diagonally into 3 mm thick slices. Peel and finely chop the onion.

2. Melt the butter in a pan and soften the chopped onion. Add the courgette and cook over a low heat for 4-5 minutes. Season with salt and pepper and sprinkle in the thyme leaves. Take off the heat, cover and keep hot.

3. Using a non-stick pan 18 cm in diameter, melt 1/4 of the butter, pour in 1/4 of the pancake batter and, over a low heat, fry on both sides to a golden brown. Take out and keep hot. Repeat three times to make 4 pancakes in total. Fill each pancake with a portion of the courgette and onion mixture and serve immediately.

Asparagus Tart

LIGHT SHORTCRUST PASTRY WITH AN ASPARAGUS AND CREAM FILLING

A subtle egg cream binds the asparagus and peas together and the final baking seals in all of the flavour. The crispy golden pastry crust makes a wonderful contrast to the softer centre.

For the pastry dough
250 g flour; 125 g butter
salt; 1-2 tbsp cold water
1 egg

For the filling
250 g fresh peas (about 125 g shelled)
700 g white asparagus

For the egg mixture
3 eggs
125 ml cream
salt; freshly ground pepper
1 egg white

In addition
1 bunch chives, snipped

When asparagus is in season this makes a wonderful party dish. It can be prepared well in advance and popped back into the oven just before serving.

1. Heap the flour onto a work surface, dot with the lightly chilled pieces of butter and work to a crumbly texture with the fingers. Make a small well in the centre and break in the egg, add the water and season with salt. Work quickly to a smooth dough, wrap in cling film and leave in the refrigerator to chill for at least 1 hour.

2. Shell the peas. Peel the asparagus and cut the spears into 4 cm long pieces. Cook in lightly salted, boiling water for 5-8 minutes, then take out and drain well.

Using a rolling pin, carefully line the flan tin with the dough.

Press the dough firmly into the bottom and sides of the tin and trim off any excess with a sharp knife.

GERMANY

3. Roll out the dough to an even 5 mm thickness, on a floured work surface and line it into a flan tin 26 cm in diameter, following the illustrated instructions opposite.

4. Blind bake the pastry case to ensure a crispy base under the moist filling. Line the pastry with greaseproof paper cut to size and fill to 1 cm below the rim with dried beans. Bake in a preheated oven at 200°C for 15 minutes, then take out and discard the paper and the beans. Leave to cool a little. Arrange the asparagus pieces and the peas on the pastry base.

5. To prepare the egg mixture, beat the eggs in a bowl with the cream and season with salt and pepper. Beat the egg white stiffly and fold it into the egg and cream. Pour the egg mixture over the vegetables and bake the tart in a preheated oven at 200°C for 35-40 minutes. Take out, leave to cool a little, then sprinkle with chives and serve.

GERMANY

Working lengthways, arrange a row of broccoli, a row of pepper and a second row of broccoli on top of the pumpkin layer. Pour over 1/4 of the pumpkin purée. For the second layer arrange 2 rows of pepper strips with 1 row of broccoli between. Cover, as before, with 1/4 of the pumpkin purée. For the third layer, repeat the pattern of the first, finishing with a final layer of pumpkin purée.

Pumpkin and Broccoli Terrine

LIGHT AND COLOURFUL, A DELICIOUS TERRINE OF BROCCOLI WITH RED PEPPERS ENCASED IN A PUMPKIN MOUSSE

750 g pumpkin flesh
20 g butter
80 g white onion, finely chopped
2 cloves garlic, finely chopped
20 g sugar; 1 tsp freshly ground ginger
5 eggs; salt; freshly ground white pepper
400 g red peppers; 300 g broccoli florets

For the red pepper sauce
450 g red peppers
20 g butter; 20 g shallots, finely chopped
1/2 clove garlic, finely chopped
salt; freshly ground white pepper
1 sprig thyme; 1 bay leaf
40 ml white wine
150 ml vegetable stock

In addition
butter and clear film for the terrine dish

Cut 1/3 of the pumpkin into 5 mm cubes and chop the remainder into small pieces. Blanch the cubed pumpkin in boiling salted water for 3 minutes, then strain and set aside. Reserve 150 ml of the cooking liquid. Melt the butter in a pan and soften the onion and the garlic. Add the chopped, raw pumpkin, sprinkle in the sugar and cook, turning from time to time, until caramelised. Slake with the reserved cooking liquid, sprinkle in the ginger and leave to simmer, covered, for 5 minutes. At the end of this time, remove the lid and continue to cook until the liquid has been completely absorbed. Leave to cool, then turn the mixture out into a blender jug, add the eggs and blend to a purée. Season with salt and pepper. Stir in the pumpkin cubes. Roast the peppers in a preheated oven at 220°C until the skins blister, then take out, put into a plastic bag and leave to sweat. Skin the peppers, working from top to bottom and pulling off the skin in strips. Halve and deseed the peppers, remove the fibres and cut the flesh, lengthways, into strips about 1.5 cm wide. Blanch the broccoli in boiling, salted water, then take out and leave to drain well. Lightly butter a 1 litre capacity terrine dish, line it with clear cooking film and spoon in 1/4 of the pumpkin mixture, then finish filling the terrine, following the illustrated instructions, above left. Tap the terrine once on the work surface to settle the contents and clear air pockets, then cover it. Place in a bain-marie and cook in a preheated oven at 150°C until it sets. To prepare the sauce, rinse, quarter and deseed the peppers, remove the fibres and dice the flesh. Melt the butter in a pan and soften the shallots and the garlic, then add the peppers and sweat these. Season with salt and pepper and add the thyme and the bay leaf. Slake with the wine and the stock and leave to simmer over the lowest possible heat until cooked through. Purée with a hand held mixer, then strain the sauce through a fine sieve. Take the terrine out of the oven, leave to cool until lukewarm, then turn out onto a chopping board and remove the clear film. Slice and serve with the sauce.

Clear cooking film helps to make a perfect terrine. Wrapped in the film it cooks firmly and is easy to turn out when the time comes.

GERMANY

Sprinkle the mixed herbs into the corn mixture, add the egg and cream, then season with salt, pepper and nutmeg and mix everything well together. Stir in the onion, courgette and carrot. Roll the mixture by hand into rolls weighing about 100 g each then flatten into cakes.

Corncakes with Cucumber Sauce

CRISPY, WHOLEGRAIN FRICADELLES – A VEGETARIAN VARIATION ON HAMBURGERS

In this country recipe, fine strips of vegetable are mixed with the cooked corn and made into cakes which are then pan fried and served with a portion of fresh cucumber in a cream sauce.

For the corncakes
1/2 litre vegetable stock; 2 cloves garlic
250 g coarse ground green corn; 80 g onion
125 g courgettes; 125 g carrots; 20 g butter
salt; freshly ground white pepper
2 tbsp mixed herbs (rosemary, thyme, basil, parsley and celery leaves), chopped
1 egg; 50 ml cream
freshly grated nutmeg; 3 tbsp vegetable oil

For the cucumber sauce
800 g large cucumbers; 100 g onions, finely chopped
40 g butter; salt; freshly ground white pepper
60 ml white wine; 100 ml cream; 2 tbsp chopped dill

In addition
4 nasturtium flowers to garnish

Nasturtium flowers make a wonderfully decorative garnish for these crispy corncakes.

The small, outdoor variety of cucumber is best for this dish, as the more common greenhouse cucumber is bland by comparison.

GERMANY

1. Bring the vegetable stock to the boil in a pan. Peel the garlic and, using a garlic press, press it into the stock. Stir in the corn, turn down the heat, cover and leave to cook for about 20 minutes, stirring from time to time, until thick and cooked through. Turn the corn mixture out into a bowl.

2. Meanwhile prepare the vegetables. Peel and finely chop the onion. Trim the courgettes, trim and scrape the carrots, and cut both into julienne strips. Melt the butter in a pan and soften the onion until just transparent. Add the carrot and sweat for 3 minutes, followed by the courgette for another 2 minutes. Season with salt and pepper.

3. Prepare the corncakes, following the illustrated instructions, opposite. Heat the oil in a pan and fry the corncakes for 4 minutes on each side, then set aside and keep hot.

4. To prepare the sauce, peel the cucumbers and halve them lengthways. Scoop out the seeds and dice the flesh into 1 cm long pieces. Melt the butter and soften the onion until just transparent. Add the cucumber pieces, season with salt and pepper and fry briefly over a high heat. When the juices start to run, add the wine and bring briefly to the boil, then turn the heat down as low as possible and leave to simmer, uncovered, for about 10 minutes until the liquid has nearly cooked away. Stir in the cream and the dill and carefully heat through. Arrange the corncakes on plates with a portion of cucumber sauce, garnish with a nasturtium flower and serve.

GERMANY

Fresh chanterelles are among the finest mushrooms available. They need to be very carefully wiped clean but are well worth the effort. Tinned chanterelles have nothing like the same taste.

Chanterelle Parcels

SERVED WITH A MUSTARD, CREAM AND HERB SAUCE, THIS TASTES AS GOOD AS IT LOOKS

Sheets of ready made Turkish *yufka* or Greek *filo* pastry are perfect for this recipe, so there is no need to go through the lengthy and difficult process of making them at home. Either can be bought, frozen, in major supermarkets.

To make 8 Chanterelle parcels
For the filling
1 kg fresh chanterelles; 100 g butter; 80 g onion
1 clove garlic; 400 g firm potatoes; 1 tbsp vegetable oil
250 g tomatoes; 80 g spring onions
2 tbsp flat leaf parsley, chopped
1 tbsp chives, snipped; 1 tsp truffle oil
salt; freshly ground black pepper
For the pastry parcels
4 sheets yufka pastry; 50 g melted butter
8 strips chive tops, for binding
For the herb and cream sauce
30 g onion; 20 g butter; 100 ml white wine
400 ml cream; 1 tbsp chopped mixed herbs
(rosemary, oregano, sage and basil)
salt; freshly ground white pepper; 1 tsp lemon juice

These Chanterelle parcels do not need an accompaniment but a few crunchily cooked baby carrots, pieces of white turnip or courgette make an ideal garnish.

In addition
butter for the baking tray

1. Wipe the mushrooms clean – it is best not to wash them. Leave the small ones whole and cut the larger ones in half. Melt the butter in a pan and evenly fry them. Take out and leave to cool.

2. Peel and finely chop the onion and the garlic. Wash and peel the potatoes and cut into 5 mm cubes. Heat the oil in a pan and sauté the garlic and the onion until just transparent. Add the potato and fry over a low heat for a further 5 minutes. Set aside to cool.

GERMANY

3. Scald, skin and deseed the tomatoes, then finely dice the flesh. Wash and trim the spring onions and slice them into thin rings.

4. Put the mushrooms, the potato mixture, tomatoes and spring onions into a bowl. Add the parsley, chives and truffle oil. Season with salt and pepper and mix well together.

5. Cut the sheets of yufka pastry in half and brush each piece with melted butter. Spread a spoonful of filling in the middle, wrap and twist the pastry into little sacks and tie the tops with a thin strip of chive top. Arrange the pastry parcels on a buttered baking tray and bake in a preheated oven at 200°C for 15-20 minutes. About 5 minutes into the cooking time, cover the parcels with a little greaseproof paper in order to stop the tops from overcooking.

6. To prepare the sauce, peel and very finely chop the onion. Melt the butter in a pan and soften the onion until just transparent. Slake with the white wine and cook to reduce to about 1/3 of the original volume of liquid. Pour in the cream and, stirring continuously over a very low heat, bring carefully to the boil. Reduce to a thick creamy consistency. Sprinkle in the mixed herbs, season with salt and pepper, add the lemon juice and, using a hand held mixer, whip to a foam. Arrange the mushroom parcels on plates, pour a portion of sauce round them and serve.

GERMANY

Peppers are a good source of vitamins and modern growing techniques now mean they are available all year round. However, winter grown peppers are not quite as aromatic as those grown in the summer.

Fried Sesame Bread with a Tomato and Pepper Salad

INSPIRED BY THE TRADITIONAL RECIPE FOR SWEET DUMPLINGS, THIS IS A FILLING WHOLEFOOD VERSION

For previous generations, waste was practically a crime and using up leftovers or slightly stale bread was common practice. For this old recipe the bread rolls are left for a day before being fried and then served with a light salad

4 wholegrain rolls, fresh the previous day
250 ml milk
salt
freshly ground white pepper
freshly grated nutmeg
2 eggs
4 tbsp breadcrumbs
5 tbsp sesame seeds
For the tomato and pepper salad
400 g tomatoes
400 g yellow peppers
1 bunch chives
3 tbsp sunflower oil
1/2 clove garlic, peeled and crushed
3 tbsp herb vinegar
salt; freshly ground black pepper
In addition
60 g butter
red basil leaves to garnish

Run a grater over the outside of the rolls and reserve the grated crust. Slice the rolls in half and lay them flat in a dish. Bring the milk briefly to the boil, season with salt, pepper and nutmeg and pour it over the bread. Leave to soak for 1 minute, then carefully turn the sliced rolls over. Beat the eggs in a bowl. Put the breadcrumbs, grated crust and sesame seeds in a second bowl and mix well. One after another, dip the rolls first in the egg and then in the breadcrumb mixture, then set aside. To prepare the salad, scald, skin and deseed the tomatoes, then dice the flesh into 1.5 cm cubes. Skin the peppers, following the illustrated instructions, below. Halve and deseed the skinned peppers, remove the fibres and slice the flesh into diamond shapes. Put the tomatoes and the peppers in a salad bowl. Wash and trim the chives, then slice them into 2 cm long pieces. Mix the oil, garlic, and vinegar together, season with salt and pepper, pour it over the tomatoes and peppers and mix well. Sprinkle with chives. Melt the butter in a large pan and slowly fry the coated rolls to a golden brown on each side. Serve the hot rolls with the salad and garnish both with basil leaves.

Roast the peppers in a preheated oven at 220 °C until the skins blister and lightly burn.

Wrap in a damp cloth or plastic bag and leave to sweat. Skin the peppers, working in strips, from top to bottom.

GERMANY

A distinctive Rheingauer Riesling is delicious with mushrooms, and so perfect for the sauce.

Mushroom Maultaschen

THIS IS A POPULAR SWABIAN RECIPE, USING MUSHROOMS INSTEAD OF THE CLASSIC MEAT AND SPINACH FILLING

Many countries have their own versions of these stuffed pasta flaps — the most famous being, of course, Italian *ravioli*. Russian *Piroggi* and, to a lesser extent, Chinese *won-tons* also fall into the same category.

For the pasta dough
250 g flour; 2 eggs; 1 egg yolk
2 tbsp oil; 1/2 tsp salt
20 g mixed herbs (sage, thyme, parsley and spring onion tops), finely chopped

For the filling
100 g onions; 1 clove garlic
600 g ceps; 40 g butter
salt; freshly ground white pepper
3 tbsp chopped parsley

For the chive sauce
20 g shallots; 20 g butter
80 ml white wine; 250 ml cream
salt; freshly ground white pepper
1 tbsp snipped chives

In addition
1 egg white; 1 tbsp snipped chives

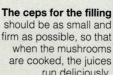

The ceps for the filling should be as small and firm as possible, so that when the mushrooms are cooked, the juices run deliciously.

1. Sift the flour onto a work surface and make a well in the centre. Put the eggs, egg yolk, oil, salt and mixed herbs into the well and work everything to a smooth dough, adding a little water as required. Wrap the dough in cling film and put in the refrigerator to stand for 1 hour.

GERMANY

2. To prepare the filling, finely chop the onions and the garlic. Wipe the mushrooms completely clean then dice them into 5 mm cubes. Melt the butter in a pan and soften the garlic and the onion until just transparent. Add the diced mushroom and sweat the mixture for a further 2-3 minutes. Season with salt and pepper, sprinkle in the parsley and set aside to cool completely.

3. To prepare the sauce, peel and very finely chop the shallots. Melt the butter in a pan and lightly soften the shallots. Slake with the white wine, then cook to reduce to about 1 tbsp. Stir in the cream and reduce again to half the volume. Season and sprinkle in the snipped chives.

4. Roll the pasta dough out thinly and evenly and, using a pastry cutter, cut into small oblong pieces 6 cm x 11 cm. Put a spoonful of filling on one end of each piece of dough, then brush all of the edges with egg white. Fold the other end up and over and press the edges together firmly to seal them. Cook the *maultaschen* in boiling, salted water for about 8 minutes. Take out, drain well and arrange on individual dishes with a coating of chive sauce. Sprinkle with the snipped chives and serve.

AUSTRIA

Autumn is the best time of year for potatoes as they taste wonderful freshly dug. However, it is possible to keep potatoes reasonably fresh for quite a while as long as they are stored in a light and airy, but frost free, place.

Potato 'Snails'

THIS SIMPLE DISH IS AN AUSTRIAN COUNTRY RECIPE WHICH IS ALSO POPULAR IN NEIGHBOURING BAVARIA

For a non-vegetarian version of the dish fry some diced, smoked ham or sausage with the onion.

For the dough
1 kg floury potatoes; 2 eggs
1 tsp salt; 250 g flour

For the filling
400 g onions
60 g butter
2 tbsp parsley, chopped
1 tbsp mixed chopped marjoram and wild marjoram
salt; freshly ground pepper

For the cream
1/4 litre cream; 3 eggs
salt; freshly ground pepper

In addition
20 g butter for the oven dish

Using a palette knife, spread the cooled onion filling evenly over the rolled out dough.

Cut the dough into strips 4 cm wide and 20 cm long. Roll these up to resemble snails.

Spoon the cream mixture around, not over, the snails. Set in the cream they cook evenly, without drying out.

Place the potatoes on a baking tray and bake in a preheated oven at 200°C for 1 hour. Take out and scoop the potato out of the skins while still hot. Press through a potato press onto a work surface and leave to cool. Make a well in the centre of the potato and put the eggs and the salt in this. Draw a little of the potato over the well and work in the eggs and salt. Sift the flour over, work everything by hand to a smooth dough and leave to stand for 15 minutes. To prepare the filling, peel and finely chop the onions. Melt the butter in a pan, add the onion, parsley and the marjoram and sweat for 5 minutes. Season with salt and pepper, then set aside to cool. Roll the dough out to an even 5 mm thickness on a floured work surface, then proceed following the first two illustrated instructions, left. Arrange the potato snails in a buttered oven dish and bake in a preheated oven at 200°C for 25 minutes. Meanwhile, prepare the cream. Beat the cream and the eggs together in a bowl and season with salt and pepper. Take the dish out of the oven, spoon in the cream, following the third illustrated instruction, left. Put the dish back into the oven and bake for a further 45 minutes at the same temperature. Serve straight from the dish.

Schwammerlknödel

AUSTRIAN MUSHROOM DUMPLINGS: A VARIATION ON TRADITIONAL BREAD DUMPLINGS

It is said that the best dumplings in the world come from Bohemia and this Austrian recipe for mushroom dumplings almost certainly has Bohemian origins, dating back to the time that the area was ruled by the Hapsburg Empire. These delicious mushroom delicacies are only served in late summer or autumn, when fresh mushrooms are available. Of course, these dumplings taste best when made with ceps or chanterelles but a variety of other mushrooms can be used instead.

For the dumplings
200 g stale white bread, without a crust
50 ml cream
100 ml milk
50 g butter, melted
3 eggs
salt
freshly ground pepper
freshly grated nutmeg
200 g ceps
200 g chanterelles
20 g shallots
1 clove garlic
50 g butter
1 tbsp chopped parsley
1 tsp chopped oregano
40 g flour
In addition
30 g butter
1 tbsp chopped mixed herbs (parsley and oregano)

Freshly chopped herbs and lightly browned butter turn these mushroom dumplings into a delicacy. A little Tyrolean hard cheese can also be sprinkled over them, if desired.

1. Finely dice the bread and place it in a bowl. Add the cream, milk and the melted butter. Break in the eggs and season with salt, pepper and nutmeg. Mix everything well, then leave to stand and soak for 1 hour.

2. Trim and thoroughly wipe both types of mushroom, then dice them into 5 mm cubes. Peel and finely chop the shallots and the garlic.

3. Melt the butter in a pan and soften the onion and the garlic over a low heat. Add both types

AUSTRIA

of mushroom and sweat for 1 minute, then sprinkle in the herbs. Set the mixture aside and leave to cool.

4. Add the cooled mushroom mixture to the soaked breadcrumbs and mix everything well. With damp hands, roll the mixture into balls, then form it into dumplings, each weighing about 70 g. Bring a pan of salted water to the boil, add the dumplings, turn down the heat and cook for 12-15 minutes. The dumplings are ready when they float to the top.

5. Melt the butter in a small pan and heat until lightly browned, then sprinkle in the chopped herbs. Arrange a portion of dumplings on individual plates, spoon a little browned herb butter over and serve immediately. A fresh green salad with raw onion, cherry tomatoes and a herb vinaigrette goes well with this dish.

AUSTRIA

Kaiserschmarren with Plum Compôte

A CLASSIC DISH FROM THE WIDE RANGE OF AUSTRIAN PANCAKE RECIPES

Kaiserschmarren are delicious, sugared pancakes which are served chopped into pieces. The most common version of this traditional recipe includes raisins, but here the *kaiserschmarren* are served with a plum compôte. In Austria and Germany sweet dishes of this kind are occasionally served as main courses, as well as desserts. This recipe is really a summer dish, as it is only then that the plum compôte can be made with fresh fruit. There is a fair amount of alcohol in the compôte but this can be reduced, or even left out altogether, if preferred.

For the batter
180 g flour
200 ml milk
100 ml cream
8 egg yolks
juice and grated zest of 1 untreated lemon
seeds from 1 vanilla pod
1 pinch salt
3 egg whites
50 g sugar

For the plum compôte
1 kg plums
50 ml water
50 ml white wine
2 cl Slivovitz (plum brandy)
80 g sugar
1 pinch cinnamon

In addition
120 g butter
icing sugar for dusting

Sieve the flour into a bowl, add the milk, cream, egg yolks, lemon juice and zest, vanilla and salt and work to a smooth batter. In a second bowl, beat the egg whites to a firm snow, gradually whisking in the sugar. Using a wooden spatula, fold the egg white into the batter. Melt a little butter in a frying pan 24 cm in diameter and fry 8 pancakes, following the illustrated instructions left. To prepare the plum compôte, wash the plums under running water, then halve and stone them. Put the water, the white wine, the slivovitz and the sugar into a pan and heat through. Add the plums and the cinnamon and leave to simmer over a very low heat for about 15 minutes, until the fruit is cooked through and the skins begin to come away from the flesh. Arrange the chopped pancakes on four dishes, dust with icing sugar, add a portion of compôte and serve immediately.

Ladle a little pancake batter into the pan and tip to spread evenly. Cook until the underside is lightly browned, then turn and fry the other side.

Using 2 spatulas, chop each pancake into pieces. Keep them hot.

SWITZERLAND

Cabbage and Chestnut Rolls

COATED IN A WHITE WINE SAUCE AND SERVED WITH MUSHROOM PASTA, THIS MAKES A LUXURIOUS AUTUMN DISH

Savoy cabbage and chestnuts make a wonderful combination. The plainness of the cabbage and the subtle flavour of the chestnuts produce a unique taste which is well worth experiencing.

For the filling
700 g chestnuts; 80 g celery
80 g onion; 1 clove garlic
140 g carrots; 50 g butter
1 tsp sugar; 1 tsp chopped thyme leaves
salt; freshly ground pepper
30 ml cream; 200 ml vegetable stock; 1 egg

In addition
4 medium savoy cabbage leaves; 30 g butter
100 ml white wine (Dézalay or Aigle)
250 ml vegetable stock; 100 ml cream
salt; freshly ground pepper
1 tsp chopped thyme leaves

Strip out the thick inner stalk from each cabbage leaf and trim the leaves evenly. Spread the leaves out on a work surface, season with salt and pepper and spread neatly with the chestnut mixture as shown. Roll up tightly, folding the sides over the centre to prevent the contents falling out during cooking.

The woods around Chiavenna are full of chestnut trees. Freshly gathered chestnuts taste great and mid-October, when they ripen, is the best time of year to prepare this recipe.

Fresh, homemade wholewheat pasta, with its subtle flavour, is the perfect accompaniment to cabbage and chestnut rolls.

SWITZERLAND

1. Score the chestnuts crosswise, then roast them in a preheated oven at 220°C for 10 minutes, take out and peel while still hot. Take care to remove the inner skins as well as the shells.

2. Trim, wash and finely dice the celery. Peel and finely dice the onion, garlic and carrots. Melt the butter in a pan, add the chestnuts and sugar and cook, turning, until glazed. Reserve 40 g carrot and add the rest of the diced vegetables and the thyme and season with salt and pepper. Pour in the cream and the stock and simmer, covered, over a very low heat for 25 minutes, stirring frequently. Turn the mix out into a bowl, stir in the egg and season to taste. Purée in a blender, then stir in the reserved carrot.

3. Cook the cabbage leaves in boiling, salted water for 8 minutes, then take out and refresh under cold running water. Make up the rolls following the illustrated instructions, opposite.

4. Melt the butter in a large pan and quickly fry the cabbage and chestnut rolls evenly on all sides. Add the white wine and the vegetable stock, then turn down the heat and leave to simmer for 15 minutes. Take the rolls out of the pan and keep them hot. Strain the sauce through a sieve into a saucepan, stir in the cream and cook to a smooth, creamy consistency. Season with salt and pepper and sprinkle in the thyme leaves. Arrange the cabbage rolls on individual plates, coat with the sauce and serve. Wholewheat pasta makes a good accompaniment to this dish.

Rösti with Scrambled Egg and Mushrooms

AN AUTUMN FEAST

Although it is often difficult to find fresh, the clavaria mushroom is a delicacy which is well worth the trouble to track down. The stalks must be trimmed and the mushrooms, with their almost undefined, club-like heads, scrupulously cleaned before use. Although they are also available dried, the flavour is not nearly as good.

For the rösti
800 g firm potatoes
salt; freshly ground pepper; 80 g butter

For the mushrooms
300 g clavaria mushrooms; 30 g butter
40 g white onion, chopped; 1/2 clove garlic, chopped
salt; freshly ground pepper; 1 tbsp snipped chives

For the scrambled egg
8 eggs; salt; freshly ground pepper; 20 g butter

In addition
1 tbsp snipped chives; coarsely ground pepper

A thin and crispy potato rösti makes the best base for this delicious scrambled egg and mushroom dish.

To make the perfect Swiss rösti it is essential to use the right sort of potatoes and to grate them to the right size. The rösti should be cooked in a heavy, iron pan.

SWITZERLAND

1. Peel the potatoes and grate them into thin strips, using a vegetable grater. Pat the strips dry and season with salt and pepper. Melt 20 g butter in a pan 15 cm in diameter. Put in 1/4 of the grated potato and press lightly to form a traditional rösti pancake. Fry to a golden brown on each side. Repeat to make 4 rösti.

2. Trim and thoroughly wash the mushrooms, then cut them into pieces. Melt the butter in a pan and lightly soften the onion and the garlic. Add the mushrooms and sauté for 2-3 minutes. Season with salt and pepper and sprinkle with chives.

3. Beat the eggs in a bowl and season with salt and pepper. Melt the butter in a large pan and scramble the eggs, stirring continuously, to a creamy consistency.

4. Arrange a hot rösti on each plate, top with a portion of scrambled egg followed by a spoonful of mushrooms. Sprinkle with chives and coarsely ground pepper and serve immediately.

ITALY

Good quality truffle oil gives that additional flavour and aroma to the risotto which makes the dish irresistible.

Saffron Risotto with Summer Truffles

SUMMER TRUFFLES MAKE AN AFFORDABLE TRUFFLE RISOTTO

Summer truffles are grown in Spain, Italy, the former Yugoslavia and North Africa and are exported fresh to most other European countries. Reasonably priced, they make an acceptable substitute for the black truffle, although the flavour and aroma are not as strong. A little grated Pecorino Toscano cheese makes a delicious garnish for this dish.

50 g shallots; 30 g celery
80 g onion; 200 g summer truffles
80 g butter; 400 g vialone rice
150 ml white wine
1 - 1 1/2 litres vegetable stock
salt; freshly ground white pepper
1 pinch saffron powder
2 tsp truffle oil
1 tbsp chopped parsley

1. Peel the shallots, trim and string the celery and finely dice both. Peel and finely chop the onion. Wash the truffles thoroughly under cold, running water, removing any trace of sand or dirt. Do not peel the truffles unless the skin is so ingrained with dirt that this is unavoidable.

2. Melt 50 g butter in a medium sized saucepan and sweat the shallot and the celery. Add the rice in a stream and, stirring continuously, cook over a low heat until it turns transparent. Slake with the white wine and cook to reduce a little. Gradually add the stock, stirring continuously, then season with salt, pepper and saffron powder. Cook the risotto for 12-15 minutes, stirring from time to time. Just before the end of cooking time, stir in 1 tsp truffle oil.

3. Heat the remaining butter and the truffle oil in a separate pan and soften the chopped onion. Pat the truffles dry then shave them razor thin and add them to the pan. Sauté briefly, until they begin to curl. Season with salt and pepper.

4. The truffles may be mixed into the risotto or served separately, according to taste. Sprinkle with parsley and serve immediately.

Being fairly bland, risotto absorbs flavours well, but it is important to use good risotto rice. It is also essential to use a pan which is large enough to stir the risotto in, without spilling any of the contents.

Fennel Risotto

SERVED WITH A TANGY GORGONZOLA TOPPING, THIS IS A REAL TREAT FOR FENNEL LOVERS

Fennel is always in season in at least one part of Europe, whatever the time of year. In the far south it is grown as a winter vegetable, whilst in spring it is cultivated in southern Italy and Sicily. Wild fennel while still retaining its characteristic aniseed flavour, is not as strong as the cultivated variety. The bulb is smaller, more elongated in shape and has more spears and leaves. If you can find it in a specialist shop, it is better to use wild fennel in this recipe.

40 g shallots
500 g fennel
80 g butter
400 g arborio rice
salt; freshly ground white pepper
150 ml white wine, preferably Sauvignon
3/4 - 1 litre vegetable stock
120 g Gorgonzola cheese
1 tbsp fennel leaves, chopped

The consistency of a risotto can vary enormously according to the cooking time and the amount of liquid used.

It is possible to recognise really fresh fennel by the light, feathery quality of the leaves and the condition of any cut ends.

ITALY

1. Peel and finely chop the shallots. Wash the fennel and dry it well. Trim the spears and strip off the tough outer leaves from the fennel bulbs, then quarter them lengthways and slice into thin, even sized strips.

2. Melt the butter in a large pan and soften the strips of fennel and chopped shallot, until just transparent. Tip the rice in and, stirring continuously, cook until it too is transparent. Season lightly with salt and pepper and slake with the white wine.

3. Cook, uncovered, until the wine is reduced to half its original volume. Pour in a little stock and cook, uncovered, for 15-20 minutes, stirring from time to time to prevent the rice sticking. Add more stock as required during cooking – the risotto should be moist but not too wet. Season to taste.

4. Cut the Gorgonzola into 4 slices. Pile the fennel risotto onto preheated plates and top each with a slice of cheese. Sprinkle with chopped fennel leaves and serve.

ITALY

Red peppers, which are rich in vitamin C, can be grown in warm sheltered gardens or even on a south facing balcony in warmer areas of the country.

Risotto with Red Peppers

A DISH WHICH PROVIDES PLENTY OF VITAMINS, ROUGHAGE AND FATTY ACIDS

For the Italians, risotto is not a special treat but an everyday dish. It can be cooked in many ways and getting the consistency of a risotto right is mostly a matter of taste. How moist should it be? Should it be cooked with the lid on, in an open pot, or even in the oven? Each cook will have a different answer to each question. Here the quantity of white wine and vegetable stock can be varied according to taste.

For the risotto
80 g onion
50 g butter
400 g arborio rice
150 ml white wine
1 - 1 1/2 litres vegetable stock
1 tsp salt
freshly ground white pepper

For the peppers
600 g red peppers
50 g shallots; 2 tbsp oil
1/2 tsp salt
freshly ground white pepper
100 ml white wine
1 tbsp tomato purée
1 tsp red pepper paste
1 tbsp mixed herbs (basil, parsley, rosemary and thyme), chopped

In addition
40 g Pecorino Sardo cheese, freshly grated or shavings

1. To prepare the risotto, peel and finely chop the onion. Melt the butter in a large pan and fry the onion until just transparent. Add the rice and, stirring continuously, cook until the rice too is transparent.

2. Slake with the white wine and leave to cook, uncovered, until the liquid has been absorbed. Add half the vegetable stock and cook over a moderate heat, stirring from time to time until all the liquid has again been absorbed. Add the remaining stock and, still stirring from time to time, leave to cook through. This will take about 20 minutes. Season with salt and pepper.

3. To prepare the red peppers, roast them in a preheated oven at 220°C until the skins blister, then take them out, put them in a plastic bag and leave to sweat. Skin the peppers, working from top to bottom and pulling off the skin in strips. Halve and deseed the peppers, remove the fibres and cut the flesh into 1.5 cm long pieces. Peel and finely chop the shallots. Heat the oil in a pan and soften the shallots. Add the red peppers and, stirring continuously, sweat these too. Season with salt and pepper. Add the wine, stir in the tomato purée and the pepper paste and leave to simmer for 2-3 minutes. Sprinkle in the mixed herbs. Ladle portions of risotto into preheated bowls, top with a serving of red peppers and sprinkle with cheese shavings to serve.

The red peppers make a decorative contrast to the white rice.

Risotto with Spinach and Gorgonzola

A TRADITIONAL CLASSIC

It is absolutely essential to use fresh, young spinach for this recipe. High quality cold pressed olive oil and, of course, the best risotto rice, such as a vialone semifino, are also critical. Carnaroli superfino, another large grain rice, can also be used for this dish but it is important to retain a slight bite to the rice in order to create a contrast with the spinach and the cheese.

The Gorgonzola should be allowed to melt into the risotto before being gently stirred in. The risotto should not be so moist that the cheese gets lost in the broth.

Gabriele Ferron, who comes from the area around Verona, is a master chef who specialises in making great risottos. He belongs to the school of thought that prefers risottos to be fairly dry.

400 g spinach; 40 g onion
2 cloves garlic; 3 tbsp extra virgin olive oil
400 g vialone rice, nano semifino grade
1 litre vegetable stock
30 g Parmesan cheese, freshly grated
salt; freshly ground pepper
200 g strong Gorgonzola cheese

1. Wash and pick over the spinach, then blanch in boiling, salted water. Take out, drain well and squeeze out any remaining moisture. Chop the

ITALY

spinach finely. Peel and finely chop the onion and the garlic.

2. Heat the olive oil in a pan and soften the onion and the garlic until just transparent. Add the spinach and sweat briefly. Pour in the rice and, stirring continuously, cook until transparent. Add the vegetable stock, bring briefly to the boil, then turn down the heat and leave to cook for 15-20 minutes, stirring from time to time so that the rice does not stick to the pan.

3. Stir the grated Parmesan into the pan and season with salt and pepper. Cut the Gorgonzola into pieces and arrange these on top of the risotto. Cover and leave just long enough for the Gorgonzola to melt slightly, then half stir it into the risotto and serve.

ITALY

Fried Polenta and Mushroom Sandwiches

AN UPMARKET VERSION OF AN ORIGINAL PEASANT DISH

Corn-on-the-cob, which originates from South America, belongs to the family of grasses. It was first brought to Europe in the 16th century by Portuguese and Spanish explorers.

In 19th century Italy, cooked maize dishes were particularly popular and economical. Today they are mostly served as accompaniments or side dishes. *Polenta* (cooked ground maize) is the main ingredient in this recipe and it is accompanied by a deliciously tangy fresh tomato sauce. If fresh mushrooms are not in season, then dried can be used for the filling instead, but only 1/3 of the quantity should be used and they should be soaked beforehand.

For the polenta
3/4 litre milk; 1/2 tsp salt; freshly grated nutmeg
80 g butter; 150 g medium grain ground maize
1 tsp olive oil

For the filling
250 g mushrooms
50 g shallots
1 clove garlic; 20 g butter
1 tbsp chopped parsley; 1 tsp snipped thyme leaves
salt; freshly ground pepper
2 tbsp cream; 80 g Fontina cheese

For the coating
flour; 2 eggs, beaten; breadcrumbs

For the tomato sauce
600 g tomatoes; 60 g onion; 1 clove garlic
3 tbsp olive oil; 1 tbsp chopped herbs
salt; freshly ground pepper

In addition
125 ml sunflower oil

1. To prepare the *polenta*, bring the milk to the boil with the salt, nutmeg and butter. Take the pan off the heat and, using a balloon whisk, whisk in the maize. Cook over the lowest possible heat for 10 minutes, stirring continuously. Spread the *polenta*, 1 cm thick, over an oiled baking tray, and leave to cool.

2. Clean, trim and roughly chop the mushrooms. Peel and finely dice the shallots and peel and crush the garlic. Melt the butter in a pan and sweat the shallots and the garlic. Add the mushrooms and sauté, stirring from time to time, until the mixture is fairly dry. Sprinkle in the parsley and thyme and season with salt and pepper. Add the cream, bring briefly to the boil, then take off the heat. Cut the cheese into small pieces and stir it into the lightly cooled mixture.

3. Cut the cold *polenta* into eight similarly-sized rectangles. Spread half of these with mushroom filling and place the remaining pieces on top. Press lightly to sandwich together. Dip the *polenta* sandwiches into the flour, beaten egg and breadcrumbs in turn, coating them evenly.

4. To prepare the tomato sauce, scald, skin and deseed the tomatoes, then dice the flesh. Peel and finely dice the onion and the garlic. Heat the oil in a pan and soften the onion and the garlic, until just transparent. Add the diced tomato and the herbs. Season with salt and pepper, bring briefly to the boil, then set aside and keep hot.

5. Heat the sunflower oil in a pan and fry the *polenta* sandwiches slowly to a golden brown on each side. Arrange on individual plates with a portion of tomato sauce and serve. A fresh wild herb salad makes a good accompaniment.

Vegetable Maccaroni Cheese

BAKED UNDER A CHEESE TOPPING, THE VEGETABLES RETAIN ALL THEIR FLAVOUR AND AROMA

The flavour of this dish comes from *cima di rapa*, a variety of Italian cabbage grown in the Campagnia and Appulia. It is occasionally available here in autumn. The stalks and flower heads (which resemble broccoli) are used, as well as the leaves. *Cima di rapa* has a slightly bitter flavour which goes particularly well with onions, garlic and tomatoes.

80 g onion; 2 cloves garlic
40 g celery
3 tbsp olive oil
400 g cima di rapa; 250 ml vegetable stock
650 g tomatoes
salt; freshly ground pepper
300 g maccheroncini
For the sauce
10 g butter; 15 g flour; 250 ml milk
salt; freshly ground white pepper
freshly grated nutmeg
1 egg yolk; 50 ml cream
20 g Casena di Valtelina cheese, freshly grated
1 tbsp cream, whipped
In addition
butter for the oven dish
30 g Pecorino cheese, freshly grated
20 g butter, in small pieces
1 tsp chopped oregano
coarsely ground pepper

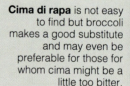

Cima di rapa is not easy to find but broccoli makes a good substitute and may even be preferable for those for whom cima might be a little too bitter.

1. Peel and finely chop the onion and the garlic. Trim, string and finely dice the celery. Heat the oil in a pan and sweat the onion, the garlic and the celery for 2 minutes.

2. Wash and trim the cima and cut the stalks into 6 cm long pieces. Cut the thicker stalks in half lengthways. Leave the young leaves and florets whole and cut up the larger leaves. Put the stalks in a pan, add the stock and leave to cook for 20 minutes. Meanwhile, scald, skin and quarter the tomatoes, then cut the quarters in half. Add the tomato wedges, the *cima* leaves and florets to the pan and boil for about 5 minutes. Season with salt and pepper.

3. Cook the maccheroncini in boiling, salted water al dente then strain and refresh in cold

water. Mix the vegetables and maccheroncini well together and turn out into a buttered oven dish.

4. To prepare the sauce, melt the butter in a pan, sprinkle in the flour and cook, stirring continuously for 1-2 minutes, without allowing it to discolour. Add the milk and stir to a smooth consistency, then season with salt, pepper and nutmeg. Stirring continuously, cook the sauce for 20 minutes. Beat the egg with the cream and stir this mix in to bind the sauce. Bring briefly to the boil, then strain the sauce through a sieve. Heat the sauce through, stir in the grated cheese and gently allow this to melt. Finally, fold in the whipped cream.

5. Pour the sauce over the pasta and vegetables, top with the Pecorino cheese and dot with pieces of butter. Bake in a preheated oven at 200°C for 20 minutes, then sprinkle with oregano and pepper to serve.

Mushroom Cannelloni

TASTY PASTA ROLLS WITH AN AROMATIC WILD MUSHROOM FILLING

This is a subtle recipe for autumn, when fresh mushrooms are readily available. The cannelloni portions may be ovenbaked in individual gratin dishes, or all together in one large oven dish.

For the pasta dough
70 g semolina; 70 g wheat flour
1 egg; 1 egg yolk; salt

For the filling
80 g onion; 1 clove garlic
300 g mixed mushrooms (chanterelles, ceps and morels)
100 g spinach; 40 g leek; 30 g butter; 100 ml cream
salt; freshly ground white pepper
1-2 small leeks

For the sauce
250 ml cream; 1 egg yolk
salt; freshly ground white pepper
1 tbsp freshly chopped parsley

In addition
4 individual gratin dishes; butter

Blanched leek leaves make a tasty wrapping for the cannelloni filling. They are laid out flat on the sheets of pasta, the filling is placed on one end and the cannelloni are then rolled up.

1. To prepare the pasta dough, mix the semolina and the flour together, add the egg, egg yolk and salt to taste and work to a smooth dough. Wrap the dough in clingfilm and leave to chill in the refrigerator for 1 hour.

2. Peel and finely chop the onion and the garlic. Clean, trim and finely dice the mushrooms. Wash and pick over the spinach. Clean and finely dice the leek.

3. Melt the butter in a pan and soften the onion and the garlic until just transparent. Add the mushrooms and sweat for a further 3 minutes. Add the spinach and the leek, sweating these until cooked through. Pour in the cream, season with salt and pepper and leave to cook for 3-4 minutes. Take the pan off the heat and leave the mushroom mixture to cool.

4. Clean the small leek (or leeks) and cut a 12 cm long section from the white part. Carefully pull off 8 strips (or leaves) and cook them in boiling salted water for 4 minutes. Take out, refresh under cold water and leave to drain well.

5. Thinly roll the pasta dough out on a floured work surface, then cut it into 8 rectangles, 9 cm by 14 cm in size. Cook the rectangles in boiling salted water for 2 minutes then remove and spread out on a damp tea towel. Lay a strip of leek on each rectangle, spread mushroom filling on top and roll up to form cannelloni.

6. To prepare the sauce, add the cream to a saucepan, bring to the boil and reduce to 1/3 its original volume. Beat the egg yolk in a small bowl, then stir in 1 tbsp of the hot cream. Add this mix to the rest of the cream in the pan and mix smoothly without allowing the sauce to come back to the boil. Season with salt and pepper and sprinkle with the chopped parsley.

7. Arrange 2 cannelloni on each individual gratin dish and coat with the sauce. Bake in a preheated oven at 200°C for 12 minutes, then pop under a hot grill for 1 minute to brown and serve.

ITALY

Wholewheat Tortelloni with Ricotta and Herbs

A FRUITY FRESH TOMATO SAUCE IS DELICIOUS WITH THE SPICY CHEESE FILLING

Ricotta, an Italian cream cheese, can be made from ewe or cow's milk. Traditionally, the runny whey was ladled into small raffia baskets but today plastic containers are used.

Pasta made from wholewheat flour is particularly tasty. However, the eggs need to be mixed with a small amount of water, as wholewheat flour absorbs liquid very quickly.

For the pasta dough
300 g wholewheat flour
3 eggs; 2 tbsp water

For the filling
400 g Ricotta cheese
1 egg; 1 egg yolk
100 g Pecorino Toscano cheese, freshly grated
3 tbsp chopped basil
2 tbsp chopped parsley
1/2 tsp snipped thyme leaves
1/2 tsp snipped oregano leaves
freshly grated nutmeg
salt; freshly ground pepper

For the sauce
500 g tomatoes; 1 tbsp olive oil
60 g shallot, finely chopped
1 clove garlic, finely chopped
1 tbsp tomato purée; 1 sprig thyme
1 bay leaf; salt; freshly ground pepper

In addition
1 egg white; 3 tbsp butter
100 g black olives
50 g Pecorino Toscano cheese shavings
1 tbsp chopped basil leaves

Work all of the pasta ingredients together to a smooth dough. Wrap in cling film and put in the refrigerator to chill for at least 1 hour. To prepare the filling, mix the Ricotta, the egg and the egg yolk together. Mix in the Pecorino cheese and all the herbs, then season with nutmeg, salt and pepper. Roll, cut and fill the dough, following the illustrated instructions, below. Set the tortelloni aside on a floured work surface and cover with cling film, until required. To prepare the sauce, scald, skin, halve and deseed the tomatoes. Heat the olive oil in a pan and soften the shallot and the garlic. Stir in the tomato and the tomato purée, add the thyme and the bay leaf and leave to simmer for 25 minutes. Discard the thyme and bay leaf and press the sauce through a fine sieve, then season with salt and pepper and set aside to keep hot. Bring a large pan of water to the boil and cook the tortelloni for about 8 minutes al dente. Strain and drain well. Melt the butter in a pan and briefly turn the pasta in this. Arrange the pasta on four plates, coat with the tomato sauce, garnish with olives and Pecorino shavings, then sprinkle with basil and serve.

Using a rolling pin or a pasta machine, roll the pasta dough out thinly, then cut it into circles 7 cm in diameter with a fluted pastry cutter.

Pipe the filling onto the centre of each pasta circle and brush the edges with egg white.

Fold the pasta over and press the edges firmly together to seal.

Egg Flan with Herbs and Mushrooms

A SMOOTH, LIGHT, NORTH ITALIAN SPECIALITY MADE WITH LOTS OF MILK AND CREAM

Adding mushrooms is a popular refinement to this Piedmontese recipe for egg flan. Normally the flan would be eaten as a starter, but when served with a green salad, it can make a delicious, light main course.

2 bay leaves; 1 sage leaf
1 small sprig rosemary; 2 stalks parsley
250 ml milk; 750 ml cream
20 g shallot; 1/2 clove garlic; 20 g butter
1 tbsp finely chopped mixed herbs (sage, rosemary, parsley, chives)
50 g Reggiano Parmesan cheese, freshly grated
6 egg yolks; 6 egg whites
1 pinch freshly grated nutmeg
salt; freshly ground white pepper

In addition
butter for the oven dish
400 g fresh mushrooms; 50 g butter
salt; freshly ground pepper
1 bunch plain leaf parsley, finely chopped

ITALY

Fresh mushrooms and herbs. Late summer and early autumn, when fresh, juicy mushrooms are in season, is the best time for making this Italian delicacy.

1. Tie the bay leaves, sage and rosemary into a bundle with the parsley stalks. Bring the milk and cream to the boil in a pan, add the herb bundle, turn down the heat as low as possible and cook until the liquid is reduced by half. Take out the herb bundle and leave the liquid to cool a little.

2. Peel and very finely chop the shallot and the garlic. Melt the butter in a small pan and lightly sweat the shallot and the garlic. Sprinkle in the mixed herbs and briefly sweat these as well.

3. Stir the herb and shallot mixture into the milk and cream. Add the grated Parmesan and the egg yolks and stir well. Beat the egg whites to a firm snow with the nutmeg and salt and pepper to taste, then fold this into the mixture. Butter a shallow, oblong oven dish, turn the mixture out into this and bake in a preheated oven at 200°C for 35-40 minutes until the top is lightly browned.

4. Meanwhile, carefully wipe the mushrooms clean but do not wash them unless it is essential. Trim and slice the stalks thinly and cut the caps into large pieces. Melt the butter in a pan and sauté the mushrooms for 4-5 minutes. Season the mushrooms with salt and pepper and sprinkle with chopped parsley. Arrange a portion of egg flan on preheated dishes, top with a spoonful of mushrooms and serve immediately.

ITALY

Pizza Verdura

THERE IS AN ENDLESS NUMBER OF POSSIBLE TOPPINGS FOR A VEGETARIAN PIZZA

Pizza was originally a vegetarian recipe made in Sicily. The traditional topping is simply tomato, cheese, garlic and oregano.

It is difficult to go wrong when making a topping for a pizza and this recipe should be used as a basic guide for making your own rather than as a fixed set of instructions.

For the pizza dough
(makes 2 oval pizzas 30 x 25 cm each)
300 g flour; 20 g yeast
125 ml water, lukewarm; 1/2 tsp salt; 2 tbsp olive oil

For the tomato sauce
250 g tomatoes; 1 peperoni
60 g onion; 1 clove garlic
2 tbsp olive oil; 1 tbsp tomato purée
salt; freshly ground white pepper
2 tbsp chopped mixed herbs (basil, parsley, rosemary and thyme)

For the vegetable topping
150 g onions; 1 clove garlic
80 g each red, yellow and green peppers
150 g aubergines; 150 g courgettes
300 g tinned tomatoes; 3-4 tbsp olive oil
salt; freshly ground pepper

In addition
50 g black olives; 200 g Mozzarella cheese, sliced
80 g Sardinian Ewe's milk cheese, roughly chopped
1 tbsp chopped mixed herbs (basil, oregano, sage and thyme)
salt; coarse ground black pepper
2 tbsp olive oil for brushing

For a good pizza the dough is as important as the topping and fresh yeast should be used to make it, whenever possible. Dried yeast can be used if fresh is not available but the taste and aroma will not be quite as good.

1. Sieve the flour into a bowl, make a well in the centre, crumble in the yeast and pour in the warm water. Sprinkle more flour over the top, then cover with a cloth and leave in a warm place to rise. Add the salt and the oil, work the mixture well together then knead to a smooth dough on a floured work surface. Leave to rise again until the dough has doubled in volume.

2. To prepare the sauce, scald, skin and deseed the tomatoes, then dice the flesh. Halve and deseed the peperoni, remove the fibres and finely chop the flesh. Peel and finely chop the onion and the garlic. Heat the oil in a pan and lightly soften the onion and the garlic. Add the diced tomato and simmer for 10 minutes. Stir in the tomato purée, season with salt and pepper, add the herbs and the peperoni and leave to simmer for a further 5 minutes.

3. To prepare the vegetable topping, peel and chop the onions into pieces. Peel and finely slice the garlic. Wash, halve and deseed the peppers, remove the fibres and cut the flesh into strips. Trim the aubergines and the courgettes, then dice the aubergines into 1.5 cm cubes and cut the courgettes into 2 mm thin slices. Quarter the tomatoes. Heat the oil in a pan and lightly soften the onion and the garlic. Add the diced aubergine and courgettes and sauté for 2-3 minutes. Stir in the peppers, season with salt and pepper and leave the mixture to cool.

4. Divide the pizza dough in half. Roll each half out into a flat oval then, with floured hands shape them to form thin bases. Using a fork, prick the pizza bases all over, then arrange them on baking trays, spread generously with the tomato sauce and spoon the vegetables on top. Arrange the olives and the Mozzarella slices on top of the vegetables, sprinkle with the chopped cheese, and mixed herbs and season with salt and pepper. Sprinkle the pizzas with olive oil, bake in a preheated oven at 220°C for 25 minutes, then serve immediately.

ITALY

A melon scoop is the perfect implement for hollowing out courgette halves, but a small sharp teaspoon will also do the job.

Polenta-stuffed Courgette

AN INEXPENSIVE AND FILLING MAIN COURSE WHICH IS TYPICALLY ITALIAN

Quick, healthy and delicious – and a dish which can be made in advance. Various ingredients can be changed, if necessary. For example, if Pecorino Toscano cheese is not available any Pecorino, other than a really strong Sardinian variety, can be used. Similarly, the polenta can be cooked with water instead of vegetable stock.

2 courgettes (about 350 g each)

For the filling
30 g dried mushrooms
50 g celery; 150 g carrots; 100 g spring onions
1 clove garlic; 2 tbsp olive oil
100 g medium grain ground maize
400 ml vegetable stock
1 tsp snipped thyme leaves
1/2 tsp chopped rosemary
salt; freshly ground white pepper

In addition
200 ml vegetable stock
50 g Pecorino Toscano cheese, freshly grated
20 g butter, in small pieces

Courgettes, filled with vegetables and polenta and baked to a golden brown, taste absolutely fabulous.

It is the ceps that give this dish its distinctive flavour. Given the shortness of the cep season it may only be possible to find them dried, but provided they are good quality and suitably soaked they are perfectly acceptable.

1. Wash and trim the courgettes, then halve them lengthways. Hollow out the halves using a melon scoop or teaspoon, leaving only a small amount of flesh around the inside. Dice the scooped-out courgette flesh.

2. Leave the mushrooms to soak in 100 ml of warm water for at least 15 minutes. Strain and reserve the liquid and chop the mushrooms. Clean, string and dice the celery. Peel and dice the carrots. Clean and trim the spring onions, then slice them into thin rings, keeping the green and white separate. Peel and finely chop the garlic.

ITALY

3. Heat the olive oil in a large pan and lightly soften the white spring onion, garlic, courgette, celery and carrot. Stir in the maize and fry lightly. Add the chopped mushroom, the reserved soaking liquid and the 400 ml vegetable stock. Bring briefly to the boil and leave to simmer over a very low heat for 15 minutes, stirring from time to time. Stir the thyme, rosemary and green spring onion into the polenta mixture, then season with salt and pepper.

4. Lightly salt the hollowed out courgettes, then fill them generously with polenta mixture. Pour the 200 ml vegetable stock into a casserole dish and sit the stuffed courgettes in this. Sprinkle with grated Pecorino Toscano cheese and dot with pieces of butter. Bake in a preheated oven at 200°C for 20-25 minutes until golden brown on top. Remove from the oven, arrange on preheated dishes and serve.

Fettucine with White Truffles

HOMEMADE PASTA AND RAZOR THIN SLICES OF TRUFFLE MAKE THIS DISH A LUXURIOUS TREAT

Served simply with a little freshly grated cheese and some melted butter, homemade fettucine is absolutely delicious. Add white truffles and it becomes an exquisite delicacy. Whilst the strong flavour is not always to everyone's taste, fresh truffles are worth trying at least once – preferably in early autumn, when they are at their very best.

The best way of shaving the white truffle over the pasta is to use a special truffle slicer. The cost of truffles is so high that it is important to get the quantities right – using not so much as to be excessively expensive but not so little that the flavour is lost. 15 g per person should be about right.

For the pasta dough
300 g fine ground wheatflour
2 eggs; 4 egg yolks
1/3 tsp salt; 1 tbsp water

Assessing the quality of fresh truffles is not easy. They should be firm, undamaged and, above all, fairly dry.

For the sauce
2 red chilli peppers; 250 ml cream; 1 tsp truffle oil
salt; freshly ground white pepper

In addition
60 g white truffles
1 tbsp snipped basil
Parmigiano Reggiano cheese, freshly grated

1. Heap the flour onto a work surface and make a well in the centre. Place the eggs, the egg yolks and the salt in the well and mix well with a fork, gradually drawing in the flour from the sides. If the mixture is too dry, add up to 1 tbsp water.

ITALY

Knead to a smooth dough, roll into a ball, then wrap in cling film and leave to stand in a cool place for 1 hour.

2. Thinly roll out the dough using a pasta machine or rolling pin, then cut it into fettucini strips 2 - 3 mm wide. Leave the strips to dry out a little.

3. Deseed the chilli peppers, remove the fibres and cut the flesh into thin strips. Heat the cream in a pan and reduce to half its original volume. Stir in the chilli strips and the truffle oil. Season with salt and pepper and keep warm.

4. Wash the truffles thoroughly under cold running water and wipe them dry immediately. The water must not be allowed to soak into the truffle. Remove any ingrained dirt or damage with the point of a sharp knife, taking care not to waste any of the truffle.

5. Cook the fettucine in boiling, salted water al dente, then strain and drain well. Arrange the pasta on preheated dishes, coat with the sauce and shave razor thin slices of truffle over the top. Sprinkle with basil and grated Parmesan cheese and serve immediately.

ITALY

Gnocchi in Fresh Tomato Sauce

THE FAMOUS ITALIAN POTATO NOODLES, COATED IN A FRUITY TOMATO SAUCE AND TOPPED WITH TANGY CHEESE

Gnocchi are a classic of Italian cuisine. As well as the traditional potato version given here, they can also be made with semolina. This recipe is a simple one which requires floury, rather than firm potatoes. They must be baked in the oven in their jackets – not boiled – as they need to be dry and crumbly to make a perfect light gnocchi dough.

For the gnocchi
900 g floury potatoes
150 g flour; 2 egg yolks; salt

For the tomato sauce
800 g fresh plum tomatoes
50 g carrot, finely diced
100 g onions; finely chopped
100 g celery, finely diced
salt
freshly ground black pepper
1 pinch sugar
4 tbsp olive oil
1 tbsp snipped red basil
1 tsp snipped thyme leaves

In addition
butter for the oven dish
40 g Pecorino Sardo cheese, freshly grated
30 g Parmesan cheese, freshly grated
20 g butter, in small pieces
red basil to garnish

Lightly flatten the rolls of dough and using a sharp knife cut into 1 cm pieces.

Roll the gnocchi, one at a time, over a grater to make a decorative pattern.

Wash and dry the potatoes, then wrap them in foil. Bake in a preheated oven at 200°C for 1 hour. Scald, skin and deseed the tomatoes, then finely dice the flesh. Add the tomato to a pan with the diced carrot, onion and celery and leave to simmer over a very low heat, covered, for about 40 minutes until the vegetables are cooked through. Using a spoon, press the vegetables through a coarse sieve into a pan. Halve the baked potatoes, scoop out the flesh and discard the skin. Pile the flour onto a work surface and make a well in the centre. Place the egg yolks and salt in the well and, using a potato press, press the hot potato over the flour. Drawing the flour and potato in gradually, work to a smooth dough. Leave the dough to stand for 10-15 minutes, then divide into 2 pieces and roll these, by hand, into 2 long rolls. Sprinkle with flour, then make the gnocchi following the illustrated instructions left. Bring a pan of salted water to the boil. Add the gnocchi, then turn down the heat and leave to cook until they rise to the surface. Take the gnocchi out and drain well. Heat the tomato sauce, season with salt and pepper and stir in the sugar. Add the olive oil, a spoonful at a time, and stir to a smooth consistency. Sprinkle in the basil and the thyme. Place the gnocchi in a buttered oven dish and cover with the sauce. Sprinkle with both kinds of grated cheese and dot with pieces of butter. Bake in a preheated oven at 200°C for 15-20 minutes. Garnish with red basil and serve.

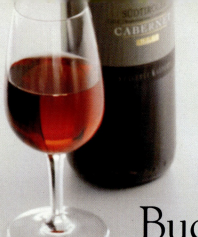

Buckwheat Dumplings

THESE VERY FILLING DUMPLINGS COME FROM THE SOUTHERN TYROL WHERE THEY ARE CALLED *SCHWARZPLENTENE KNÖDEL*

There are two distinct culinary styles in the southern Tyrol. The heavier, country style cuisine originated in the Alps, whereas the lighter, fresher style of cookery came from further south in Italy. This dish combines the two to great effect. Filling dumplings are served with a light Italian salad. For true authenticity, the dumplings should be made with *schüttelbrot* which can be bought, dried, from specialist shops.

For the dumplings
100 g rolls, fresh the previous day
80 g dried schüttelbrot
150 ml milk, lukewarm
20 g butter
1 clove garlic, finely chopped
60 g onion, finely chopped
50 g leek, cut into fine strips
2 tbsp chopped mixed herbs (parsley, chives and lovage)
freshly grated nutmeg
2 eggs; 60 g buckwheat flour
salt; freshly ground white pepper
180 g south Tyrolean cheese; about 90 g butter

For the tomato salad
600 g tomatoes; 3 tbsp oil
40 g shallots, finely chopped
100 g celery, cut into thin strips
2 tbsp red wine vinegar
salt; freshly ground pepper
1 tbsp chopped celery leaves

Tangy cheese from the south Tyrol adds taste and texture to the dumplings.

Buckwheat flour is quite different from ordinary wheat flour. The grain is three cornered and resembles beech nuts, which is probably where the name originates, as buck is another word for beech.

1. Thinly slice the rolls and finely crumble the *schüttelbrot*. Put both in a bowl, pour in the milk and leave to soak for at least 15 minutes. Melt the butter in a pan and lightly soften the garlic, onion and leek, then take out and add to the bowl of soaked bread. Add the mixed herbs, nutmeg, eggs

ITALY

and flour, season with salt and pepper and work to a firm dough. Cut the cheese into small pieces and work these into the dough as well. Make 12 small dumplings out of the dough mixture.

2. Bring a pan of salted water to the boil and add the dumplings. Turn down the heat immediately and leave the dumplings to cook for 12-15 minutes, without allowing the water to come to the boil again.

3. Blanch, skin and deseed the tomatoes, then dice the flesh. Heat the olive oil in a pan and lightly sweat the shallots. Add the celery and leave to sweat for 3 minutes. Add the tomato and simmer for a further 2 minutes. Add the vinegar, season with salt and pepper and sprinkle with the chopped celery leaves.

4. Using a draining spoon, remove the dumplings from the pan and drain well. Lightly brown some butter in a pan. Arrange the dumplings on preheated plates, spoon a generous amount of butter over and serve with the lukewarm salad.

Slovenia

Pearl Barley with Pumpkin

COOKED AS A RISOTTO, THIS IS A PARTICULARLY DISTINCTIVE VEGETARIAN DISH

Though more commonly found added to soups or stews, pearl barley can make a delicious and unusual main course. The amount of stock and wine are not set in stone and you can vary the quantities depending on how moist you like the barley to be.

800 g pumpkin
130 g onions
1 clove garlic
70 g butter
about 3/4 litre vegetable stock
300 g pearl barley
250 ml dry white wine, preferably Sauvignon
100 g Parmesan cheese, freshly grated
salt
freshly ground white pepper
vegetable stock as required
In addition
2 tbsp vegetable oil
16 small sage leaves
30 g Parmesan cheese, freshly shaved

1. Peel and deseed the pumpkin, then cut 1/3 of the flesh into 1.5 cm cubes and roughly chop the rest. Peel and finely chop the onions. Peel the garlic.

2. Melt 20 g of butter in a pan and soften 50 g of the onion. Add the roughly chopped pumpkin and leave to sweat briefly. Pour in 1/2 litre vegetable stock, cover and leave to cook for 10 minutes, then purée in a food processor and strain through a fine sieve.

3. Melt the remaining butter in a large pan and soften the remaining onion until just transparent. Using a garlic press, press the garlic over the onion and stir briefly. Add the pearl barley and allow it to sweat briefly, then pour in the wine. Cook until the liquid has been reduced to half its original volume. Stir in the pumpkin purée and, stirring continuously, simmer over a very low heat for 20 minutes. Add more vegetable stock from time to time, as required.

4. Mix in the diced pumpkin and leave to cook for a further 10 minutes. Stir in the grated Parmesan and season with salt and pepper.

5. Heat the oil in a pan and briefly sauté the sage leaves. Ladle portions of the pearl barley risotto into individual bowls, garnish with sage leaves and fresh Parmesan shavings and serve.

Crisply fried sage leaves and Parmesan cheese add the finishing touches to this pearl barley risotto.

CROATIA

Pumpkin Flowers with Red Pepper Sauce

A DECORATIVE AND ARTISTIC VEGETARIAN DISH

Pumpkin is a popular vegetable in the Balkans and there is a wide range of recipes for cooking it. The flowers make an unusual but attractive ingredient, although they are only available during the summer.

300 g courgettes; 40 g shallots
20 g butter; salt; freshly ground pepper
freshly grated nutmeg
25 ml white wine; 25 ml vegetable stock
1 egg yolk; 70 g fresh crustless white breadcrumbs
1 tbsp chopped young pumpkin leaves
12-16 pumpkin flowers

For the red pepper sauce
450 g red peppers; 1/2 clove garlic; 30 g shallots
20 g butter; salt; freshly ground pepper; 1 sprig thyme
1 bay leaf; 40 ml white wine; 200 ml vegetable stock

In addition
20 g butter for the oven dish; 20 g shallot, chopped
50 ml white wine; 80 ml vegetable stock

Pumpkin flowers have no flavour of their own and therefore make a suitably neutral case for a filling. They also make an elegant and decorative garnish.

1. Wash, trim and finely dice the courgettes. Peel and finely chop the shallots. Melt the butter in a pan and soften the shallots until just transparent. Add the courgette and sweat briefly. Season with salt, pepper and nutmeg. Add the white wine, reduce a little, then add the stock. Cook until the vegetables are cooked through and almost dry.

2. Using a food processor, purée the hot vegetables to a paste, together with the egg yolk, breadcrumbs and pumpkin leaves. Season to taste, then leave to cool.

3. Carefully open the tops of the pumpkin flowers and scrape out the centres with a spoon, without

CROATIA

separating or damaging the petals. Pipe the filling into the flowers. Twist the end of each flower together to close it.

4. Melt the butter in a flameproof oven dish and soften the shallot. Arrange the stuffed flowers on top and season with salt and pepper. Pour in the wine, reduce slightly, then add the vegetable stock. Cover the oven dish with foil, put in a preheated oven at 180°c and bake for 10 minutes.

5. To prepare the sauce, cut the red peppers into quarters. Deseed them, remove the fibres and dice the flesh. Peel and finely dice the garlic and shallots. Melt the butter in a pan and soften the shallots and garlic. Add the red pepper and sweat this, then season with salt and pepper and add the thyme and the bay leaf. Slake with the wine and the stock. Leave the sauce to simmer over a very low heat until the liquid has been reduced by half. Using a hand held mixer, purée the sauce, then put it through a fine sieve and season to taste. Arrange two stuffed pumpkin flowers on each plate, surround with a little sauce and serve. Long grain rice or plain risotto makes a good accompaniment to this dish.

Millet with Vegetables

TOMATOES, PAPRIKA AND PARMESAN CHEESE TASTE AS GOOD WITH MILLET AS THEY DO WITH PASTA OR RICE

Time consuming to prepare, this dish is still well worth the trouble it takes to make it.

For the millet
80 g white onion; 1 clove garlic
2 tbsp vegetable oil; 250 g millet
600 ml vegetable stock
salt; freshly ground pepper

For the vegetables
50 g white onion; 1 clove garlic
80 g spring onions; 600 g tomatoes
400 g mild red peppers; 2 tbsp vegetable oil
1 tbsp chopped basil
1 tbsp chopped red basil
salt; freshly ground pepper

In addition
40 g Parmesan cheese, freshly shaved

1. To prepare the millet, peel and finely dice the onion and the garlic, heat the oil in a pan and soften these until just transparent. Sprinkle in the millet and cook over a low heat for 2-3 minutes. Slake with the stock, then bring to the boil and season with salt and pepper. Turn down the heat and leave to simmer for 25-30 minutes, stirring from time to time.

2. Meanwhile, prepare the vegetables. Peel and finely chop the onion and the garlic. Clean and trim the spring onions and slice these diagonally into 1 cm long pieces. Scald, skin and deseed the tomatoes, then dice the flesh. Wash and deseed the peppers, remove the fibres and cut the flesh into 1 cm squares.

3. Heat the oil in a pan and and soften the onion and the garlic. Add the peppers and sweat for 5 minutes. Add the tomato, spring onion and both types of basil and leave to simmer for a further 3 minutes. Season with salt and pepper.

4. Arrange the millet in preheated bowls and top with the vegetables. Sprinkle with the fresh Parmesan shavings and serve immediately.

Two kinds of basil – red and green – give the vegetables a distinctive flavour in this unusual recipe.

Lahaniká Yahní

A VARIATION ON THE CLASSIC VEGETABLE STEWS WHICH ARE FOUND ALL ROUND THE SHORES OF THE MEDITERRANEAN

Stews are not always simple to make; preparation of the individual vegetables can require time and care, as in this recipe. Okra, in particular, needs to be carefully cooked as it tends to turn into a mush if over done. It has a fairly neutral flavour but may be an acquired taste for some.

20 g dried tomatoes
250 g okra
100 ml wine vinegar
salt
400 g aubergines
300 g onions
250 g Turkish peppers (dolmas)
1 Charleston peperoni (about 20 g)
250 g young courgettes
400 g fresh tomatoes
3 cloves garlic, peeled
5 tbsp vegetable oil
1/2 tsp sugar
100 ml Greek white wine (non-resinous)
100 ml vegetable stock
1/2 tsp snipped mountain thyme leaves
1/2 tsp chopped kreta marjoram or oregano
1 tbsp chopped parsley
1 bay leaf; 1 small cinnamon stick
4 cloves; freshly ground pepper
100 g Kalamata olives

In addition
150 g ewe's milk feta cheese, in large pieces
1 tbsp chopped parsley

Soak the dried tomatoes in 50 ml boiling water. Clean and prepare the okra following the illustrated instructions, below left. Add the wine vinegar to a casserole dish and season with salt, then add the okra and leave to stand in a warm place (ideally in the sun) for 2 hours. Rinse the okra thoroughly, leave to drain well, then cut in halves. Trim and chop the aubergine into 2 cm cubes and leave for 30 minutes to disgorge in strongly salted water. Peel and chop the onions. Deseed the peppers and the peperoni, remove the fibres and cut the peppers into 3 cm long pieces and the peperoni into thin rings. Halve the courgettes lengthways and cut into 1 cm thick slices. Scald, skin, halve and deseed the fresh tomatoes, then cut the flesh into bite-sized pieces. Slice the peeled garlic razor thin. Take the aubergine out of the salt water, drain well and pat dry. Strain the dried tomatoes and cut them into strips. Heat the oil in a flameproof casserole and sauté the onion until just transparent, then sprinkle with the sugar and leave to lightly caramelise. Add the aubergine and fry to a golden brown. Stir in the garlic and the remaining vegetables, except for the fresh and dried tomatoes, and sauté for 5 minutes, turning and stirring continuously. Add the wine and the stock followed by all the herbs and spices, season with pepper, then leave to simmer, covered, for 40 minutes. Add the tomatoes and the olives 5 minutes before the end of the cooking time. Sprinkle with feta cheese and parsley and serve.

Remove the fine hairs between the ridges of the okra by rubbing them gently with a damp tea towel.

Using a sharp knife, cut the stalks off the okra, being careful not to damage the pod.

GREECE

Moussaka with Tomatoes in Olive Oil

A VARIATION ON THE TRADITIONAL CASSEROLED MOUSSAKA – THIS ONE IS COOKED IN A TERRINE

Moussaka is often perceived to be a purely Greek dish, but variations on this recipe can also be found in various regions throughout the Balkans, as well as Turkey. Aubergines are, of course, the most important ingredient and most variations include onions, courgettes and tomatoes. This recipe for a vegetarian version cuts out the lamb mince, usually the other main ingredient in a moussaka, and is wrapped in strips of courgette. It is served sliced and may be eaten cold with a chunk of crusty bread or hot with a little rice.

500 g aubergines; 6 tbsp olive oil
salt; freshly ground black pepper
500 g courgettes; 500 g beef tomatoes
250 g floury potatoes
80 g shallots; 2 cloves garlic
1 tbsp chopped oregano; 1 tbsp chopped basil
30 g tomato purée; 100 g fresh goat's cheese

For the tomatoes in olive oil
500 g tomatoes; 7 tbsp olive oil; 2 tbsp lemon juice
salt; freshly ground pepper
1 tbsp coriander leaves, chopped

In addition
250 g courgettes to line the terrine dish
greaseproof paper

The lemon juice adds a piquant touch to the tomatoes whilst the goat's cheese is a perfect accompaniment to the vegetables in the moussaka.

1. Halve the aubergines lengthways and brush the cut sides with 1 tbsp of the olive oil, then season with salt and pepper. Place the aubergine halves on a baking tray and bake in a preheated oven at 190°C for 40 minutes. Take out, scoop out the cooked flesh, then finely dice it.

2. Trim and finely dice the courgettes. Scald, skin and deseed the beef tomatoes, then dice the flesh. Peel the potatoes and finely dice these too. Blanch the diced potato for 1 minute in boiling, salted water then strain and drain well. Peel and finely chop the shallots and the garlic.

3. Heat the remaining oil in a pan and sweat all the vegetables and the garlic. Add the herbs, stir in the tomato purée and simmer for 20 minutes, or until the juices have cooked away. Season with salt and pepper, then leave to cool a little. Finely grate the goat's cheese and fold into the mixture.

GREECE

4. To prepare the courgette strips for the lining trim the courgettes then slice them, lengthways, into 2 mm thin slices. Blanch the strips briefly in boiling water and drain them well. Line a 20 cm long and 7 cm deep terrine dish with lightly dampened greaseproof paper, then lay out the courgette strips to form a second lining arranging them so that they overlap, and leaving the ends to overhang the sides of the dish. Pack firmly with the vegetable mixture and fold the overhanging strips of courgette over the top. Put the terrine in a bain-marie and cook in a preheated oven at 160°C for about 40 minutes.

5. Take the terrine out and leave to cool a little. Meanwhile scald, skin and deseed the tomatoes for the accompaniment, then dice the flesh into about 1 cm cubes. Heat the olive oil in a pan, then take the pan off the heat, add the lemon juice, then mix in the diced tomato. Season with salt and pepper and sprinkle with the chopped coriander leaves.

6. Turn out the moussaka, cut it into slices and serve with a portion of tomatoes in olive oil.

Aubergine and Spicy Rice Rolls

KEFALOTIRI, THE FAMOUS GREEK CHEESE WHICH CAN BE MADE FROM EITHER GOAT OR EWE'S MILK, GIVES THIS DISH ITS UNIQUE FLAVOUR

The filling is the most important part of this recipe and, whenever possible, green Turkish dolma peppers should be used. The slim sivri peppers provide the hot, spicy note which is deliciously offset by the yoghurt sauce. If kefalotiri cheese is unavailable, pecorino can be used instead.

1 kg aubergines; 6 tbsp vegetable oil

For the filling
80 g long grain rice; 120 g onions; 1 clove garlic
200 g dolma peppers; 1 hot sivri pepper or peperoni
300 g plum tomatoes; 70 g kefalotiri cheese
2 tbsp vegetable oil; 1 tbsp chopped flat leaf parsley
salt; freshly ground pepper

For the yoghurt sauce
2 cloves garlic; 150 g Greek yoghurt
2 tbsp crème fraîche; salt; freshly ground pepper

In addition
butter for the oven dish; 50 g butter, chilled, in pieces
flat leaf parsley, chopped, to garnish

1. Wash and trim the aubergines, then slice them lengthways into 1 cm thin slices. Put the slices in a bowl, cover with salt water and set aside to disgorge.

2. To prepare the filling, cook the rice in plenty of boiling, salted water, for about 20 minutes, then strain and set it aside. Meanwhile, peel and finely chop the onions and the garlic. Halve and deseed the dolma and sivri peppers (or peperoni) and remove the fibres. Chop the dolma peppers into 5 mm cubes and finely dice the sivri pepper. Scald, skin, and deseed the tomatoes, then finely dice the flesh. Finely dice the cheese.

3. Heat 2 tbsp oil in a pan and lightly soften the onion and the garlic. Add both the peppers and sweat for a further 5 minutes. Stir in half of the chopped tomato, add the parsley, then take the pan off the heat. Leave the mix to cool a little, then stir in the cheese and the rice and season with salt and pepper.

4. Take the aubergine slices out of the salt water, drain and carefully pat them dry. Heat 6 tbsp oil in a non-stick pan and brown the aubergine slices evenly on each side. Take out and put a heaped tablespoonful of filling on one end of each slice. Roll up carefully and arrange in a shallow buttered oven dish. Spread the remaining chopped tomato over the top of the rolls, dot with pieces of chilled butter and pour in a cup of salt water. Cover and cook in a preheated oven at 180°C for 20-25 minutes.

5. Meanwhile, to prepare the yoghurt sauce, peel the garlic and, using a garlic press, press it over the yoghurt. Stir in the crème fraîche and season with salt and pepper. Take the aubergine rolls out of the oven, sprinkle with parsley and serve with the yoghurt sauce.

Greece boasts all kind of fresh goat and ewe's milk cheeses, ranging from hard to creamy.

Stuffed Eggs with White Bean Salad

THESE MAKE DELICIOUS STARTERS OR PARTY SNACKS

Turkish cuisine includes a wide range of dishes which mix eggs with beans and other pulses, and this one is particularly good. The beans have to be soaked overnight so it is essential to plan the recipe in advance. The finished bean salad needs to stand for 30 minutes before being served.

For the bean salad
300 g dried white haricot beans; salt; 250 g onions
20 g black olives, stoned
4 tbsp freshly chopped parsley; 6 tbsp olive oil
juice of 1/2 lemon; 3 tbsp white wine vinegar
1 tbsp water; salt; freshly ground black pepper
2 tsp hot paprika powder

Fill the hard boiled egg whites with the hard boiled yolk mixture, pressing it in firmly but leaving a small mound on top.

Dip the eggs in the flour and then, with the help of a spoon, in the egg yolk, coating all over.

Heat the vegetable oil to 180°C and, using a draining spoon, carefully deep fry the eggs for 3 minutes.

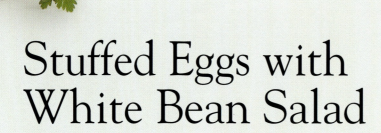

Fried in a crispy coating these stuffed eggs taste delicious with a tangy bean salad. Turkish pitta bread makes a good accompaniment.

For the eggs
8 eggs; 3 tbsp parsley, freshly chopped
80 g ewe's milk cheese (for example, feta)
salt; freshly ground black pepper
1 tsp mild paprika powder

In addition
2 egg yolks; 20 g flour
1/2 litre vegetable oil for frying

1. Soak the beans overnight in cold water, then strain and rinse well. Bring 1/2 litre of water to the boil in a saucepan with a pinch of salt. Add the beans, turn down the heat to medium and leave

TURKEY

to cook for 30-40 minutes, until cooked through but not too soft. Strain, drain and leave to cool.

2. Peel and thinly slice the onions, then sprinkle them generously with salt and leave to draw for 10 minutes. Carefully squeeze the salt and liquid from the onion slices, one by one, and put them into a salad bowl with the beans, olives and parsley. Mix well. In another bowl, stir the olive oil, lemon juice, white wine vinegar and water together, season with salt, pepper and paprika, then pour this dressing over the salad. Mix well and leave to stand for 30 minutes.

3. Hard boil the eggs for a good 10 minutes, then run them under the cold tap, shell and cut in half lengthways. Carefully scoop out the yolks, put them in a bowl with the parsley and the crumbled cheese, season with salt, pepper and paprika and mix well.

4. Beat the uncooked egg yolks in one bowl and put the flour in a second. Proceed, following the illustrated instructions opposite.

5. Drain the eggs well on kitchen paper and serve with a portion of bean salad.

TURKEY

Fresh goat and ewe's milk cheeses have been made in Turkey for over a thousand years. Their natural salt content helps them to keep for longer.

Warm Aubergine Salad

A LUXURIOUS MEDITERRANEAN SALAD WHICH MAKES A DELICIOUS LIGHT SUMMER MEAL

Aubergines are one of the most frequently used vegetables in classic Mediterranean cuisine. They can be served in a wide variety of elaborate ways, including puréed in a dip, or simply sliced, fried and served in a little olive oil. Aubergines are delicious hot or cold and sometimes, as here, are surprisingly good served warm. With such tangy ingredients as garlic, mint and feta cheese the flavour of the aubergine is really brought out.

250 g red peppers
400 g tomatoes
800 g aubergines
300 g courgettes
50 g white onion
2 cloves garlic
1-2 mild Charleston peperoni
6 tbsp olive oil; salt
freshly ground pepper
2 tsp mild paprika powder
1 tsp star aniseed, ground
juice of 1 lemon; 3 tbsp mint, chopped
200 g feta cheese

A perfect balance of flavours and textures, this freshly made, lightly cooked salad must be served immediately.

1. Roast the red peppers in a preheated oven at 200°C until the skins blister, then take out, put in a plastic bag and leave to sweat for 10 minutes. Skin the peppers, working from top to bottom, then halve and deseed them, remove the fibres and cut the flesh into thin strips.

2. Scald, skin and deseed the tomatoes, then finely dice the flesh. Wash and trim the aubergines and the courgettes and cut both into 1 cm cubes. Peel and finely chop the onion and the garlic. Deseed the peperoni and slice it thinly into rings.

3. Heat the olive oil in a large pan and fry the aubergine for 5 minutes, stirring continuously. Add the courgette and fry for 3 minutes, then add the onion and the garlic and fry for 1 minute more. Season with salt and pepper, stir in the paprika and the star aniseed, sprinkle the peperoni on top and stir in the lemon juice.

4. Add the peppers and the tomato to the pan and sweat these briefly. Quickly stir in the mint, season with salt and pepper to taste and crumble the feta cheese over the salad. Serve with hot pitta bread.

TURKEY

Cracked Wheat with Mushrooms

FRESH BOLETUS MUSHROOMS AND DRIED CEPS COMBINE TO MAKE A TASTY BUT UNCOMPLICATED DISH

In Turkey, risotto type dishes are often made with *bulgur*, a specially treated whole grain wheat. The wheat is cooked, then dried and cracked before being sold. It is then cooked in twice its volume of boiling water. Cracked wheat is rich in protein and therefore a good choice for vegetarian dishes. Served, as here, with choice mushrooms and fresh parsley, it is also delicious.

10 g dried ceps; 900 ml vegetable stock
80 g onion; 1 clove garlic
50 g carrots; 30 g root parsley
50 g leek; 30 g butter
250 g cracked wheat, ready to cook
salt; freshly ground black pepper
1 tbsp parsley, chopped
For the mushrooms
400 g boletus mushrooms
30 g butter
salt; freshly ground black pepper
1 tbsp chopped parsley

1. Soak the dried ceps in 100 ml of the vegetable stock for 10 minutes. Strain and reserve both ceps and stock. Finely chop the ceps. Peel and finely dice the onion, garlic, carrots and root parsley. Trim, wash and finely dice the leek.

2. Melt the butter in a medium sized pan and soften the onion and the garlic over a low heat. Add the ceps, carrot, root parsley and leek and sweat briefly.

3. Add the cracked wheat to the pan and fry for about 3 minutes, then pour in the stock, including the 100 ml used to soak the ceps. Season with salt and pepper. Bring briefly to the boil, then turn down the heat, cover and cook for about 20 minutes, stirring from time to time, until the wheat is cooked and the liquid absorbed. Sprinkle in the parsley and season again to taste.

4. Wipe the boletus mushrooms clean, then either halve or quarter them, according to size. Melt the butter in a pan and sauté the mushrooms for 3-4 minutes, then season with salt and pepper and sprinkle with parsley. Serve the cracked wheat in bowls, spoon a serving of mushrooms on top, and serve immediately.

To add a tang to this dish, stir a little grated cheese (about 40 g) into the wheat before serving.

MOROCCO

Fresh vegetables and herbs are always available in the Medina, from the strongest garlic to the lightest variety of tomatoes.

Spicy Vegetables

SERVED WITH COUSCOUS OR HOT PITTA BREAD THIS MAKES A GREAT SAVOURY MEAL

Good quality olive oil, fresh vegetables and the right spices all add up to a very tasty dish. This is a typical example of everyday eating in Moroccan cuisine, in which vegetables always play a large part. The assortment of vegetables is interesting, including as it does different kinds of peppers, tomatoes and potatoes which all originated in America rather than Africa.

250 g dolma peppers
150 g mild red chilli peppers
150 g onions
400 g tomatoes
300 g aubergines
300 g courgettes
2 cloves garlic
6 tbsp olive oil
2 tsp mild paprika powder
1/2 tsp chilli powder
salt; freshly ground black pepper
1 tsp lemon juice
1 tbsp chopped parsley
1 tbsp chopped mint

1. Roast the dolma and chilli peppers in a preheated oven at 200°C until the skins blister, then take out, put in a plastic bag and leave to sweat for 10 minutes. Skin the peppers, working

The mild red chilli pepper still has a strong flavour but it is milder than most other chillies. In North Africa it is known as the *felfel*.

MOROCCO

from top to bottom, then halve and deseed them, remove the fibres and cut the flesh into roughly 1 cm squares.

2. Peel and roughly chop the onions. Scald, skin and deseed the tomatoes, then dice the flesh. Trim the aubergines and the courgettes and dice both into roughly 1 cm cubes. Peel and finely chop the garlic.

3. Heat the olive oil in a pan and briefly sauté the aubergine and the courgette. Add the garlic, paprika and chilli powder and season with salt and pepper. Leave to simmer for 5 minutes.

4. Add the peppers and the onion to the pan and cook over a low heat for 3 minutes. Fold in the tomato and simmer for 1 minute more. Stir in the lemon juice, sprinkle with parsley and mint, season to taste and serve.

MOROCCO

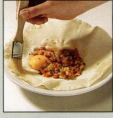

Briks

A CRISPY PASTRY ENVELOPE SEALS IN A SPICY VEGETABLE AND EGG FILLING

In Morocco the wrapping is made of sheets of flaky *warkha* pastry. This is baked on a charcoal grill and is wonderfully crispy. It can be found over here in a few specialist shops but filo pastry or Turkish *yufka* would make an acceptable substitute for this recipe.

16 sheets warkha or filo pastry, 22 cm in diameter
2 egg whites
For the filling
350 g mild red chilli peppers
250 g light green courgettes
1 green peperoni
120 g white onions; 2 cloves garlic
2 tbsp olive oil; salt; freshly ground pepper
1/4 tsp ground star aniseed
1 tsp mild paprika powder
1 tbsp chopped parsley
1 tbsp chopped coriander leaves; 8 eggs
In addition
oil for frying

Lay 2 sheets of pastry, one on top of the other, on a plate. Spoon 1/8 of the vegetable mixture into the middle and break 1 egg carefully on top. Brush the edges of the pastry with egg white and fold the pastry in half to cover the filling. Brush the edges with egg white and fold in half once more.

Lightly sautéed vegetables are cooked until dry and the egg carefully slid onto them so that no moisture can spoil the crispness of the cooked pastry.

MOROCCO

1. Halve and deseed the chilli peppers, trim the courgettes and very finely dice both of them. Deseed the peperoni, remove the fibres and finely chop the flesh.

2. Peel and finely chop the onions and the garlic. Heat the oil in a pan and sauté the onion and the garlic until just transparent. Add the peppers, courgette and peperoni and simmer until the juices have cooked away. Season with salt and pepper, stir in the star aniseed, paprika, parsley and coriander leaves and leave to cool.

3. Fill and wrap the pastry envelopes following the illustrated instructions opposite. Heat the oil to 180°C in a frying pan and fry the pastries for about 2 minutes on each side, until golden brown. Take out with a draining spoon and leave to drain on kitchen paper.

4. The following makes a delicious dressing for the *briks*: finely chop 100 g stoned green olives with 30 g white onion, add to a bowl and stir in 4 tbsp olive oil, 2 tbsp white wine vinegar, salt, freshly ground black pepper, a squeeze of lemon juice, 1 tbsp chopped parsley and 1 tbsp chopped coriander leaves.

Pepper Jelly is more spicy than sweet. It makes a delicious relish and will keep for a long time in sealed preserve jars.

Pan-fried Pepper Bread

SERVED WITH A SWEET AND SPICY JELLY WHICH ORIGINALLY CAME FROM THE SOUTHERN STATES OF THE USA

Modern Israeli cookery is truly international, having, unsurprisingly, been shaped by a multitude of different influences. However, in the last 40 years there has been a conscious effort to protect traditional Israeli cuisine, which is known as 'sabre' cookery after the cactus plant that is the symbol of native-born Israelis.

For the pepper jelly
500 g cooking apples
zest of 1/2 untreated lemon, grated
900 g sugar; 125 ml apple vinegar
75 g each red and green chilli peppers, deseeded and finely chopped
50 g onion, diced

For the pepper bread
500 g red peppers; 10 tbsp olive oil
50 g onion, finely chopped
salt; freshly ground white pepper
8 slices thick cut wholemeal bread
150 ml milk; 2 eggs
1/2 tsp mild paprika powder
1 tbsp chopped mixed herbs (parsley and thyme)
2 sprigs thyme

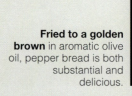

Fried to a golden brown in aromatic olive oil, pepper bread is both substantial and delicious.

1. To prepare the pepper jelly, wash and quarter the apples. Bring 250 ml water, the lemon zest and 300 g sugar to the boil in a pan and add the apples. Turn down the heat, cover and leave to cook for 45 minutes. Strain the cooked apple through a muslin lined sieve, without pressing any of the fruit through. Bring the vinegar, chilli peppers, onion and remaining sugar to the boil in a pan, stirring well to prevent sticking. Add the apple juice, return briefly to the boil, turn down the heat and leave to cook, uncovered, for 5-10 minutes. Test to see if the jelly has reached the right consistency to set. Take the pan off the heat, turn the jelly out into jars and leave to cool, covered, stirring from time to time to stop the chilli pieces falling to the bottom.

2. Roast the peppers in a preheated oven at 220°C until the skins blister, then take out, put in a plastic bag and leave to sweat for 10 minutes. Skin the peppers, working from top to bottom, then

ISRAEL

halve and deseed them, remove the fibres and finely dice the flesh.

3. Heat 2 tbsp of the oil and lightly soften the onion. Stir in the diced peppers, season with salt and pepper and leave to sweat for 10 minutes.

4. Cut the crusts off the bread. Put the milk in a bowl and soak the slices of bread for 1 minute, then lay them on a work surface. Spread half the slices with the filling, leaving the edge clear all round. Cover with the other halves, pressing the edges together lightly to seal the sandwiches.

5. Beat the eggs in a bowl with the paprika and herbs. Heat the remaining oil in a pan and add the sprigs of thyme. Dip the pepper sandwiches in the egg, coating them all over, then fry in the hot oil for 3 minutes on each side. Serve with the pepper jelly.

Falafels

A SPICY SNACK, USUALLY EATEN WITH THE FINGERS, WHICH IS VERY POPULAR IN ISRAEL

Chickpeas are rich in protein and are everyday eating in the Middle East and the Mediterranean.

These delicious chickpea snacks are made all over the Middle East. In Israel, they can be bought from every food stall. Served with a yoghurt sauce and a salad, the following recipe can also be used as a main course.

For the falafels
300 g dried chickpeas
80 g onion
2 cloves garlic
1/2 tsp ground star aniseed
1/2 tsp ground coriander seeds
1/4 tsp chilli powder
salt; freshly ground black pepper
1 tsp lemon juice
2 tbsp chopped parsley
1 egg

For the sauce
250 g thick, plain yoghurt
150 g cucumber
salt; freshly ground black pepper
1/4 tsp ground caraway seeds
1 pinch paprika
1 pinch sugar
1 tsp chopped coriander leaves

In addition
vegetable oil for deep frying

Deliciously refreshing on a hot day, yoghurt and cucumber sauce goes perfectly with falafels.

1. Soak the chickpeas overnight in a bowl with enough water to cover. Strain through a sieve and wash thoroughly. Bring them to the boil in a pan with 1 1/2 litres water. Turn the heat down slightly, cover and leave to cook for 50-55 minutes, until cooked through. Strain the

Crispy falafels are delicious cold or hot.

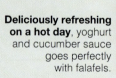

ISRAEL

chickpeas, reserving 80 ml of the cooking liquid, and drain well.

2. Peel and finely chop the onion. Put it in a food processor, together with the chickpeas and the reserved 80 ml liquid, and purée to a paste. Peel and finely chop the garlic and add it to the chickpea mixture, together with the spices, sesoning, lemon juice, parsley and egg and work to a smooth dough. Working with dampened hands, form the mixture into 24 balls, each weighing about 30 g.

3. Using a chip pan or deep fat fryer, heat the oil to 180°C and fry the *falafels* for 3-4 minutes until crispy on the outside. Take out with a draining spoon and leave to drain on kitchen paper.

4. To prepare the sauce, whisk the yoghurt smoothly in a bowl. Peel and very finely dice the cucumber and fold this into the yoghurt. Season with salt and pepper and sprinkle in the caraway seeds, paprika, sugar and coriander leaves. Serve the *falafels* with the sauce and a green salad.

IRAN

Asafoetida, the dried and crushed resin of an oriental plant, is sold as a spice powder in India and the Middle East. Its rather bitter taste and powerful garlic-like smell led the Germans to call it *Teufelsdreck* or 'devil's dung'.

Vegetable Patties with Lentils

EXOTIC SPICES GIVE THESE LITTLE VEGETABLE CAKES A TYPICALLY MIDDLE EASTERN FLAVOUR

Vegetarian cookery has always been popular in the Middle East, mainly due to religious influences. Pulses, which are good at providing the protein that meat usually adds to the diet, are widely used.

For the patties
1 kg firm cooking potatoes
250 g red peppers; 100 g carrots
150 g onions; 3 green chilli peppers
300 g fresh peas (about 150 g shelled)
3 tbsp vegetable oil; salt; 1 tsp garam masala
1/4 tsp asafoetida; 1 tbsp lemon juice

For the lentils
300 g red lentils (masoor dal)
15 g fresh ginger; 100 g onions
2 tbsp vegetable oil; 1/2 tsp black mustard seeds
1/2 tsp ground turmeric; 1/2 tsp garam masala
1/4 tsp sugar; 1 tbsp lemon juice; salt

In addition
100 g breadcrumbs; vegetable oil for frying

1. Wash the potatoes and bring them to the boil in a pan with enough water to cover, then turn down the heat and leave to cook for 20 minutes. Drain and lightly wipe the potatoes dry, then peel and mash them.

2. Wash, halve and deseed the peppers, then remove the fibres and finely dice the flesh. Peel and finely dice the carrots and the onions. Deseed the chilli peppers, remove the fibres and finely dice the flesh. Shell the peas, blanch them in boiling water, then refresh under cold running water and leave to drain well.

3. Heat the oil in a pan and fry the onion to a golden brown. Add the red pepper and carrot and fry for 5 minutes. Next, add the chilli pepper, peas and potato and mix well together. Season with salt, add the *garam masala* and asafoetida, sprinkle in the lemon juice and continue to cook for a further 5 minutes, then set aside to cool.

4. Rinse the lentils and add them to a pan with 600 ml of water. Bring to the boil and cook for 15-20 minutes. Peel and finely chop the ginger and the onions. Strain the lentils, reserving 100 ml of the cooking liquid. Heat the oil in a pan and fry the ginger and the onion to a golden brown. Add the spices, sugar and lemon juice, season with salt and sauté briefly. Stir in the lentils and the reserved liquid, then mix everything together and keep hot.

5. Make 12 patties from the vegetable mixture. Turn these in the breadcrumbs, coating them evenly all over. Heat the oil in a pan and fry the patties for about 4 minutes on each side, until golden brown. Arrange on plates and serve with a portion of lentils.

Fried Cauliflower

THE PERFECT STARTER FOR AN INDIAN OR FAR EASTERN MEAL

Vegetables coated in a tasty batter and deep fried are common to many Eastern cuisines. They may be served with a spicy sauce or, as here, with a refreshing yoghurt dip. They are delicious as a party snack or as part of a vegetarian meal. Served with hot bread or rice they can also be eaten as a light meal.

1 cauliflower (about 1.5 kg)
juice of 1/2 lime
salt
For the batter
150 g buckwheat flour
50 g flour
1 tsp salt
2 tsp curry powder
1 tsp turmeric
15 g ginger, freshly ground
250 ml water
1 egg yolk
For the yoghurt sauce
50 g spring onions
2 red chilli peppers
200 g yoghurt (3.5% fat content)
50 g crème fraîche
1 clove garlic, finely chopped; salt
1 tbsp chopped
1 tbsp chopped coriander leaves
1 tbsp lime juice
In addition
1/2 litre oil for frying

Wash the cauliflower, cut out the stalk and break up the head into medium sized florets. This should leave you with about 800 g of cauliflower. Bring a pan of water to the boil with the lime juice and salt to taste. Add the cauliflower and blanch for 5 minutes, then take it out with a draining spoon, refresh under cold running water and leave to drain. To prepare the batter, mix both kinds of flour and the salt and spices in a bowl. Add the water and the egg yolk and mix to a smooth consistency. Cover and leave to stand for 30 minutes. To prepare the yoghurt sauce, wash, trim and thinly slice the spring onions into rings. Halve and deseed the chilli peppers, remove the fibres and finely chop the flesh. Stir the yoghurt and the crème fraîche smoothly together in a bowl, add the spring onions, chilli peppers and chopped garlic. Season with salt, add the parsley, coriander and lime juice and stir well. Heat the oil in a wok or frying pan to 180°C and fry the cauliflower, following the illustrated instructions, below. Serve immediately with the yoghurt sauce.

Spear the cauliflower florets with a fork and dip them into the batter, coating them evenly all over.

Fry the florets in hot oil, suspended in a wire basket or ladle, for 2-3 minutes, until golden brown. Take out and leave to drain.

INDIA

Okra and Mixed Vegetable Curry

A SUBTLE AND DELICIOUSLY FLAVOURED CURRY

Okra, which originally came from Ethiopia, is now grown in nearly all the sub-tropical areas of the world. Like the hibiscus, okra belongs to the genus *malvaceae* and, with its unique, though fairly bland flavour, it makes an excellent vegetable for a mixed stew or curry.

20 g tamarind seeds; 300 g firm potatoes
200 g large carrots; 350 g okra
6 green chilli peppers
250 g aubergines; 250 g yams; 4 tbsp vegetable oil
1 tsp fenugreek seeds
1 tsp star aniseed
20 g fresh ginger, peeled and chopped
12 fresh curry leaves
1/4 tsp asafoetida (see page 136)
60 g chickpea flour
1/2 tsp chilli powder; 1 tsp ground turmeric
1 tsp sugar; 1 tsp chopped mint; salt

In addition
1 tsp chopped coriander leaves

The various kinds of vegetables are added to the curry in stages according to the amount of cooking time they need. This way the curry does not turn into a mushy stew.

1. Soak the tamarind seeds in 125 ml water for 20 minutes, then strain them through a sieve, discard the seeds and reserve the water.

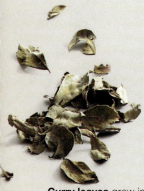

Curry leaves grow in India and Sri-Lanka and are rarely available fresh in this country. They can be bought dried, in which case twice the quantity given should be used.

2. Peel the potatoes and cut them into 2 cm cubes. Peel the carrots and cut them into pieces 2 cm by 4 cm. Wash the okra and trim off the stalks with a sharp pointed knife, without damaging the pods. Deseed 2 of the chilli peppers, remove the fibres and finely chop the flesh. Trim the aubergines and cut them into 2 cm cubes. Peel the yams and cut them into 1.5 cm cubes.

3. Heat the oil in a large, flameproof casserole. Add the fenugreek

INDIA

seeds and the star aniseed and sauté briefly over a moderate heat. Add the ginger, chopped chilli peppers and curry leaves and sauté for 1 minute further. Stir in the asafoetida and the chickpea flour and, stirring continuously, cook for 4-5 minutes. Stir in the chilli powder and the turmeric and, still stirring, sweat these for 2-3 minutes. Gradually add 1.2 litres of water, stirring this in carefully. Leave to cook for another 10 minutes.

4. Add the yams and cook for 5 minutes, then add the potatoes and cook for another 10 minutes. Next add the carrot and the aubergine and cook for 5 minutes. Finally, add the okra and leave the vegetable curry to stew for a further 10 minutes.

5. Add the remaining chilli peppers, sugar, reserved tamarind water and chopped mint, season with salt to taste, stir well, heat through and serve.

INDIA

Kath Katha

AN INDIAN DISH MADE WITH PLENTY OF FRESH VEGETABLES, CHOICE HERBS AND THE BEST SPICES

No curry is complete without the hand-pulled Indian bread known as *nan*.

Spices play an enormous role in Indian cuisine and the various spice mixtures that are blended together are known as *masalas*. The spices in this recipe are critical and for the best results the spice mixture should be cooked for a while before the vegetables are added. This way they really absorb the full flavour.

For the curry paste
80 g onion; 6 dried red chilli peppers
2 tbsp vegetable oil; 80 g freshly grated coconut
2 tbsp coriander seeds; 4 cloves
10 white peppercorns; 1 stick cinnamon

For the vegetables
100 g onions; 1 clove garlic
2 tbsp vegetable oil
1/2 tsp brown mustard seeds; 1/2 tsp star aniseed
1/2 tsp ground turmeric; 1 bay leaf
1 nutmeg flower; salt
200 g carrots; 300 g sweet potatoes
300 g firm potatoes
250 g green beans
300 g fresh peas (about 150 g shelled)

In addition
250 g brown Basmati rice; salt
chopped coriander leaves

1. To prepare the curry paste, peel and thinly slice the onion into rings. Trim the stalks from the chilli peppers and scoop out the seeds through the hole. Heat 1 tbsp oil in a non-stick pan, add the coconut and, stirring continuously, fry this for 5 minutes, then remove the coconut and reserve it. Add the remaining oil, heat it, then add the chilli peppers and the coriander seeds. After 3 minutes add the cloves, the peppercorns and the cinnamon and, stirring continuously, fry for 2-3 minutes. Put the coconut back into the pan and mix everything together. Finally, add the onion rings and 125 ml water. Turn the mixture out and, using a pestle and mortar or a food processor, grind to a paste.

2. To prepare the vegetables, peel and finely chop the onions and the garlic. Heat 2 tbsp of oil in a large flameproof casserole and briefly fry the mustard seeds, the star aniseed and the turmeric in this for 1 minute, then add the bay leaf, garlic and onions and leave to simmer over the lowest possible heat for 10 minutes. Stir in the curry paste, add the nutmeg flower and leave to simmer for a further 10 minutes. Add 3/4 litre of water, season with salt, bring briefly to the boil, stir well, cover and leave to simmer over a very low heat.

3. Meanwhile, peel the carrots, sweet potatoes and potatoes and dice all three into 1.5 cm cubes. Wash and trim the beans, then cut these into 3 cm long pieces. Shell the peas.

4. Rinse the rice in a sieve, under cold, running water and leave to drain. Bring the rice to the boil in a pan with 1/2 litre of water. Turn down the heat, season with salt, cover and leave to cook for about 15 minutes, until the rice has absorbed all the liquid.

5. Add the carrots to the casserole dish and cook for 5 minutes. Next add both kinds of potato and cook for 10 minutes, then, finally, add the beans and peas and cook for a further 3 minutes. Sprinkle with coriander leaves and serve with the Basmati rice.

Mango and Banana Curry

SPICED FRUIT IS COMMONLY USED IN INDIAN COOKERY AND ESPECIALLY IN HOT CURRIES

One of the most distinctive features of Indian cuisine is the way in which it stops at nothing when it comes to mixing ingredients. This especially applies to spices and while, in true Indian cookery, home ground mixes would be used, there are many excellent ready ground curry powders and *masalas* available from supermarkets and specialist shops. These are specially prepared for different types of curry and some will be suitable for fish or shellfish, others for meat, others for poultry and some, of course, for vegetables. However, these may lack the extra spiciness and flavour achieved by using fresh ingredients or homemade mixes.

100 g onions; 1 clove garlic
10 coriander seeds; 2 red chilli peppers
3 tbsp vegetable oil; 5 g ground turmeric
6 fresh or 12 dried curry leaves
400 ml coconut milk; 200 ml vegetable stock
2 green mangoes (about 800 g)
500 g green bananas
150 g green peppers
salt; freshly ground white pepper

Peel the mangoes very thinly. This is best done with a vegetable peeler. Then take a thick slice of fruit off the back and again off the front of the stone, and finally cut the remaining fruit from the stone.

INDIA

In addition
50 g coconut, freshly grated

1. Peel and finely chop the onions and the garlic. Grind the coriander seeds with a pestle and mortar. Halve and deseed the chilli peppers and remove the fibres. Heat the oil in a pan and lightly soften the onion and garlic. Add the coriander, turmeric, curry leaves and chilli peppers and sauté for 1-2 minutes. Pour in the coconut milk and vegetable stock, turn down the heat and leave to simmer for 15 minutes.

2. Prepare the green mangoes, following the illustrated instructions, opposite. Dice the mango flesh into 2 cm cubes. Peel and slice the bananas, diagonally, into 1.5 cm thick slices. Halve and deseed the green peppers, remove the fibres and dice the flesh into 1 cm cubes. Add the peppers to the curry and leave to cook for 3 minutes, then finally add the mango and the banana and cook for a further 5 minutes. Season with salt and pepper. Sprinkle the grated coconut over the curry and serve. If desired the coconut may be dry fried to a golden brown first.

The best kind of bananas for a curry are the small, rounder bananas, sometimes known as apple bananas. Under no circumstances should plantain bananas be used for this recipe – ordinary everyday fruit bananas are fine, providing they are still fairly green. However, neither the bananas nor the mangoes should be too hard and unripe.

Cauliflower Curry

A SIMPLE BUT EXCITING CURRY FROM SOUTHERN INDIA, BEST SERVED WITH EITHER RICE OR BAGEES

Panch foron is the Indian 5 spice mixture which is used in many basic curry mixes. The ingredients include mustard seeds, fennel seeds, star aniseed and onions and it can be bought ready mixed in Asian supermarkets.

The word curry can mean different things depending on where you are. In England it once simply meant a stew to which curry powder had been added, although, thanks to the spread of really good Indian cuisine here, this is now rarely the case. In the East it refers to a whole range of culinary styles, from *Tandoori* to *Balti,* and to individual dishes as well as whole meals. A connoisseur of Indian food should be able to tell, just from the ingredient mix, which part of India or Pakistan the curry comes from.

1 cauliflower (about 1 kg)
500 g firm cooking potatoes
120 g spring onions; 15 g fresh ginger
250 g tomatoes; 2 chilli peppers
300 g fresh peas (150 g shelled)
5 tbsp vegetable oil; 1 tbsp panch foron (see left)
10 g turmeric, freshly grated
1 tsp ground star aniseed
2 tsp mild paprika
salt; freshly ground pepper
400 ml vegetable stock
1 tbsp chopped coriander leaves
80 g yoghurt; 1 tsp garam masala

1. Wash the cauliflower, cut out the stalk and divide the head into medium size florets. Rinse these again. Peel and dice the potatoes into 3 cm cubes. Wash and trim the spring onions and thinly slice them into rings. Peel and finely chop the ginger. Scald, skin and deseed the tomatoes, then chop into quarters. Halve and deseed the chilli peppers, remove the fibres and cut the flesh into thin strips.

2. Heat the oil in a large pan, add the *panch foron* and, stirring, sweat this briefly. Add the spring onion and cook over a low heat until it turns transparent. Add the potato, cauliflower and chilli peppers and sauté over a moderate heat for 3-4 minutes. Stir in the turmeric, ginger, star aniseed and paprika and season with salt and pepper. Leave to cook for 3-4 minutes, stirring from time to time.

3. Pour in the vegetable stock and leave the curry to cook over a moderate heat for about 20 minutes, until the cauliflower and potatoes are cooked through. Five minutes before the end of the cooking time, add the tomato and the peas and sprinkle in the coriander leaves.

4. Spoon the yoghurt on top of the curry, sprinkle with garam masala and serve.

Papaya and Sweet Potato Curry

A COMBINATION OF HOT SPICES AND SWEET VEGETABLES

Coconut palms are among the most productive agricultural crops in southern India.

In southern India, coconut is the favourite flavouring for mixed vegetable curries. This original recipe is for a delicious curry in which the sweet potato and the coconut milk make a wonderful foil for the hot spices. If vegetable papayas are unobtainable they can simply be replaced by unripe fruit papayas.

50 g onion; 2 cloves garlic
1 piece lemon grass (15 g)
2 red chilli peppers
20 g fresh ginger
1/2 tsp black peppercorns
1 tbsp chopped coriander leaves
700 g sweet potatoes
600 g vegetable papayas
300 g fresh peas (150 g shelled)
1 tbsp vegetable oil; 300 ml vegetable stock
400 ml coconut milk; salt
30 g coconut, freshly grated

Sweet potato and papaya are two exotic vegetables that make a wonderfully out of the ordinary curry.

1. Peel and finely chop the onion and the garlic. Chop the lemon grass into thin rings. Halve and deseed the chilli peppers, remove the fibres and finely chop the flesh. Peel and finely grate the ginger. Put the onion, garlic, chilli peppers, lemon grass, ginger, peppercorns and coriander leaves into a mortar and grind to a paste.

2. Peel the sweet potatoes and dice them into 1.5 cm cubes. Peel and halve the papayas, scoop out the seeds, then cut out and dice the flesh into 2 cm cubes. Shell the peas, blanch them in boiling, salted water then strain and refresh.

3. Heat the oil in a large pan and, stirring continuously, fry the curry paste for 3 minutes.

INDIA

4. Add the papaya to the pan, pour in the stock and the coconut milk and give everything one careful stir. Turn down the heat and leave to simmer for 20 minutes. Add the sweet potato and cook for a further 15 minutes, then finally add the peas and cook for a final 5 minutes. Season with salt to taste.

5. Using a non-stick pan, dry fry the grated coconut to a golden brown. Ladle the curry into individual preheated dishes, sprinkle with the coconut and serve. Basmati rice makes a good accompaniment to this curry.

Fried Rice in Pineapple

KNOWN AS MAO YONG IN THAILAND, THIS DISH IS DECORATIVELY SERVED IN THE PINEAPPLE SHELL

For perfect fried rice it is best to use rice which has been part cooked the day before. This dish therefore requires a bit of forward thinking. It is essential to use a really good, ripe pineapple, although these may be more expensive than the green ones normally sold in the shops here.

350 g jasmine scented Thai rice
1 tsp salt
50 g shallots; 3 cloves garlic
200 g white cabbage leaves
100 g Chinese straw mushrooms
2 small pineapples
4 tbsp peanut oil
1 tsp ground turmeric; 1 tsp curry powder
1 tsp sugar
salt; freshly ground pepper

1. Put the rice in a bowl and cover it with water, then leave to soak for 30 minutes. Strain the rice through a sieve and rinse it under cold, running water until the liquid runs clear. Bring 600 ml of water to the boil in a flameproof casserole. Quickly add the rice and the salt, turn down the heat, cover and leave to cook for 10 minutes. Take the casserole off the heat and put it in a preheated oven at 150°C for 30 minutes to finish cooking. Take out, leave to cool, then place in the refrigerator for 24 hours.

2. Peel and thinly slice the shallots. Peel and finely chop the garlic. Strip the centre stalks out of the cabbage leaves and cut the leaves into 1 cm squares. Clean and halve the mushrooms. Cut the pineapples in half lengthways, slicing right through the leaf crowns. Hollow out the pineapple halves and dice the scooped out fruit into 1 cm cubes. Reserve the pineapple halves.

3. Heat the oil in a wok until it begins to lightly smoke, then fry the shallots and the garlic to a golden brown. Stir in the turmeric and the curry powder. Add the pineapple pieces, mushrooms, cabbage leaf squares and sugar and, stirring continuously, fry for 5 minutes. Add the precooked rice from the day before and stir fry for a further 5 minutes. Season with salt and pepper.

4. Fill the pineapple halves with the fruit and rice mixture and cook in a preheated oven at 180°C for 10 minutes. Take out and serve.

A wide range of fresh vegetables is always available in the markets of Thailand.

THAILAND

The air in this Thai market is heady with the scent of exotic tropical fruit and vegetables.

Fried Vegetables with Egg Noodles

A THAI SPECIALITY IN A SPICY SAUCE

Stir frying is the most popular method of cooking in Thailand, not least because of the way it preserves vitamins and the texture of the food.

For the vegetables
400 g cauliflower; 300 g broccoli
100 g mangetout; 200 g mangold
100 g baby sweetcorn
2 cloves garlic; 2 red chilli peppers
10 g fresh ginger; 60 g spring onions
5 tbsp peanut oil; 125 ml vegetable stock
2 tbsp vegetarian oyster sauce; 3 tbsp light soy sauce
1 tsp ground Szechuan pepper; salt
1 tsp cornflour
In addition
200 mee (egg noodles); salt
1 tbsp chopped coriander leaves

1. Discard the cauliflower leaves, cut out and discard the stalk and chop the head into medium sized florets. Divide the broccoli into florets and cut the stalks into 1 cm long pieces. Clean and trim the mangetout. Rinse the mangold, pull off and chop up the leaves, then string and cut the stalks into 4 cm long pieces.

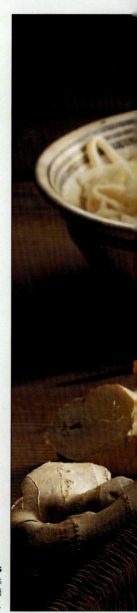

Crispy, fresh vegetables and soft egg noodles make a simple and delicious meal.

2. Cook the cauliflower and the baby sweetcorn in boiling, salted water for 10 minutes. Five minutes into the cooking, add the broccoli and the mangetout. Take all of the vegetables out with a draining spoon and leave to drain well.

3. To prepare the sauce, peel and finely slice the garlic. Trim the chilli peppers and slice them into rings, discarding the seeds. Peel and cut the ginger into julienne strips. Clean and trim the spring onions and cut them into 2 cm long pieces.

4. Cook the egg noodles in plenty of boiling salted water al dente. Strain, drain and keep hot.

THAILAND

5. Heat the oil in a wok and stir fry the cauliflower and the sweetcorn for 5 minutes, then take out and reserve them. Add the broccoli, mangetout and mangold stalks and stir fry these for 3 minutes, then add the mangold leaves and stir fry for a further 2 minutes, then remove all four and reserve.

6. Using the same oil stir fry the garlic, chilli pepper, ginger and spring onions for 1 minute. Add the vegetable stock reserving 1 tbsp. Sprinkle in the vegetarian oyster sauce, soy sauce and Szechuan pepper. Season with salt. In a bowl, stir the cornflour to a smooth paste with the reserved stock, then stir this into the sauce to bind it and bring briefly to the boil. Put all of the vegetables back into the pan and briefly heat through.

7. Ladle the vegetables into preheated bowls and sprinkle with coriander leaves. Serve with the noodles in a separate bowl.

THAILAND

Tofu, also known as bean curd is one of the basic ingredients of Chinese cooking and is similarly popular in Thailand, where it can always be bought fresh.

Fried Tofu with Peanuts and Vegetables

MARINATED AND THEN STIR FRIED IN A WOK WITH GINGER AND GARLIC

In Southeast Asia many everyday dishes are vegetarian. Some, like this recipe with tofu, contain no animal protein at all. Basmati rice makes a good accompaniment to this dish.

500 g tofu
1 tbsp dark soy sauce; 2 tbsp light soy sauce
1 tsp cornflour; salt
150 g fresh peanuts, in the shell
2 green chilli peppers; 10 g ginger
2 cloves garlic
150 g red peppers
100 g spring onions
For the sauce
200 ml vegetable stock
1 tbsp dark soy sauce
2 tbsp light soy sauce
1 tsp white rice vinegar
1 tsp cornflour
1/2 tsp Szechuan peppercorns
In addition
1/2 litre vegetable oil for frying
1 tbsp snipped Chinese chives

1. Cut the tofu into 2 cm cubes. Put both kinds of soy sauce, the cornflour and salt to taste in a bowl and stir well. Turn the tofu in this mixture, cover and leave to marinate for 30 minutes.

2. To prepare the vegetables, shell and skin the peanuts. Halve and deseed the chilli peppers, remove the fibres and cut the flesh into thin strips. Peel and finely chop the ginger and the garlic. Halve and deseed the peppers, remove the fibres and dice the flesh into 5 mm cubes. Clean and trim the spring onions and slice them diagonally into 2 cm long pieces.

3. To prepare the sauce, put the vegetable stock, both kinds of soy sauce, vinegar and cornflour in a bowl and beat well. Grind the peppercorns with a pestle and mortar and stir into the sauce.

4. Heat the oil in a wok to 180°C. Take the tofu out of the marinade, drain well, and fry for 2 minutes until golden brown. Take out. Fry the peanuts in the same oil for 1 minute then take out and drain.

5. Pour off all but 2 tbsp oil from the wok and briefly stir fry the chilli strips, ginger and garlic. Add the peppers and spring onions and stir fry for a further 2 minutes. Pour in the sauce, bring briefly to the boil, then add the tofu and the peanuts and cook for 1 minute. Ladle into individual bowls, sprinkle with Chinese chives and serve immediately.

INDONESIA

Candle nuts have a very individual, delicate flavour and are used in many Asian dishes. Like macadamia nuts they will keep in the refrigerator, though not for long. They keep better whole than shelled but need a strong nutcracker to break the exceptionally hard shell.

Vegetable Fried Rice with Eggs

AT FIRST SIGHT THIS LOOKS LIKE NASI GORENG, BUT IT ACTUALLY TASTES QUITE DIFFERENT

Unlike the national dish, *nasi goreng*, the vegetables are the main ingredient in this recipe, rather than the rice. Hard boiled eggs are served with it but these should not be too hard – the yolks should remain slightly soft in the centre.

400 g basmati rice; 1 tsp salt
4 eggs; 50 g shallots; 2 cloves garlic
15 g fresh ginger; 2 red chilli peppers
60 g spring onions; 200 g green beans
150 g carrots; 80 g celery
250 g tomatoes; 5 tbsp vegetable oil
100 ml vegetable stock
2 tbsp vegetarian oyster sauce; 3 tbsp light soy sauce
salt; freshly ground pepper
1/2 tsp ground turmeric
40 g candle nuts, chopped and roasted
grated zest and juice of 1/2 lime
1/2 tsp palm sugar
coriander leaves

Rice fields at the foot of Mount Agung in eastern Bali. The island is covered in picture book views like this one and while Bali is a long journey away, it is worth it, not only for the scenery, but for the cuisine as well.

1. Using a sieve, rinse the rice thoroughly. Bring 1 litre of water to the boil in a pan with the salt, pour in the rice and bring briefly back to the boil. Turn down the heat, cover and leave to cook for 15-20 minutes. Rinse through a sieve again and leave to drain well.

2. Bring a pan of water to the boil, add the eggs and boil for 8 minutes, then rinse

INDONESIA

under cold running water. Peel the eggs and set them aside in warm water.

3. Peel and finely chop the shallots, garlic and ginger. Trim and slice the chilli peppers into thin rings, discarding the seeds. Wash and trim the spring onions, then slice into thin rings. Wash and trim the green beans and cut them into 3 cm long pieces. Peel the carrots and cut them into 4 cm long julienne strips. Wash and slice the celery. Scald, skin and deseed the tomatoes, then dice the flesh into 1 cm cubes.

4. Heat 2 tbsp of the oil in a wok. Stir fry the rice for 2-3 minutes, then take out and set aside. Add the remaining oil to the wok, heat this and fry the shallots, garlic and ginger for 1 minute. Add the spring onions, beans, carrots, chilli pepper and celery and stir fry for 3 minutes. Pour in the vegetable stock and cook for 5 minutes. Add the tomatoes and cook for a further 2 minutes, then add the oyster and soy sauces and season with salt, pepper and turmeric. Put the fried rice back into the wok and add the candle nuts, zest of lime, lime juice and palm sugar. Mix everything carefully together and season to taste. Put the vegetable rice into individual bowls, slice the eggs lengthways and arrange 2 halves on top of each bowl. Sprinkle with coriander leaves and serve.

Banana and Vegetable Stuffed Egg Pancakes

EXOTIC VEGETABLES AND AROMATIC RICE AND SPICES GIVE THIS DISH A DISTINCTIVE CHARACTER

Plantain bananas are not unlike potatoes in their floury consistency and should not be confused with fruit bananas. They can be cooked in a number of ways, including fried and baked but should never be eaten raw. Fruit bananas can be used for this recipe if you cannot find any of the plantain variety.

A spicy sweet and sour sauce is perfect with these pancakes. 1 red pepper (about 180 g) is ground in a mortar with 5 Thai red chilli peppers (seeds and fibres removed) and 2 cloves garlic. The resultant paste is put into a pan with 250 ml water, 8 tbsp vinegar, 400 g sugar and 1/2 tsp salt and brought to the boil. It is then simmered over a very low heat for about 30 minutes to produce a spicy sauce with a creamy consistency.

400 g scented Thai rice
3/4 litre water; salt
2 chilli peppers
15 g fresh ginger
10 g lemon grass
80 g spring onions
80 g celery; 100 g white cabbage
100 g carrots; 200 g red peppers
400 g ripe plantain bananas
flour for dipping
5 tbsp vegetable oil
1 tsp ground Szechuan pepper
150 ml vegetable stock; 3 tbsp light soy sauce
1/2 tsp Vietnamese coriander, chopped
For the egg pancakes
100 g flour; 125 ml water; 2 eggs; salt
freshly ground white pepper; 2 tbsp vegetable oil

1. Boil the rice, covered, in the lightly salted water, for 10 minutes in a flameproof and ovenproof casserole. Put the casserole in a preheated oven at 200°C and cook for 10 minutes.

2. To prepare the pancakes, mix the flour and the water together in a bowl to a smooth batter. Using a balloon whisk, whisk in the eggs. Season with salt and pepper and leave to stand for 30 minutes.

3. Halve and deseed the chilli peppers, remove the fibres, then finely chop the flesh. Peel and finely chop the ginger. Slice the lemon grass into thin rings. Wash and trim the spring onions and slice into thin rings. Slice the celery thinly and cut the cabbage into thin strips. Peel the carrots and cut these into 4 cm long julienne strips. Halve and deseed the peppers, remove the fibres and slice the flesh into lozenge shapes about 1 cm thick. Peel and slice the bananas, then dip them in the flour, lightly coating them all over.

4. To fry the pancakes, heat a little oil in a 20 cm diameter omelette pan. Pour in 1/4 of the batter and fry to a golden brown on each side. Make 3 more pancakes in the same way.

5. Heat the oil in a wok and briefly fry the spring onions and the Szechuan pepper. Add the prepared vegetables and stir fry for 6-8 minutes, then take out. Stir fry the bananas in the wok for 2-3 minutes, then add the rice and the vegetable mixture and fry everything together for 2 minutes. Stir in the stock and the soy sauce. Season to taste and sprinkle with coriander.

6. Arrange the egg pancakes on individual dishes, fill them generously with the vegetable mixture, fold them up and serve.

Rice with Sweet Potato and Tofu

SLICES OF GOLDEN BROWN TOFU, STIR-FRIED IN A WOK, ARE SERVED ON A BED OF VEGETABLES WITH A SPICY SAUCE

Rice and vegetable dishes are very popular in Malaysian cookery. Here, scented white rice from Thailand, perhaps the best rice in the world, is used, but because of the delicacy of the aroma and flavour of the rice, it is important to be careful when using spices so as not to overwhelm it. For the same reason, care must be taken with the rice vinegar too. It should contain only 3% acidity but most rice vinegars contain much more.

A Malaysian food market with its vast array of exotic fruit and vegetables. The banana flowers in the foreground are eaten as vegetables.

120 g sweet potatoes
240 g scented Thai rice
salt

This extremely decorative Malaysian dish is particularly cheap to make.

120 g mangetout
100 g tofu
150 g fresh peas (about 40 g shelled)
3 tbsp vegetable oil
1/4 tsp sugar
1/4 tsp ground ginger
1 stalk lemon grass, snipped
coarse ground Szechuan pepper
1 tbsp chilli sauce; 1/2 tsp light soy sauce
3 tbsp tomato ketchup; 1/2 tsp rice vinegar
In addition
a few coriander leaves
bean curd sticks
oil for frying

MALAYSIA

1. Wash and peel the sweet potatoes, then dice them into 1 cm cubes. Using a sieve, rinse the rice thoroughly under cold running water. Bring a pan of lightly salted water to the boil, add the rice and the sweet potato and leave to cook over a moderate heat for 15-20 minutes.

2. Wash and trim the mangetout and partly split them open, to about halfway. Chop the tofu into slices 1 cm thick. Shell the peas, blanch them in boiling water, strain and leave to drain.

3. Heat the oil in a wok and fry the tofu to a golden brown on all sides, then take out and keep hot. Add the mangetout to the pan and stir-fry for 1 minute, then take out. Using the same oil, add the sugar, ginger, lemon grass, pepper to taste, chilli sauce, soy sauce, ketchup and rice vinegar and stir to a sauce.

4. Pile the rice and sweet potato onto the centre of individual, preheated dishes, surround with mangetout, peas and tofu and sprinkle generously with the sauce. Garnish with coriander leaves and pre-soaked and fried bean curd sticks and serve.

Biryani Rice with Aubergines

AUBERGINE COOKED IN TWO DIFFERENT WAYS ON A BED OF EXOTICALLY SPICED BASMATI RICE

Some of the ingredients for this recipe can only be found in specialist Asian supermarkets. If no fresh curry leaves are available, dried ones may be used instead. If this is the case, the quantity needs to be doubled as the flavour is not as strong.

50 g shallots; 3-4 red chilli peppers
3 cloves garlic; 20 g fresh ginger
400 g aubergines; 4 tbsp peanut oil
20 g ground turmeric; 80 g candle nuts, chopped
1 panicle curry leaves (10-14 leaves)
30 ml vegetable stock; 200 ml coconut milk; salt

For the rice
30 g shallots; 60 g ghee (or margarine)
10 g cinnamon; 8 cardamom seeds; 6 cloves
30 g fresh ginger, peeled and chopped
3 cloves garlic, finely chopped; 400 g basmati rice
salt; 40 ml rose water; 1 pinch saffron

For the aubergine crisps
100 g aubergines; 200 ml vegetable oil for frying

Served with aromatic rice, the coconut, turmeric and fresh curry leaves turn these aubergines into a Far Eastern treat.

Instead of climbing the tree himself, this man uses a more agile monkey on a lead to pick the ripe coconuts

1. Peel and thinly slice the shallots. Halve and deseed the chilli peppers, remove the fibres and finely chop the flesh. Peel and finely chop the garlic and the ginger. Wash, trim and dice the aubergines into 2 cm cubes.

2. Heat the oil in a pan and, stirring continuously, fry the shallots, garlic, chilli peppers, ginger, turmeric and candle nuts for 2 minutes. Add the diced aubergine and fry for 5 minutes, then the curry leaves and cook for a further 3 minutes. Slake with the vegetable stock. Pour in the coconut milk, season with salt and leave to simmer for 10-15 minutes. Keep hot.

MALAYSIA

3. To prepare the rice, peel and thinly slice the shallots. Heat the ghee or margarine in a flameproof casserole and, stirring continuously, sauté the cinnamon, cardamom and cloves for 2 minutes. Add the ginger, garlic and shallots and sauté until lightly browned. Add the rice and fry for 3-4 minutes, stirring continuously. Slake with 800 ml water, season with salt, bring briefly to the boil, then leave to simmer, stirring from time to time, until most of the liquid has been absorbed and the rice is just moist.

4. Take the rice off the heat, cover the casserole and cook for 20 minutes in a preheated oven at 150°C. Meanwhile, mix the rose water with the saffron in a pan and cook for 1 minute. Sprinkle the rose water over the rice 5 minutes before the end of the cooking time.

5. To prepare the aubergine crisps, wash and trim the aubergines and slice them razor thin. Heat the oil to 180°C in a chip pan or deep fat fryer and briefly and crisply fry the aubergine slices. Take out and drain well on kitchen paper.

6. Ladle the rice into individual bowls, top with a portion of the curried aubergine mixture, garnish with a few aubergine crisps and serve.

Rice-stuffed Pumpkin

SMALL PUMPKINS MAKE ATTRACTIVE SERVING DISHES AS WELL AS BRINGING OUT THE FULL FLAVOUR OF THE DISH

Small varieties of yellow fleshed pumpkin, such as Hokkaido, are ideal for this recipe. The pumpkin should be firm fleshed but not too hard.

1 tbsp vegetable oil; 250 g jasmine whole grain rice	
500 ml vegetable stock; salt	
2 Hokkaido pumpkins (about 1 kg each)	
For the filling	
40 g fresh ginger; 2 cloves garlic	
80 g spring onions; 2 small red chilli peppers	
80 g celery; 150 g mangetout	
350 g tomatoes	
2 tbsp vegetable oil; 1 tsp turmeric	
1/2 tsp ground star aniseed	
3 cardamom pods; 1 stick cinnamon	
salt; freshly ground pepper	
1 tsp Chinese herbs	

1. Heat the oil in a pan and fry the rice until just transparent. Add the stock, season with salt, and leave to cook for 15 minutes.

2. Slice a 'lid' from the top of the pumpkin and scoop out the seeds with a spoon. If the centre of the pumpkin is a bit small for the filling, scrape some of the flesh away with a spoon. You can dice these trimmings and add them to the filling.

3. To prepare the filling, peel and finely chop the ginger and the garlic. Clean, trim and slice the spring onions into rings. Halve and deseed the chilli peppers, remove the fibres and cut the flesh into thin strips. Trim the celery and the mangetout, then slice the celery thinly and halve the mangetout. Scald, skin and blanch the tomatoes, remove the seeds, then dice the flesh.

4. Heat the oil in a wok and briefly stir fry the turmeric, star aniseed, cardamom and cinnamon. Add the ginger, garlic, spring onions and chilli pepper strips and stir fry for 1 minute. Add the celery, mangetout and any diced pumpkin and stir fry for a further 2 minutes. Finally, add the tomato and the rice, season with salt and pepper, sprinkle in the herbs and mix everything well.

5. Fill the pumpkin halves with the rice mixture and place the lid on top. Tie the pumpkins firmly shut with kitchen string. Fill a wok 1/3 full with water and place a bamboo steamer over the top. Place the pumpkins in the steamer, bring the water to the boil, then reduce the heat and steam for 1 1/2 hours, adding more water as needed. Serve in preheated dishes.

Head Chef Tony Khoo steams his pumpkins in a bamboo basket set over a wok, as described above.

CHINA

Lay the pastry sheets on a work surface with one corner facing you. Put 2 tbsp of filling in the centre. Fold the far corner over this and brush the upturned edges with egg white. Fold the left and right hand corners over, then brush the remaining flap and the edges above with egg white and close the envelope, pulling and pressing firmly to seal.

Tofu Envelopes

CRISPY TREATS WITH A SPICY PEANUT SAUCE

Water chestnuts are very popular in Far Eastern cookery and particularly in Chinese cuisine. Despite their name, they bear no botanical relationship to other types of chestnut. Water chestnuts are specially cultivated and, being hand picked, they can rarely be bought fresh here. They are available in bottles or tins though, but in this case the amount should be reduced to 100 g.

For the filling
30 g dried shitake mushrooms; 3 cloves garlic
80 g spring onions; 150 g carrots; 100 g leeks
200 g water chestnuts; 3 tbsp vegetable oil
100 g beansprouts; salt; freshly ground pepper
3 tbsp vegetarian oyster sauce
4 tbsp light soy sauce; 350 g tofu; 1 egg

For the peanut sauce
1 red chilli pepper; 100 g roasted peanuts
10 g fresh ginger
2 tbsp vegetable oil; 250 ml coconut milk
juice of 1/2 lime; 4 tbsp light soy sauce
1/2 tsp palm sugar (or brown sugar)
salt; freshly ground black pepper

In addition
12 sheets spring roll pastry (25 cm x 25 cm)

1. Soak the dried mushrooms in hot water for 20 minutes, then take out, drain and squeeze out the excess moisture. Trim off the stalks and slice the caps into strips. Peel and finely chop the garlic. Trim and slice the spring onions into rings. Peel the carrots, wash and trim the leeks and cut both into thin strips. Prepare the water chestnuts, following the illustrated instructions, opposite.

2. Heat the oil in a wok and soften the garlic and the spring onion. Add the carrot, leek and

Wash the water chestnuts then peel them with a sharp knife, exactly as if you were peeling an apple. Trim off the hard stalk and slice them into small pieces.

CHINA

mushrooms and stir fry for 1 minute. Add the water chestnuts and stir fry for 2 minutes. Stir in the beansprouts, season with salt and pepper and flavour with the oyster and soy sauces. Turn the mixture out into a bowl and leave to cool.

3. Meanwhile, finely dice the tofu. Beat the egg in a bowl and stir this and the tofu into the mixture. Season with salt and pepper to taste.

4. To prepare the peanut sauce, halve and deseed the chilli pepper, remove the fibres and cut the flesh into thin strips. Grind the peanuts with a pestle and mortar. Peel and finely grind the ginger. Heat the oil in a pan and, stirring continuously, fry the ginger and the ground peanuts over a moderate heat for 2 minutes. Add the coconut milk, lime juice, soy sauce, palm sugar and chilli pepper strips, turn the heat right down and simmer, still stirring, for about 5 minutes. Season with salt and with pepper.

5. Make up the envelopes, following the illustrated instructions, opposite, top. Heat the oil in a chip pan or deep fat fryer to 180°C and fry the filled envelopes until crispy. Serve the peanut sauce separately.

Spring roll pastry, in ready made sheets, is now available in most supermarkets. When taken out of the packet, the sheets must be covered with a damp cloth, to prevent them drying out.

Basmati rice is one of the best varieties of rice. Lightly aromatic, it is best to use whole grain rice for this recipe.

Fried Aubergine with Tofu

SERVED WITH MIXED VEGETABLES AND AROMATIC BASMATI RICE

The small round variety of aubergine which is grown in Asia is the best type to use when stir frying in a wok, as they only need to be halved beforehand. They come in white, purple and yellow fleshed varieties, all of which are equally tasty. This type of aubergine is difficult, but not impossible, to find here but sliced, European varieties can be used instead.

20 g dried mu-err (Chinese mushrooms); 250 g tofu
2 tbsp light soy sauce; 1 tbsp vegetarian oyster sauce
400 g small round aubergines
150 g mangetout; 150 g red peppers
50 g small red onions; 4 tbsp peanut oil

In China, making tofu is an art and here the workers in this factory are preparing the bean curd at great speed.

Stir fried vegetables should remain slightly crunchy and the short cooking time means all the goodness is sealed in. The bland tofu is particularly good at absorbing the full flavour of the spicy sauce.

For the sauce
150 ml vegetable stock; 2 tbsp vegetarian oyster sauce
3 tbsp light soy sauce; 1 tsp cornflour
salt; freshly ground pepper

For the rice
250 g basmati whole grain rice; salt

In addition
1 tbsp chopped coriander leaves

1. Rinse the rice under cold running water, bring it to the boil in 600 ml water, then season with salt. Turn down the heat as low as possible and leave to cook for about 40 minutes.

CHINA

2. Soak the dried mushrooms in 125 ml of water for 30 minutes. Take out, lightly drain and cut them into smaller pieces, if necessary.

3. Dice the tofu into 1.5 cm cubes, then put it in a bowl, add the soy and oyster sauces, and mix well. Leave to marinate for 15 minutes then take out and drain.

4. Trim and halve the aubergines. Wash and trim the mangetout. Halve and deseed the peppers, remove the fibres, then dice the flesh into 1 cm cubes. Peel and finely chop the onions.

5. Heat the oil in a wok and fry the tofu to a golden brown on all sides, then take out and reserve. Add the onions to the pan and soften, then add the aubergine and stir fry for 3 minutes. Next add the mangetout, peppers and mushrooms and stir fry for a further 4 minutes. Finally, fold in the tofu.

6. To prepare the sauce, mix the stock, oyster and soy sauces and cornflour smoothly together. Turn this into a wok and bring briefly to the boil. Season with salt and pepper. Pile the vegetable and tofu mixture onto preheated plates, pour over the sauce and sprinkle with coriander leaves. Serve the basmati rice separately.

Mixed Vegetables with Quail's Eggs

CANTONESE CUISINE IS FULL OF RECIPES FOR INTERESTING COMBINATIONS OF VEGETABLES

In the southern regions of China, where the climate is ideal for growing vegetables, there are an endless number of different vegetarian recipes. In this recipe, pumpkin, carrots and mushrooms are stir fried in a wok with garlic, onion and spices. Quail's eggs are delicious with this dish but hard boiled hen's eggs, cut into wedges, would be almost as good.

Vegetarian oyster sauce and white bean sauce are both made from a soya bean base. The first is flavoured with a concentrate of shitake mushrooms and the second is lightly thickened with cornflour, but both are quite spicy.

12 quail eggs
2 cloves garlic; 50 g onion
60 g spring onions
300 g Hokkaido pumpkin
150 g carrots
80 g shitake mushrooms
100 g cultivated white mushrooms
200 g tomatoes; 3 tbsp vegetable oil
1 tsp tomato purée
180 ml vegetable stock
2 tsp white bean sauce
2 tbsp vegetarian oyster sauce
salt; freshly ground pepper
coriander leaves

1. Put the quail eggs in a pan, cover with hot water and cook for 4 minutes, then take out and refresh under cold water.

2. Peel and slice the garlic. Peel and finely chop the onion. Wash and trim the spring onions and slice them into rings. Peel, halve and deseed the pumpkin, slice it into 3 mm slices, then cut the slices into 1.5 cm long diamond shapes. Peel the carrots and cut them into 4 cm long matchsticks. Cut the stalks off the shitake mushrooms and chop the caps in half. Wash, trim and quarter the white mushrooms. Scald, skin and deseed the tomatoes and finely dice the flesh.

3. Heat 2 tbsp of oil in a wok and briefly stir fry the garlic, onion and spring onions. Add the pumpkin and carrot and stir fry for 4 minutes, then take out the garlic and all of the vegetables. Add the remaining oil to the wok, heat it and stir fry both kinds of mushrooms for 2 minutes, then take out. Add the tomato, simmer briefly, then stir in the tomato purée and pour in the stock. Finally, stir in the bean sauce and the vegetarian oyster sauce and leave to cook for 3 minutes.

4. Shell and slice the quail eggs lengthways and add them to the sauce, together with the vegetables, mushrooms and garlic. Mix everything carefully together, season with salt and pepper and briefly reheat. Divide between individual bowls, sprinkle with coriander and serve.

Asparagus and Pak Choi

PLAIN, STICKY CHINESE BOILING RICE GOES WELL WITH THIS DISH

The Chinese practice of stir frying vegetables enables them to retain as much goodness as possible. The bowl shape of the wok enables the vegetables to be cooked evenly over a high heat, in very little fat or oil, and in a very short time.

400 g Pak choi (Chinese cabbage), Shanghai variety
400 g thin, green asparagus; 10 g fresh ginger
30 g Thai red onions or shallots
1 clove garlic
80 g spring onions
2 small chilli peppers; 4 tbsp vegetable oil
salt; freshly ground pepper

For the rice
250 g Chinese boiling rice; 1/2 litre salted water

For the sauce
100 ml vegetable stock; 3 tbsp rice wine
3 tbsp light soy sauce; 1 tbsp dark soy sauce
grated zest and juice of 1/2 lime
1/2 tsp cornflour; 1 tsp chopped coriander leaves

In addition
coriander leaves to garnish

Though you may not be able to find a Chinese shop in the UK quite like this one, specialist Asian supermarkets do sell almost the same range of products.

Pak choi, also known as Chinese cabbage, is slightly spicy and is readily available here. The Shanghai variety, with its firm and juicy stalks, is the best type for stir frying

1. Wash and trim the Pak choi and cut it into 1.5 cm long strips. Trim the tough ends off the asparagus and peel the lower stalks, if necessary, then cut the spears into 5 cm long pieces. Peel and finely chop the ginger, onions and garlic. Wash and trim the spring onions and slice them into rings. Trim the chilli peppers and slice them into rings, removing the seeds.

CHINA

2. Rinse the rice thoroughly in a sieve, leave to drain, then put it in a pan with the salted water and bring to the boil. Turn down the heat, cover and leave to cook for about 10 minutes. When the liquid has been completely absorbed, take the pan off the heat and leave it to stand, covered, for a further 10 minutes.

3. To prepare the sauce, thoroughly mix all of the ingredients together in a small bowl.

4. Heat the oil in a wok and stir fry the ginger, onions and garlic over a low heat. Add the asparagus and stir fry for 2 minutes. Finally add the Pak choi, spring onions and chilli pepper rings and stir fry for 3 minutes. Add the sauce and bring briefly to the boil. Season with salt and pepper. Serve in individual bowls, sprinkled with coriander leaves. Serve the rice separately.

CHINA

Chilli peppers, galingale and ginger are always available fresh in Chinese shops. Here too, there is a wide range of Asian produce to be found, not only in specialist shops but also in supermarkets.

Rice Noodles with Mixed Vegetables

THIS IS VEGETARIAN COOKERY AT ITS BEST – CRISPY FRIED VEGETABLES, DONE TO A TURN

A perfect example of Far Eastern country cooking, this recipe has hundreds of variations and is usually made with whatever vegetables happen to be fresh in the market that day. Texture is important in this dish and both crispy and softer cooked vegetables should be included, in order to give it the right contrast.

140 g medium-size rice noodles; salt
50 g Thai red onions or shallots
1 clove garlic
10 g fresh galingale or ginger
1 stalk lemon grass (about 10 g)
2 small chilli peppers; 100 g baby sweetcorn
100 g mangetout
200 g small round aubergines
150 g red peppers; 100 g shitake mushrooms
4 tbsp peanut oil; freshly ground pepper
4 tbsp chopped Thai basil, chopped
For the sauce
100 ml vegetable stock; 2 tbsp soy sauce
2 tbsp vegetarian oyster sauce; 1 tbsp mirin
1/2 tsp cornflour
In addition
a few leaves Thai basil

Noodles made with rice flour are usually sold in tagliatelle style shapes. For this recipe, medium-wide noodles are best. If no fresh Chinese rice noodles are available the dish could be made with European pasta instead, although it would then lose some of its Chinese character.

1. Cook the rice noodles in boiling, salted water al dente, then strain, refresh and reserve.

2. Peel and finely chop the onions, garlic and galingale. Cut the lemon grass into thin strips. Halve and deseed the chilli peppers, remove the fibres and cut the flesh into thin strips.

3. Blanch the baby sweetcorn for 2 minutes, then strain, refresh and cut

CHINA

into halves. Wash and trim the mangetout and trim and quarter the aubergines. Halve and deseed the peppers, remove the fibres and slice the flesh into 1.5 cm thick diamond shapes. Cut the stalks off the mushrooms and either halve or quarter the caps, according to size.

4. To prepare the sauce, mix the vegetable stock, soy sauce, vegetarian oyster sauce, mirin and cornflour smoothly together in a small bowl.

5. Heat the oil in a wok and stir fry the onions, garlic, galingale, lemon grass and chilli pepper strips until the juices run. Add the sweetcorn, and stir fry briefly, then add the mangetout, aubergines, peppers and mushrooms and stir fry for 5-6 minutes. Pour in the sauce and bring briefly to the boil. Carefully fold in the cooked rice noodles and briefly heat through. Season with salt and pepper and stir in the chopped basil. Ladle into individual bowls, garnish with basil leaves and serve.

CHINA

Healthy, vitamin-rich vegetables are cheap to buy and simple to prepare. Chinese markets boast a wider range of vegetables than any other country.

Choisum and Paprika with Rice Noodles

ANOTHER DELICIOUS CHINESE STIR FRIED VEGETABLE DISH THAT IS SLIGHTLY SPICIER THAN USUAL

Choisum is one of the many varieties of Chinese cabbage which play such an important role in the cookery of China and South East Asia. It is grown here, where it is known as Chinese flowering cabbage, and it is an economical vegetable, since every part of the cabbage is used.

For the vegetables
20 g mu-err mushrooms; 200 g choisum
200 g each red and green peppers
150 g carrots; 1 chilli pepper, finely chopped
1 tsp sesame seed oil; 3 tbsp vegetable stock
3 tbsp vegetarian oyster sauce
1 tbsp dark soy sauce; salt; freshly ground pepper
1/2 tsp cornflour

For the rice noodles
200 large rice noodles; salt; 3 tbsp oil
1 tbsp dark soy sauce

In addition
vegetarian 'prawns' to garnish; oil for frying

Vegetarian 'prawns' make a wonderful garnish as they are as tasty as they are decorative. They usually come from Japan, are made mainly of flour and can be bought, frozen, in Asian supermarkets.

Rice noodles can be boiled and/or fried and can be used in a number of ways. For example, the small, thin, vermicelli style rice noodle is perfect for soups and the larger, flat, wide noodle goes well with vegetables.

CHINA

1. Soak the mushrooms in 125 ml lukewarm water for 20 minutes. Take out, drain well and either halve or quarter, according to size.

2. Trim, wash and chop the choisum. Halve and deseed the peppers, remove the fibres and slice the flesh into 1.5 cm long pieces. Peel the carrots and cut them into slices 5 mm thick. Carve these slices into flower shapes, then cut them in half.

3. Cook the noodles in lightly salted, boiling water al dente. Strain, refresh under cold running water and leave to drain. Heat the oil in a wok and stir fry the noodles for 1-2 minutes, then stir in the soy sauce. Using a draining spoon, take the noodles out of the wok and set aside.

4. Heat the oil for the vegetables in the wok, add the peppers, chilli pepper, mushrooms and the carrots and stir fry for 4 minutes. Add the choisum and stir fry for 1 minute more. Take all the vegetables out.

5. Add the stock and the oyster and soy sauces to the wok and season with salt and pepper. Mix the cornflour to a smooth paste with a little water, then stir this into the sauce, and bring briefly to the boil. Turn the noodles and the vegetables back into the wok and keep hot. Cook the 'prawns' in lightly salted, boiling water for 2-3 minutes, leave to cool a little, then briefly stir fry them in a separate pan. Ladle the vegetables, noodle and sauce mixture into individual, preheated bowls, garnish with 'prawns' and serve.

JAPAN

In Japan the shops are full of exotic produce, most of which is now well known to European palates. Even seaweed and shitake mushrooms are now available over here.

Tofu and Vegetable Nimono

JAPANESE CUISINE IS ALWAYS FULL OF SURPRISES

Japanese cookery is noted not only for its simplicity and its relatively few ingredients, but also for its recipes with spicy, clear soup foundations as here. In this recipe, the *dashi* broth, normally flavoured only with fish stock, is replaced by a clear *dashi* which is flavoured with seaweed, mushrooms and soy sauce.

For the dashi
20 g kombu (dried seaweed); 1 litre water
10 g dried shitake mushrooms
salt; freshly ground pepper
2-3 tbsp light soy sauce

For the omelette
1 red chilli pepper; 4 eggs; 1/2 tsp salt
freshly ground white pepper; 20 g cornflour
1 tbsp Japanese parsley, chopped
30 g fresh shitake mushrooms, chopped and stalks removed
2 tbsp vegetable oil for frying

In addition
150 g mangetout; 200 g white cabbage
300 g tofu; 3 tbsp vegetable oil
a few Japanese parsley leaves to garnish

First prepare the *dashi* broth, following the illustrated instructions, right. To prepare the omelette, halve and deseed the chilli pepper, remove the fibres and finely chop the flesh. Beat the eggs well with the salt, the pepper and the cornflour, then stir in the parsley, mushrooms and chilli pepper. Fry 8 omelettes, one after the other in a little oil, then leave them to cool a little and fold them in half. Roll up each omelette tightly, working from the short side, then slice them into 4 cm thick slices. Spear the omelette rolls with wooden cocktail sticks to hold them in place, then set aside. Trim the mangetout. Quarter the cabbage, cut out the stalk and cut the head into thin strips. Heat the *dashi* in a pan and simmer the cabbage in this, over the lowest possible heat, for 10 minutes. Add the mangetout and simmer for 3-4 minutes. Dice the tofu into 3 cm cubes. Heat the oil in a pan and fry the tofu to a golden brown, then stick each cube with a cocktail stick. Season the broth to taste, ladle it into individual bowls, add the tofu and omelette sticks, sprinkle with parsley and serve.

Wipe the seaweed with a damp cloth. Add it to 1 litre cold water in a pan and simmer over a very low heat for 10-15 minutes, bringing it very slowly to the boil.

Test the top leaves with a thumbnail to see if they are cooked through, if not cook for another 1-2 minutes. Using a draining spoon, take out the seaweed.

Add 80 ml of cold water to the cooking liquid, leave it to cool and add the shitake mushrooms. Reheat the broth, turning down the heat the minute it comes to the boil.

Leave the *dashi* to stand for 10 minutes, then take the pan off the heat and strain it through a muslin lined sieve. Season with salt, pepper and soy sauce.

Root stocks for the Shiraz grape were imported more than a century ago to the Hill of Grace vineyards in Australia from Germany, where they prospered wonderfully. Today hundreds of vines produce very good Australian Shiraz in numerous vineyards.

Spaghetti with a Shallot and Red Wine Sauce

PASTA MAKES THE IDEAL BASE FOR THIS KIND OF SAUCE, ALLOWING THE AROMA OF THE WINE TO REALLY COME OUT

Shiraz is unique to Australia and the country's reputation for producing wine has grown to such an extent that it is internationally recognised as a great wine. Wine is fast taking over from sherry and many aperitifs as a drink to be enjoyed without food as well as with. The best Australian vineyards are found in the southern part of Australia from Adelaide to Melbourne and compete favourably with any in the world.

250 g spaghetti
For the sauce
100 g shallots
20 g butter
250 ml Shiraz
600 g tomatoes
salt; freshly ground white pepper
In addition
40 g hard ewe's milk cheese
1 tbsp chopped parsley

1. Peel and finely chop the shallots. Melt the butter in a pan and soften the shallots until just transparent. Slake with the red wine and leave to cook, uncovered, until the liquid has reduced to about 50 ml.

2. Scald, skin and deseed the tomatoes, then chop the flesh into 5 mm pieces. Add the tomato to the sauce and simmer, over the lowest possible heat, for 3-4 minutes. Season with salt and pepper to taste.

3. Cook the spaghetti in boiling, salted water al dente. Strain and leave to drain well.

4. Divide the spaghetti between 4 individual dishes, top with the sauce, followed by shavings of goat's cheese, sprinkle with parsley and serve.

Risotto with Peas and Asparagus

MANY POPULAR AMERICAN RECIPES ARE ITALIAN INSPIRED

American cuisine is as multicultural as the population of the country and in this recipe the Italian influence is obvious. The vegetables are certainly very American though – peas and asparagus – and the wine is wholly so. A dry Chardonnay from the Sonoma valley in California, where the white wines are lighter and sweeter than those of the Napa valley, is perfect both as an ingredient in the risotto and as an accompaniment to it.

---
250 g green asparagus; salt
1/2 litre vegetable stock
300 g fresh peas (150 g shelled)
50 g shallots
40 g butter
300 g arborio rice
150 ml dry white wine (preferably Chardonnay)
freshly ground white pepper
1 tbsp parsley, chopped
50 g Monterey Jack cheese, freshly grated
50 g butter, in small pieces

Freshly grated cheese and a knob of butter are the finishing touches for this delicious risotto. An American cheese such as Montery Jack is perfect for this but Parmesan can also be used if necessary.

1. Trim the hard ends from the asparagus spears and peel the bottom quarter of each stalk. Cut the spears into 3-4 cm long pieces. Bring a pan of lightly salted water to the boil, add the asparagus – which should just be covered by the water – and leave to cook for 10-12 minutes. Using a draining spoon, take out the asparagus. Pour off 1/2 litre of the cooking liquid and mix it with the vegetable stock. Shell the peas and cook them for 3 minutes in boiling, salted water, then strain and refresh.

2. Peel and finely chop the shallots. Melt the butter in a pan and soften the shallots. Add the

rice and, stirring continuously, cook until transparent. Slake with the wine, season with salt and pepper and leave to cook, uncovered, stirring occasionally, until the liquid has been absorbed. Pour in half the stock mixture and, stirring occasionally, leave the rice to cook until the liquid is almost cooked away, then add the remaining stock and stirring occasionally leave to cook until the risotto is of the required consistency, neither too dry nor too wet. More stock may be added if necessary, during cooking.

3. Fold the pieces of asparagus, peas and chopped parsley into the risotto and reheat briefly. Sprinkle the grated cheese over, dot with pieces of butter and cover the pan. Heat gently for a minute so that the cheese and butter melt into the risotto, stir once again and serve immediately.

Green Bean Stew

A TYPICALLY AMERICAN DISH, SERVED WITH POTATOES AND GLAZED VEGETABLES AND GARNISHED WITH RYE BREAD CROUTONS

Beans and other pulses were staple foods for both the American Indians and the early pioneers. They remain popular throughout the country and are cooked in a wide variety of ways, particularly in casseroles and stews.

For the vegetables
700 g green beans; 300 g firm cooking potatoes
salt; 200 g turnips; 100 g carrots
100 g shallots; 4 tbsp sunflower oil; 15 g sugar
freshly ground white pepper

For the sauce
25 g butter; 30 g flour; 400 ml milk
2 bay leaves; 2 sprigs savory
salt; freshly ground white pepper
freshly grated nutmeg

In addition
4 tbsp vegetable oil; 1 clove garlic, finely chopped
150 g crustless rye bread, diced
1 tsp chopped savory

1. Wash and trim the beans, then slice them into 2 or 3 pieces, according to size. Peel the potatoes, dice them into 1.5 cm cubes, then cook in lightly salted, boiling water for 5 minutes. Add the beans and cook for a further 8 minutes. Strain and set aside, reserving 1/2 litre of the cooking liquid.

2. Peel and dice the turnips and carrots into 1 cm cubes. Peel and quarter the shallots. Heat the oil in a pan and lightly brown the sugar, add the carrot, shallot and turnip and, stirring, sauté until lightly glazed. Season with salt and pepper, then take out all of the vegetables.

3. To prepare the sauce, melt the butter in the same pan, sprinkle in the flour and stir to a smooth roux, without allowing it to discolour. Add the milk and the reserved cooking liquid. Stir well until the sauce is of a smooth consistency. Add the bay leaf and the savory. Season with salt, pepper and nutmeg, turn down the heat and leave to simmer for 10 minutes. Add the glazed vegetables and simmer for a further 20 minutes, then add the potato and the green beans and cook for a final 10 minutes. Season to taste.

4. Heat the oil in a second pan and fry the garlic and croûtons to a golden brown. Sprinkle over the bean stew, together with the chopped savory and serve immediately.

Savory – known in some countries as bean herb – is particularly good at bringing out the flavour of green beans. Dried savoury can be used instead of fresh but it will not be quite as effective.

USA

It is these small green mung beans that produce the ever popular bean sprouts. They can be bought in this state and the sprouts forced. However the process, while simple, is long and involves days of wrapping, washing, soaking, straining and rinsing the beans.

Bean Sprout Patties

A REALLY TASTY WHOLEFOOD RECIPE – JUICY PEPPERS MAKE A GREAT ACCOMPANIMENT TO THESE UNUSUAL PATTIES

Mung, or mungo beans as they are known in America, produce the bean sprouts that are so widely used in Far Eastern cookery. For this recipe, the sprouts must be ripe and really fresh. Instead of peppers, a green salad with herb dressing could also make a good accompaniment.

190 g bean sprouts
120 g white onions; 1 small red chilli pepper
100 g wholegrain wheatflour; 4 eggs
2 tbsp chopped mixed herbs (basil, parsley and thyme)
salt; freshly ground pepper

For the peppers
150 g each red and green peppers
60 g white onion; 1 clove garlic
2 tbsp vegetable oil; 1/4 litre vegetable stock
1 tsp thyme leaves; 20 g butter, diced and chilled
salt; freshly ground white pepper

In addition
vegetable oil for frying
4 nasturtium flowers to garnish

1. Rinse the fresh bean sprouts, pick them over, then rinse again. Leave to drain well. Peel and finely chop the onions. Deseed the chilli pepper, remove the fibres and finely chop the flesh. Mix the flour and the eggs well together in a bowl. Add the onion, chilli pepper, bean sprouts, and the mixed herbs, season with salt and pepper and mix everything to a smooth dough. Leave to stand for 15 minutes in a cool place.

2. To prepare the peppers, roast them in a preheated oven at 220°C until the skins blister. Wrap in a damp cloth, or in a plastic bag, and leave to sweat, then skin them, working in strips, from top to bottom. Halve and deseed the peppers, remove the fibres and dice them into 5 mm cubes. Peel and finely chop the onion and the garlic.

3. Heat the oil in a pan and lightly soften the onion and the garlic. Add the peppers and sweat these. Pour in the stock, turn down the heat and leave to cook for 15 minutes. Sprinkle in the thyme and gradually stir in the pieces of chilled butter to lightly bind the vegetables. Season with salt and pepper.

4. Form the dough into 12 small, flat patties. Heat the oil in a frying pan and fry the patties for 3 minutes on each side, to a golden brown. Arrange the bean sprout patties on preheated plates with a portion of peppers and garnish with a nasturtium flower. Serve immediately, as the patties lose their crispness quite quickly.

Oatmeal Soufflé

SERVED WITH A FRESH GREEN SALAD THIS LIGHT SOUFFLÉ MAKES A WONDERFUL MAIN COURSE

The problem with making any soufflé that includes cereal is the difficulty of ensuring that it is evenly and smoothly mixed with the other ingredients. The final soufflé must rise lightly without ending up with a heavy base. It is also more important than ever that this soufflé is served the minute is cooked. Freshly crushed oats are better than the precooked kind, as they add much more flavour to the dish.

30 g shallots; 60 g butter
50 g oats, fine ground
40 g oatmeal flour
250 ml milk; salt
freshly ground pepper
freshly grated nutmeg
1/2 tsp ground coriander seeds
4 tbsp cream; 1 egg
1 tbsp chopped parsley; 1/2 tbsp chopped oregano
1 tbsp chopped sage leaves
4 egg yolks
100 g American Colby or Chester cheese, freshly grated
4 egg whites
In addition
softened butter
oatmeal flour for the soufflé dish

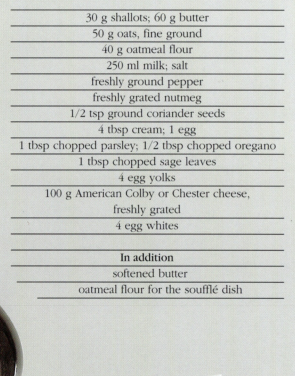

The cheese and herbs make this a really tasty soufflé. Tangy American Colby or Chester cheese can, if necessary, be replaced by a good mature Cheddar.

1. Peel and finely chop the shallots. Melt the butter in a pan and briefly fry the ground oats and the shallots. Add the oatmeal flour and, stirring continuously, cook over the lowest possible heat for 2-3 minutes. Gradually add the milk and stir to a smooth consistency. Season with salt, pepper and nutmeg, stir in the coriander and bring briefly to the boil. Turn down the heat and leave to cook for 10 minutes. Using a balloon whisk, whisk the

USA

mixture away from the sides of the pan to prevent it sticking or settling. Carefully fold in the cream and the egg.

2. Take the pan off the heat and stir in the herbs, followed, one at a time, by the egg yolks. Ensure each yolk has been completely absorbed into the mixture before adding the next. Stir in the grated cheese, then turn the mixture out into a bowl and leave to cool a little.

3. In a bowl, beat the egg whites to a firm snow. Using a spatula, fold these into the cheese and oatmeal mixture while it is still warm. Butter a 1.2 litre capacity soufflé dish with the softened butter and sprinkle the base and sides with oatmeal flour. Tip out any excess flour and fill the dish 2/3 full with the soufflé mixture, so that it has room to rise. Bake in a preheated oven at 180°C for 40-45 minutes. Serve immediately.

Vegetable Gratin

DRIED WHITE HARICOT BEANS PREPARED WITH A MIXTURE OF OTHER FRESH VEGETABLES

In America they love simple, filling dishes like this vegetable gratin. This is a dish which can be partly cooked well in advance, if required. The final 15 minutes cooking, however, must be done just before the dish is due to be served and the breadcrumbs must not be sprinkled on until the gratin is ready to go into the oven.

For the beans
250 g white cannellini beans
salt; 1 bay leaf; 3 sprigs thyme

For the mixed vegetables
100 g onions; 2 cloves garlic
500 g swedes; 350 g pumpkin; 300 g savoy cabbage
2 tbsp olive oil; 250 ml vegetable stock
salt; freshly ground pepper; 300 g tomatoes

In addition
25 g breadcrumbs; 3 tbsp olive oil; salt

The breadcrumb topping gives the dish a particularly crunchy finishing touch. Grated Parmesan, or another tasty hard cheese, can be mixed with the crumbs if desired.

All the vegetables, except the tomatoes, must be precooked before the gratin is baked in the oven.

USA

1. Soak the dried beans overnight in plenty of cold water. Strain, pick over and drain well. Put the beans in a pan with 1 litre salted water, add the bay leaf and the thyme and bring to the boil. Turn down the heat and leave the beans to cook for 1 hour, until cooked through.

2. Peel and slice the onions into rings. Peel and finely chop the garlic. Peel the swedes. Halve the pumpkin, scoop out the seeds and fibres, then peel the halves. Chop the pumpkin halves and the swedes into 4 mm thick matchsticks. Pull the tough outer leaves off the cabbage, cut out the main stalk and strip out the thicker leaf stalks and veins. Chop the leaves into 5 mm long pieces.

3. Heat the oil in a pan and lightly soften the onion and the garlic. Add the swede, pumpkin and cabbage, pour in the stock and leave to cook over a moderate heat for 15 minutes. Season with salt and pepper. Meanwhile, scald, skin and deseed the tomatoes and cut them into quarters.

4. Strain the beans and discard the thyme and the bay leaf. Mix the tomato and the beans into the pan with the vegetables, then turn out into a casserole dish. In a bowl, mix the breadcrumbs with the oil and the salt and then spread them evenly over the vegetables. Bake in a preheated oven at 200°C for 15 minutes and serve.

Sweetcorn and Vegetable Hotpot

AUTUMN, WHEN THE SWEETCORN HAS JUST RIPENED, IS THE SEASON FOR SERVING THIS AMERICAN VEGETABLE STEW

In this dish, the quality of the vegetables is more important than the actual combination. If calabrese (a green flowering variety of broccoli) is not available, cauliflower can be used instead.

250 g dried red kidney beans
2 corn-on-the-cob (about 250 g each)
600 g calabrese
200 g celeriac
600 g sweet potatoes
100 g spring onions
1 peperoni
2 tbsp vegetable oil
600 ml vegetable stock
salt; freshly ground pepper
cayenne pepper
1 tbsp chopped parsley
2-3 tbsp grated fresh horseradish
1/2 tsp cornflour mixed with 1 tbsp water

1. Soak the beans overnight in plenty of cold water, then strain, pick over and drain. Bring the beans to the boil with 1 litre salted water, turn down the heat and simmer until cooked through, but not mushy.

2. Pull the fibrous leaves and threads off the corn-on-the-cobs, then cook them in salted water for 35 minutes. Take out, leave to cool a little, then cut into 1 cm thick slices. Wash the calabrese, divide it into florets and discard the stalks.

3. Peel and dice the celeriac into 1 cm cubes. Peel and dice the sweet potatoes into 1.5 cm cubes. Clean and trim the spring onions, then slice them into 3 cm long pieces. Halve and deseed the peperoni, remove the fibres and cut the flesh into thin strips.

4. Heat the oil in a large stew pot, and sweat the celeriac and the sweet potato. Add the vegetable stock, season with salt, pepper and cayenne pepper, cover and leave to cook for 10 minutes. Add the sweetcorn and the calabrese and cook for a further 8 minutes. Finally add the spring onion, the peperoni and the red kidney beans and cook for a further 3 minutes.

5. Sprinkle in the parsley and the fresh, grated horseradish and season to taste. Smoothly stir in the cornflour paste and simmer briefly to thicken the stew. Serve with a chunk of crusty bread.

It is freshly grated horseradish which gives this dish its unique flavour. Do not use horseradish sauce or creamed horseradish as they will not have the same effect.

Sweetcorn Pasta with a Vegetable Sugo

THIS EXCEPTIONAL PASTA DISH OWES ITS SUCCESS TO THE ROQUEFORT CHEESE AND FRESH CREAM

The pasta for this dish is a reminder of the early pioneer years in America, being made with 50% maize flour. As a result, the dough has a unique consistency and is particularly light to work with.

For the pasta dough
150 g maize flour; 150 g wheatflour; 3 eggs
3 egg yolks; 1 tbsp olive oil; 1/2 tsp salt

For the sauce
80 g shallots; 1 clove garlic; 50 g carrots; 50 g leeks
200 g fresh peas (about 80 g shelled)
1 corn-on-the-cob (about 230 g)
200 g green asparagus; 100 g Roquefort cheese
150 ml cream; 150 ml vegetable stock; 20 g butter
1 tbsp chopped mixed herbs (thyme, basil, oregano and parsley)
salt; freshly ground pepper

1. Prepare the pasta dough, following the illustrated instructions, left and below. Roll the dough into a ball, wrap in cling film and leave to stand for 1 hour in the refrigerator. Using a pasta machine, roll out the dough to the required thickness and cut into 2 cm wide strips. Lay these on a cloth and leave to dry out a little.

Sift both kinds of flour together onto a work surface, make a well in the centre and place the eggs, egg yolks, oil and salt inside.

Mix the ingredients in the well with fork, then gradually draw in the flour from the sides and mix well together.

Knead the dough to a smooth, firm consistency.

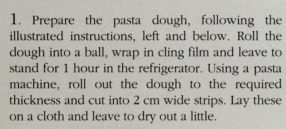

USA

Corn plays a dual role in this tasty recipe – as sweetcorn in the sauce and as maize flour in the pasta dough.

2. Peel and finely chop the shallots and the garlic. Wash, peel and finely dice the carrots. Wash, trim and finely dice the leeks. Shell the peas. Trim the corn-on-the-cob and scrape off the corn with a sharp knife. Wash the asparagus, and trim the stalk ends. Thinly peel the bottoms, then cut the spears into 3 cm long pieces.

3. Cook the sweetcorn in boiling, salted water for about 10 minutes. Add the asparagus and cook for a further 5 minutes, then add the peas and cook for another 3 minutes. Strain and refresh all three in ice cold water.

4. Dice the Roquefort. Heat the cream and the vegetable stock together in a pan, add the cheese, and, stirring continuously, cook until the cheese is melted. Melt the butter in a separate pan and sweat the shallots and the garlic. Add the diced leek and carrot and sweat for a further 5 minutes. Pour in the Roquefort sauce, add the asparagus, sweetcorn and peas and simmer for 3 minutes. Stir in the mixed herbs and season with salt and pepper. Cook the pasta in boiling, salted water al dente, then strain and divide between individual bowls. Top with the sauce and serve.

Radicchio di Treviso, with its white stalks and leaf veins and its long leaves, might be described as a designer vegetable. It is perfect for this recipe – both in colour and taste. Being slightly bitter it makes a good contrast to the blander lentils. If radicchio is not available, spinach can be used instead.

Lentils with Radicchio

A RAINBOW OF COLOURS, FROM LIGHT ORANGE LENTILS TO DARK RED RADICCHIO

Lentils were eaten in ancient Egypt and are among the oldest recorded foods known to man. The red lentils used here are already shelled, and so do not need to be soaked. They should only be cooked for a short time as they quickly turn mushy. The dish is accompanied by a creamy sauce, flavoured with raspberry vinegar.

For the sauce
50 g onion; 20 g butter
20 g young corn kernels
200 ml vegetable stock
250 ml cream; 1 tsp raspberry vinegar
salt; freshly ground white pepper
For the lentils
200 g red lentils, ready to cook; salt
80 g onion; 1 clove garlic
1 small red chilli pepper
500 g tomatoes
300 g radicchio di Treviso
2 tbsp olive oil
freshly ground white pepper
2 tbsp chopped mixed herbs (parsley, lemon thyme),

1. To prepare the sauce, peel and finely chop the onion. Melt the butter in a pan and lightly fry the onion until just transparent. Stir in the corn and leave to sweat briefly. Add the vegetable stock and the cream. Bring briefly to the boil, stirring well. Turn down the heat and leave the sauce to simmer for about 20 minutes, until it reaches a creamy consistency. Stir in the raspberry vinegar and season with salt and pepper. Purée the sauce in a blender.

2. Rinse the lentils in a sieve and drain well. Bring 1/2 litre salted water to the boil in a pan, add the lentils, turn down the heat and leave to cook for 15 minutes. Strain and drain well.

3. Peel and finely chop the onion and the garlic. Deseed the chilli pepper and slice it into rings. Scald, skin and deseed the tomatoes, then cut the flesh into quarters. Clean and trim the radicchio and cut it into 2 cm long strips.

4. Heat the oil in a pan and briefly sweat the onion, garlic and chilli pepper. Add the raddicchio and the tomato and simmer for 3 minutes. Season with salt and pepper, then stir in the lentils. Sprinkle in the mixed herbs, divide between individual preheated plates and serve with a spoonful of sauce.

A simple and extremely decorative dish with its amazing combination of different colours.

Pumpkin with Spicy Rice

A TRADITIONAL AMERICAN PUMPKIN RECIPE SERVED WITH SPICY RICE FROM THE FAR EAST

Once the pumpkin was considered a poor man's vegetable, but today the reverse is true and it has become highly sought after. The seeds are also the source of an inexpensive oil.

For the rice
5 g fresh ginger
1 chilli pepper
750 ml water
300 g long grain rice; salt

For the pumpkin
1 kg pumpkin
100 g spring onions
80 g onion
10 g fresh ginger

Spicy rice is the perfect accompaniment to this extremely tasty pumpkin dish.

2 chilli peppers; 3 tbsp vegetable oil
1/2 tsp cardamom seeds; 3 cloves
1 level tsp ground star aniseed
1 level tsp ground coriander seeds; salt; 300 ml water
freshly ground black pepper

In addition
1 tbsp chopped parsley or coriander leaves

Pumpkins have other uses as well as being good to eat, most notably on Hallowe'en night when children decorate them or carve them into imaginative lamps.

Photograph: Oliver Brachat

1. To prepare the rice, peel the ginger. Halve and deseed the chilli pepper and remove the fibres. In a pan, bring the water to the boil with the rice, salt, chilli pepper and ginger. Turn down the heat, and leave to cook for 15-20 minutes until cooked through.

USA

2. Peel the pumpkin, scoop out the seeds and dice the flesh into 2 cm cubes. Wash and trim the spring onions and slice them into 3 cm long pieces. Peel and finely chop the onion and the ginger. Halve and deseed the chilli peppers, remove the fibres and finely chop the flesh.

3. Heat the oil in a pan and lightly sweat the chopped onion, chilli and ginger. Add the cardamom seeds and the cloves and fry until the aroma of the spices is released. Add the pumpkin, stir in the star aniseed and the coriander and season with salt. Pour in the water and leave to cook for 10-12 minutes. Add the spring onions and cook for a further 3 minutes, then season with salt and pepper to taste. Take the chilli pepper and ginger out of the rice and discard. Fold the rice into the vegetable mixture, sprinkle with parsley or coriander and serve.

Broccoli and Potato Gratin

A SUBSTANTIAL DISH FROM THE NEW WORLD, FLAVOURED WITH GARLIC AND FRESH THYME

Layer the potato mixture on the bottom of the casserole dish, then layer the broccoli on top. Dot with the peeled, cooked garlic and spoon the tomato sauce over. Sprinkle with the grated cheese, place in a preheated oven at 190°C and bake for 15-20 minutes until the top has turned a golden brown.

Purple sprouting broccoli can vary in shade from a light reddish violet to dark purple, depending on the variety. However, it gradually loses its colour as it cooks.

For the fresh tomato sauce
700 g tomatoes; 80 g onion; 30 g carrot
30 g leek; 2 tbsp vegetable oil; 1 sprig thyme
salt; freshly ground pepper
1 tbsp chopped mixed herbs (thyme, parsley and basil)

For the broccoli and potato
700 g purple sprouting broccoli; 600 g potatoes
100 g onions; 150 g root parsley
2 tbsp vegetable oil; salt; freshly ground pepper
1 tbsp chopped thyme

In addition
8 cloves garlic; 1 sprig thyme
1 tbsp vegetable oil for the oven dish
30 g Monterey Jack cheese, freshly grated

1. Scald, skin and deseed the tomatoes, then cut the flesh into small pieces. Peel the onion and the carrot, wash and trim the leek, then finely dice all three vegetables.

2. Heat the oil in a pan and fry the onions until just transparent. Add the tomato, carrot, leek and sprig of thyme and season with salt and pepper. Cover and leave to simmer over the lowest possible heat for about 40 minutes. Strain through a sieve, stir in the mixed herbs and season to taste with salt and pepper.

3. Divide the broccoli into florets and wash and drain these well. Cut off and discard the thicker stalks, peel the thinner ones and cut them into 2 cm long pieces. Cook the stalks in boiling, salted water for 2 minutes, then add the florets and cook for a further 5 minutes. Take out, strain and refresh. Drain the broccoli well and reserve it.

4. Peel the potatoes and dice them into 1 cm cubes. Peel and chop the onions. Peel and cut the root parsley into quarters, then slices. Heat the oil in a pan and fry the diced potato for 10 minutes. Add the onion and the root parsley and fry for a further 5 minutes. Season with salt and pepper and sprinkle in the chopped thyme.

5. Add the unpeeled garlic and the sprig of thyme to a shallow casserole dish, pour over the oil and roast in a preheated oven at 190°C for 15 minutes. Take the dish out. Discard the thyme, leave the garlic to cool a little, then peel it. Finish the gratin preparation, following the illustrated instructions, top left. Serve on preheated plates.

USA

When buying artichokes, check that the stalks are intact. This way you can be sure that the first time the artichoke is cut into is just before it is cooked.

Fried Artichokes in Batter

SERVED WITH GUACAMOLE – A SPICY TOMATO AND AVOCADO SAUCE

This recipe is a typical example of Californian nouvelle cuisine, a style of cooking which concentrates on really fresh produce, imaginatively prepared. This dish undoubtedly gets its inspiration from South America, as *guacamole* is, of course, a popular Mexican dip. The *guacamole* needs to be made as late as possible, as avocado quickly discolours.

8 globe artichokes with stalks (about 60 g each)
juice of 1 lemon; salt

For the batter
1/4 lampion chilli pepper, deseeded
200 g flour
1/8 litre white wine
100 ml milk
2 eggs; salt

For the guacamole
120 g tomatoes
50 g white onion
1/2 lampion chilli pepper, deseeded
2 avocado pears
salt; juice 1/2 lime
freshly ground pepper
3 tbsp vegetable oil
1 tbsp coriander leaves, chopped

In addition
oil for frying; coriander leaves to garnish

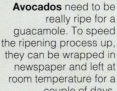

Avocados need to be really ripe for a guacamole. To speed the ripening process up, they can be wrapped in newspaper and left at room temperature for a couple of days.

1. Slice the stalks off the artichokes directly under the base and brush the base immediately with lemon juice. Pull off the small, tough lower leaves and trim the points off the remainder with kitchen scissors, then slice the top off the artichoke using a sharp knife.

2. Bring a large pan of water to the boil with the remaining lemon juice and a pinch of salt. Add the artichokes and cook for 15 minutes. Take out of the water and drain, upside down. Halve the artichokes lengthways and scoop out the choke with a spoon.

3. To prepare the batter, finely chop the lampion chilli pepper. Sieve the flour into a bowl and mix well with the white wine and the milk. Add the

USA

eggs, chilli pepper and salt to taste and beat well. Leave the batter to stand for about 20 minutes.

4. To prepare the *guacamole,* scald, skin and deseed the tomatoes, then finely chop the flesh. Peel and finely chop the onion. Finely chop the chilli pepper. Halve the avocados lengthways and prise out the stones. Scoop out the flesh with a spoon and roughly mash it with a fork.

5. One after the other, carefully mix the tomato, onion, chilli pepper and avocado together. Season with salt, flavour with the lime juice and season with pepper if desired. Stir in the oil and the coriander leaves.

6. To fry the artichokes, heat the oil in a chip pan or deep fat fryer to 180°C. Dip the artichokes, one at a time, into the batter then fry them in the hot oil to a golden brown.

7. Take the artichokes out and drain well on kitchen paper. Arrange on plates with a portion of *guacamole,* garnish with coriander leaves and serve immediately.

MEXICO

Salsa Verde

HERE THE SPICY SAUCE MADE FROM GREEN TOMATOES AND CHILLI PEPPERS IS USED AS A TORTILLA FILLING

Mexican cookery without the *tortilla* would be unthinkable. Generally, *tortillas* are made from maize flour, except in northern Mexico, where they are often made from wheat flour. They can always be bought ready made in the markets.

In Mexico, *salsa verde* is served with a wide variety of simple dishes, including *tortillas*. It is made, not with ordinary unripe tomatoes but with tomatillos, the so-called green tomato which is actually a member of the *physalis* family. If these are not available, then ordinary, unripened tomatoes can be used instead.

For the tortilla dough
400 g wheat flour; 1 tsp salt
60 g melted butter; 150 ml lukewarm water

For the salsa verde
500 g tomatillos; 4 cloves garlic
60 g white onion; 2 dried Serrano chilli peppers
1 dried chilli pasilla; 1/2 litre water
1 tbsp coriander leaves, roughly chopped; salt

In addition
2 tbsp vegetable oil; 80 g white onion, chopped
250 g Mexican cream cheese or Ricotta
salt; coriander leaves to garnish

1. Rub the flour, melted butter and salt together in a bowl. Add the water and work to a smooth dough. Wrap in cling film and leave to stand for 1/2 hour. Divide the dough into 16 pieces, then thinly roll these out to form tortillas, 16 cm in diameter. Dry fry these in a non stick pan for 1-2 minutes on each side and keep hot.

2. Wash and quarter the tomatillos. Peel the garlic. Peel and finely chop the onion. Wash both types of chilli pepper thoroughly, under cold running water. Cut off the stalks and deseed the chilli peppers through the hole. Bring the water to the boil, add the tomatillos, onion, chilli peppers and 2 of the garlic cloves, turn down the heat and simmer for 20 minutes. Strain, reserving the cooking liquid, and leave to drain.

3. Grind the remaining garlic with the coriander leaves in a mortar. Season with salt. Add the tomato and chilli mixture and grind everything to a paste. If the salsa is too dry, add a little of the reserved cooking liquid.

4. Heat the oil in a pan and sweat the chopped onion. Add the *salsa* and simmer over a low heat for 10 minutes. Take off the heat, leave to cool a little, then stir in the cheese. Season with salt.

5. Lay one tortilla on each plate, spread with the *salsa verde* and top with a second *tortilla*. Sprinkle with coriander leaves and serve.

Stuffed Pancakes with Vegetables

CONTRASTING COLOUR AND FLAVOUR IS PROVIDED BY THE BLACK BEAN SAUCE

This is a different way to serve mixed vegetables from the usual stew or gratin – in parchment thin pancakes with a black bean sauce.

For the black bean sauce
100 g black beans; 1 tbsp vegetable oil
50 g shallots, chopped; 1/2 litre vegetable stock
50 ml red wine; 2 tbsp light soy sauce
salt; freshly ground black pepper
1 level tsp cornflour

For the pancakes
90 ml milk; 30 ml water; 50 g flour
1 egg, 1 egg yolk; 10 g butter, melted; salt
butter for frying

For the vegetables
150 g red peppers; 150 g mangold
100 g yellow peppers; 100 g green courgettes
50 g white onion; 1 chilli pepper; 3 tbsp vegetable oil
100 ml vegetable stock; salt; freshly ground pepper
1 tsp chopped Mexican oregano

In addition
1 tbsp sesame seeds, roasted
Mexican oregano leaves to garnish

1. Soak the black beans overnight in plenty of cold water. Strain and drain well.

2. Heat the oil in a pan and soften the shallots until just transparent. Add the beans. Pour in the vegetable stock and the red wine, bring to the boil, turn down the heat and leave to cook for about 50 minutes. Flavour with the soy sauce and season with salt and pepper. In a bowl, stir the cornflour to a smooth paste with a little water, then stir it into the sauce to thicken it.

3. To prepare the pancakes, mix the milk and the water together in a bowl. Sift the flour into a second bowl and, using a balloon whisk, whisk in the milk and water. Add the egg, egg yolk, melted butter and salt to taste and whisk quickly to a smooth batter. Cover and leave to stand for 1 hour. Stir the batter again just before you use it.

4. To prepare the vegetables, halve and deseed the peppers, remove the fibres and dice the flesh into 1 cm cubes. Rinse the mangold and slice the leaves into 1 cm wide strips and the stalks into 4 cm long, julienne strips. Trim the courgettes, halve them lengthways and cut into slices. Peel and thinly slice the onion into rings. Halve and deseed the chilli pepper, remove the fibres and finely chop the flesh.

5. Heat the oil in a pan and fry the onion until just transparent. Add the peppers and the mangold stalks and sweat for 4 minutes. Stir in the chilli pepper and the courgette, add the stock and simmer for 2 minutes. Finally, add the mangold leaves, season with salt and pepper, sprinkle in the oregano and leave to simmer for a further 3 minutes.

6. Melt a knob of butter in an omelette pan, 18 cm in diameter. Tipping the pan slightly, pour in a little batter and gradually tip the pan to spread it thinly and evenly over the bottom. Cook evenly on each side, using a pan slice to turn the pancake. Make 3 more pancakes the same way.

7. Roll each pancake into a cornet shape, lay it on a plate and fill it generously with the vegetables. Sprinkle with sesame seeds and oregano leaves, ladle the bean sauce round and serve.

Quinoa Seed Risotto with Beetroot

A VEGETARIAN RECIPE FROM THE HIGH ANDES

Quinoa seeds, which come from a plant that is virtually unknown here, are an important foodstuff in Peru. Thanks to the popularity of vegetarian cookery however, these seeds are becoming better known and more readily available in this country.

For the beetroot
700 g beetroot; 60 g spring onions
40 g butter; 1 heaped tsp flour
300 ml vegetable stock; 50 ml cream
salt; freshly ground pepper

For the quinoa seed risotto
50 g white onion; 70 g celery; 30 g leek
30 g root parsley; 2 tbsp oil
200 g quinoa seeds; 800 ml vegetable stock
salt; freshly ground pepper; 1 tbsp parsley, chopped

Cooked as a risotto, the quinoa seeds swell to resemble rice. Served with a creamy beetroot accompaniment, this is an unusual and delicious recipe.

1. Scrub the beetroot under cold running water. Trim the leaves to within 2-3 cm of the root, to prevent bleeding. Cook in boiling salted water for 1 hour.

2. Test the beetroot with a wooden cocktail stick, to ensure it is cooked through. Take out, refresh under cold water and leave to cool a little. Skin and trim the beetroot. Using a decorative

PERU

vegetable cutter, slice the beetroot into 1.5 cm long sticks. Set aside.

3. To prepare the risotto, peel and finely chop the onion. Trim and wash the celery and the leek. Peel the root parsley. Finely dice all four of these.

4. Heat the oil in a pan and sweat the diced vegetables for a few minutes, add the quinoa seeds and fry briefly. Pour in the stock and season with salt and pepper. Bring briefly to the boil, turn down the heat, cover and leave to cook for 30 minutes, stirring occasionally. Sprinkle in the parsley and season to taste.

5. To finish the beetroot, trim and thinly slice the spring onions. Melt the butter in a pan and lightly soften the spring onion. Sprinkle in the flour and leave to lightly colour. Add the stock, and stirring continuously, cook for 10 minutes. Stir in the cream, season with salt and pepper and mix in the beetroot. Ladle portions of quinoa seed risotto and beetroot onto individual plates and serve.

ARGENTINA

Ragout of Mushrooms with Polenta

SERVED IN A SMOOTH SAUCE MADE WITH WHITE WINE, DRY VERMOUTH AND LOTS OF CREAM

In South America, maize, or corn as it would be called here, is an important foodstuff that can be used as an ingredient in any number of different recipes. For this dish it is ground as semolina, made into polenta and then diced and fried.

For the polenta
625 ml vegetable stock
80 g butter; 1/2 tsp salt
180 g medium ground semolina
1 tbsp vegetable oil

For the sauce
50 g shallots; 20 g butter
100 ml white wine
50 ml dry vermouth (Noilly Prat)
200 ml cream
150 ml crème fraîche
salt; freshly ground white pepper

For the mushrooms
300 g field mushrooms
300 g shitake mushrooms
50 g shallots
1 tbsp vegetable oil
30 g butter
salt; freshly ground white pepper
1 tbsp chopped parsley

1. To prepare the polenta, bring the vegetable stock to the boil in a pan with 40 g butter and the salt. Stirring continuously, add the semolina in a thin stream, ensuring that the stock does not go off the boil or that any lumps form. Cook the polenta for about 20 minutes, stirring continuously in one direction to stop it sticking to the sides of the pan. Using a palette knife, spread the cooked polenta out evenly to about 1 cm thick on a board. Leave it to cool and then cut it into 2.5 cm square pieces.

2. To prepare the sauce, peel and finely chop the shallots. Melt the butter in a pan and soften the shallots until just transparent. Slake with the white wine and the vermouth and cook to reduce the liquid by about 2/3. Stir in the cream and the crème fraîche and cook, over the lowest possible heat, to a creamy consistency. Season with salt and pepper, then strain through a fine sieve and set aside.

3. To prepare the mushrooms, clean and either quarter or halve the field mushrooms, according to size. Halve the shitake mushrooms and trim the ends off the stalks. Peel and finely chop the shallots. Melt the oil and the butter in a pan and soften the shallots. Add both types of mushroom and, stirring continuously, sauté for 5 minutes. Season with salt and pepper and sprinkle with chopped parsley.

4. In a second pan, heat the oil and remaining butter and fry the polenta cubes to a golden brown on all sides. Briefly reheat the sauce and whisk it with a hand-held mixer. Arrange portions of mushrooms and polenta squares on individual preheated dishes, coat with the sauce and serve.

UTENSILS

The range of utensils needed for vegetarian cookery is much the same as that normally used in any kitchen, although there are a few specialist tools which may be useful. However, these are not essential.

1. Cereal grinder
2. Cereal grinding attachment for food processor
3. Blender jug
4. Wok with basket steamer
5. Wire draining spoon for use with a wok
6. Pasta machine
7. Cutting attachment for pasta machine
8. Mandolin grater
9. Whisking bowls
10. Spatula for use with a wok
11. Vegetable graters
12. Vegetable slicer with set of blades
13. Shallow casserole dishes
14. Terrine dish
15. Chopping board and chopping blade
16. Citrus fruit juicer
17. Set of sieves
18. Potato press
19. Pastry wheel
20. Melon baller
21. Vegetable peeler
22. Asparagus peeler
23. Garlic press
24. Grater for slicing truffles
25. Wooden spoon
26. Balloon whisk
27. Hand held electric mixer

Index

References to information on ingredients or techniques are written in italics. All other entries in the index are for recipes.

A
Artichokes with an Egg Vinaigrette 26
Artichokes, Fried, in Batter, 202
Asafoetida 136
Asparagus and Pak Choi 173
Asparagus Tart 60
Asparagus with Poached Eggs 42
Asparagus, Risotto with Peas and, 182
Aubergine and Spicy Rice Rolls 120
Aubergine Salad, Warm, 124
Aubergine, Fried, with Fresh Tomato Sauce 12
Aubergine, Fried, with Tofu 169
Aubergines, Biryani Rice with, 162
Avocados, ripening, 202

B
Banana and Vegetable Stuffed Egg Pancakes 158
Banana Curry, Mango and, 144
Bananas for curry 145
Batter, Fried Artichokes in, 202
Bean Sprout Patties 186
Bean sprouts, forcing 9
Bean Stew, Green, 184
Beetroot, Quinoa Seed Risotto with, 208
Biryani Rice with Aubergines 162
Blinis 50
Briks 130
Broccoli and Potato Gratin 200
Broccoli Terrine, Pumpkin and, 62
Buckwheat Dumplings 108

C
Cabbage and Chestnut Rolls 78
Candle nuts 156
Cannelloni, Mushroom, 94
Carrots, chopping 9
Cauliflower Curry 146
Cauliflower, Fried, 138
Ceps 102
Ceps with Potato Noodles 52
Chanterelle Parcels 66
Cheese Balls, Rice and, 48
Cheese, Vegetable Macaroni, 92
Cheeses, Portuguese, 12
Chestnut Rolls, Cabbage and, 78

Chickpea snacks 134
Choisum and Paprika with Rice Noodles 176
Comté cheeses 24
Corncakes with Cucumber Sauce 64
Corn-on-the-cob 90
Courgette Gratin 18
Courgette, Polenta-Stuffed, 102
Cracked Wheat with Mushrooms 126
Cucumber Sauce, Corncakes with, 64
Curry leaves 140
Curry, Cauliflower, 146
Curry, Indian vegetable, 142
Curry, Mango and Banana, 144
Curry, Okra and Mixed Vegetable, 140
Curry, Papaya and Sweet Potato, 148

D
Dumplings, Buckwheat, 108
Dumplings, mushroom, 74

E
Egg and vegetables, spicy, in pastry 130
Egg Bake, Vegetable and, 14
Egg Flan with Herbs and Mushrooms 98
Egg Noodles, Fried Vegetables with, 152
Egg Pancakes, Banana and Vegetable Stuffed, 158
Egg Vinaigrette, Artichokes with an, 26
Eggs, free range, 14
Eggs, Poached, Asparagus with, 42
Eggs, Stuffed, with White Bean Salad 122
Eggs, Vegetable Fried Rice with, 156

F
Falafels 134
Fennel Risotto 84
Fettucine with White Truffles 104
Flan, Egg, with Herbs and Mushrooms 98
Fried Cauliflower 138

G
Garlic Mushrooms 22

Gnocchi in Fresh Tomato Sauce 106
Goat's milk cheeses 36
Gorgonzola, Risotto with Spinach and, 88
Gouda cheeses 46
Gratin, Broccoli and Potato, 200
Gratin, Courgette, 18
Green Bean Stew 184
Guacamole 202

H
Herb Pancakes 58
Herbs and Mushrooms, Egg Flan with, 98
Herbs, Wholewheat Tortelloni with Ricotta and, 96
Hot Vegetable Quiche 24
Hotpot, Sweetcorn and Vegetable, 192

J
Jacket Potatoes with a Spicy Filling 54

K
Kaiserling Mushrooms, Stuffed, 28
Kaiserschmarren with Plum Compôte 76
Kath Katha 142

L
Lahaniká Yahní 116
Lentils with Radicchio 196
Lentils, Vegetable Patties with, 136

M
Macaroni Cheese, Vegetable, 92
Mango and Banana Curry 144
Mangold Stuffed Pancakes 32
Mediterranean vegetable stew 116
Millet Pancakes 46
Millet Risotto, Vegetable 'Tagliatelle' with, 44
Millet with Vegetables 114
Mimolette cheese 44
Mixed Vegetables 16
Moussaka with Tomatoes in Olive Oil 118
Mung bean sprouts 186

INDEX

Mushroom Cannelloni 94
Mushroom dumplings 74
Mushroom Maultaschen 70
Mushroom Sandwiches, Fried Polenta and, 90
Mushrooms, Cracked Wheat with, 126
Mushrooms, Egg Flan with Herbs and, 98
Mushrooms, Garlic, 22
Mushrooms, Ragout of, with Polenta, 210
Mushrooms, Rösti with Scrambled Egg and, 80
Mushrooms, Stuffed Kaiserling, 28

N
Nimono, Tofu and Vegetable, 178

O
Oatmeal Soufflé 188
Okra and Mixed Vegetable Curry 140
Onions, chopping 9
Oyster sauce, vegetarian, 170

P
Paella, Vegetarian, 20
Pak Choi, Asparagus and, 173
Pancakes with plum compôte 76
Pancakes, Banana and Vegetable Stuffed Egg, 158
Pancakes, Herb, 58
Pancakes, Mangold Stuffed, 32
Pancakes, Millet, 46
Pancakes, Stuffed, with Vegetables 206
Panch foron spice mixture 146
Pan-Fried Pepper Bread 132
Papaya and Sweet Potato Curry 148
Paprika with Rice Noodles, Choisum and, 176
Pasta, Sweetcorn, with a Vegetable Sugo 194
Pastry, spicy egg and vegetables in, 130
Pasty, Tomato, 30
Patties, Bean Sprout, 186
Patties, Vegetable, with Lentils 136
Peanuts and Vegetables, Fried Tofu with, 154
Pearl Barley with Pumpkin 110
Peas and Asparagus, Risotto with, 182
Pepper Bread, Pan-Fried, 132
Pepper jelly 132
Pepper Salad, Fried Sesame Bread with a Tomato and, 68

Pineapple, Fried Rice in, 150
Pizza Verdura 100
Plum Compôte, Kaiserschmarren with, 76
Polenta, Fried, and Mushroom Sandwiches 90
Polenta, Ragout of Mushrooms with, 210
Polenta-Stuffed Courgette 102
Potato 'Snails' 72
Potato Gratin, Broccoli and, 200
Potato Noodles, Ceps with, 52
Potato Terrine, Hot, with Cold Ratatouille 36
Potatoes, Jacket, with a Spicy Filling 54
Provençal Vegetables, Red Rice with, 34
Pulses, soaking 9
Pumpkin and Broccoli Terrine 62
Pumpkin Flowers with Red Pepper Sauce 112
Pumpkin with Spicy Rice 198
Pumpkin, Pearl Barley with, 110
Pumpkin, Rice-Stuffed, 164

Q
Quail's Eggs, Mixed Vegetables with, 170
Quiche, Hot Vegetable, 24
Quinoa Seed Risotto with Beetroot 208

R
Radicchio, Lentils with, 196
Ragout of Mushrooms with Polenta 210
Ratatouille, Cold, Hot Potato Terrine with, 36
Red Pepper Sauce, Pumpkin Flowers with, 112
Red Peppers, Risotto with, 86
Red Rice with Provençal Vegetables 34
Red Wine Sauce, Spaghetti with a Shallot and, 180
Rice and Cheese Balls 48
Rice Noodles 174, 176
Rice Noodles with Mixed Vegetables 174
Rice Noodles, Choisum and Paprika with, 176
Rice Rolls, Spicy, Aubergine and, 120
Rice with Sweet Potato and Tofu 160
Rice, Fried, in Pineapple 150

Rice, Spicy, Pumpkin with, 198
Rice, Vegetable Fried, with Eggs, 156
Rice-Stuffed Pumpkin 164
Ricotta 96
Ricotta and Herbs, Wholewheat Tortelloni with, 96
Riesling Sauce. Vegetables in, 56
Risotto with Peas and Asparagus 182
Risotto with Red Peppers 86
Risotto with Spinach and Gorgonzola 88
Risotto, Fennel, 84
Risotto, Millet, Vegetable 'Tagliatelle' with, 44
Risotto, Quinoa Seed, with Beetroot 208
Risotto, Saffron, with Summer Truffles 82
Rösti with Scrambled Egg and Mushrooms 80

S
Saffron 20
Saffron Risotto with Summer Truffles 82
Salad, Warm Aubergine, 124
Salsa Verde 204
Savory 184
Schwammerknödel 74
Scrambled Egg and Mushrooms, Rösti with, 80
Sesame Bread, Fried, with a Tomato and Pepper Salad 68
Shallot and Red Wine Sauce, Spaghetti with a, 180
Soufflé, Oatmeal, 188
Spaghetti with a Shallot and Red Wine Sauce 180
Spicy Filling, Jacket Potatoes with a, 54
Spicy Rice Rolls, Aubergine and, 120
Spicy Rice, Pumpkin with, 198
Spicy sweet and sour sauce 158
Spicy Vegetables 128
Spicy vegetables and egg in pastry 130
Spinach and Gorgonzola, Risotto with, 88
Spinach Tartlets 40
Stock, Vegetable 8
Stuffed Eggs with White Bean Salad 122
Stuffed Kaiserling Mushrooms 28 ???
Sugo, Vegetable, Sweetcorn Pasta with, 194

INDEX

Sunflower crisps 56
Sweet Potato and Bean Curd, Rice with, 160
Sweet Potato Curry, Papaya and, 148
Sweetcorn and Vegetable Hotpot 192
Sweetcorn Pasta with a Vegetable Sugo 194

T
Tart, Asparagus, 60
Tartlets, Spinach, 40
Terrine, Hot Potato, with Cold Ratatouille, 36
Terrine, Pumpkin and Broccoli, 62
Tofu and Vegetable Nimono 178
Tofu Envelopes 166
Tofu, Fried Aubergine with, 169
Tofu, Fried, with Peanuts and Vegetables 154
Tofu, Sweet Potato with Rice and, 160
Tomato and Pepper Salad, FriedSesame Bread with a, 68
Tomato Pasty 30
Tomato Sauce, Fresh, Fried Aubergine with, 12
Tomato Sauce, Fresh, Gnocchi in, 106
Tomatoes in Olive Oil, Moussaka with, 118
Tortelloni, Wholewheat, with Ricotta and Herbs 96
Truffles, Saffron Risotto with Summer, 82
Truffles, White, Fettucini with, 104

V
Vegetable 'Tagliatelle' with Millet Risotto 44
Vegetable and Egg Bake 14
Vegetable Fried Rice with Eggs 156
Vegetable Gratin 190
Vegetable Macaroni Cheese, 92
Vegetable Patties with Lentils 136
Vegetable stew, Mediterranean, 116
Vegetables, Fried, with Egg Noodles, 152
Vegetables in Riesling Sauce 56
Vegetables, Millet with, 114
Vegetables, Mixed, 16
Vegetables, Mixed, with Quail's Eggs 170
Vegetables, Mixed, with Rice Noodles 174
Vegetables, Spicy, 128
Vegetables, Stuffed Pancakes with, 206
Vegetables, Yorkshire Pudding with, 38
Vegetarian 'prawns' 176
Vegetarian Paella 20
Vinaigrette, Egg, Artichokes with an, 26

W
White Bean Salad, Stuffed Eggs with, 123
White bean sauce 170
White Truffles, Fettucini with, 104
Wholewheat Tortelloni with Ricotta and Herbs 96

Y
Yeast pancakes, filled, 50
Yorkshire Pudding with Vegetables 38

ACKNOWLEDGEMENTS

The publishers gratefully acknowledge the help and advice of all those invloved in the production of this book, in particular
Rachid Sabir, Al Baraka Restaurant, Marrakesh, Morocco; Gabriele Ferron, Antica Riseria, Isola della Scala, Italy; Yim Chee Peng, Culinary Studios Pte. Ltd., Singapore; M. Schmidt and Mme Ager, Ferme des Embêts, Lapoutroie, France; Edoardo Ferrarini, Firma Slogan immagine e comunicazione, Bologna, Italy; MM. Droutet and Barbier, Fromagerie Vacherin du Mont d'Or, Frasne, France; M. Griotto, Mas de Nans, Arles, France; James Koh and Abdul Salam, Imperial Hotel, Singapore; Tony Khoo, Konrad Hilton Hotel, Singapore; Herrn Georg Schütterle Jun., Untereschach, Germany.

PICTURE CREDITS

48 (bottom left) Lennard, Dänisches Fremdenverkehrsamt, Hamburg, Germany
198 (bottom left) Oliver Brachat, Füssen, Germany

TEUBNER EDITION

Copyright	© 1997 by Teubner Edition Postfach 1440 • D-87620 Füssen, Germany
Procurement and styling	Pascale Veldboer, Angelika Mayr
Studio cooks	Barbara Mayr, Walburga Streif, Oliver Brachat, Helena Brügmann
Photography	Christian Teubner, Odette Teubner, Oliver Brachat, Julia Christl, Bettina Gousset, Kerstin Mosny, Christoph Tumler
Editors	Veronika Storath, Pascale Veldboer, Katrin Wittmann, Birgit Kahle
Layout/DTP	Christian Teubner, Gabriele Wahl, Dietmar Pachlhofer
Production	Gabriele Wahl
Reproduction	Studio Europa, Trento, Italy

TIME-LIFE BOOKS

Editor	Mark Stephenson
Editorial	Anton Wills-Eve, Kate Cann
Design	Dawn McGinn
Translated from German by	Carole Fahy
Production	Justina Cox
Copyright	Authorized English language edition published by Time-Life Books BV, 1066 AZ, Amsterdam 1997 Time-Life Books BV First English language printing 1997

All rights reserved. No part of this publication may be reproduced, stored in a retrieval system or transmitted in any form or by means, electronic, mechanical, photocopying, recording or otherwise, without the permission of the publishers and copyright holders.

ISBN 0-7054-3552-0

MOTORCYCLE RACING

MOTORCYCLE RACING

BILL HOLDER

PHOTOGRAPHY BY
BOB FAIRMAN

MAGNA BOOKS

Published by Magna Books
Magna Road
Wigston
Leicester LE18 4ZH

Produced by Bison Books Ltd
Kimbolton House
117A Fulham Road
London SW3 6RL

Copyright © 1994 Bison Books Ltd

All rights reserved. No part of this publication may be reproduced, stored in a retrieval system or transmitted in any form by any means, electronic, mechanical, photocopying or otherwise, without first obtaining the written permission of the copyright owner.

ISBN 1-85422-574-X

Printed in Spain

Page 1: High-flying Georges Jobe, a top-flight European Motocross competitor, gets some 'air-time' on his way to winning the 500cc race at the Belgian Motocross Grand Prix.

Previous pages: Two-time World Superbike champion Fred Merkel from the United States shows his championship form.

These pages: Italian Luca Cadalora takes his Yamaha to victory in the 500cc race at the British Motorcycle Grand Prix, Donington Park, 1993.

Overleaf: Spaniard Alex Criville defies gravity as he leans his NSR500 Honda over during the Japanese Grand Prix at Suzuka circuit.

CONTENTS

ROAD RACING	**6**
DIRT TRACKING	**38**
MOTOCROSS	**50**
DRAG RACING	**70**
HILLCLIMBING	**86**
ICE RACING, DESERT RACING, AND MORE	**96**
INDEX AND ACKNOWLEDGMENTS	**112**

Dedication

This book is dedicated to AMA road racers James Adamo, who was fatally injured in the 1993 Daytona 200, and Wayne Rainey, who was seriously injured in the 1993 Italian Grand Prix.

ROAD RACING

MOTORCYCLE RACING

Without a doubt, the ultimate expression of speed and performance on two wheels is road racing. Whether on esoteric Grand Prix machinery or production motorcycles, every weekend somewhere in the world leather-clad warriors take themselves to the limit in search of an unimaginable thrill. No matter what level of competition, only a racer knows the 'buzz' that comes from competing and being in total harmony with the bike, as he screams around the world's great racetracks at mind-boggling speeds. Through the turns, the bikes are laid over almost horizontally, seemingly defying the laws of physics, gripping the road with massive tires specially made for the job.

Road racing takes place on most of the same tracks worldwide that Formula One, Indy Cars and NASCAR use — famous world championship courses such as Daytona (USA), Donington Park (Great Britain), Hockenheim (Germany), Le Mans (France), Suzuka (Japan), Brno (Czechoslovakia), Eastern Creek (Australia), and others. The sport has been popular in Europe, and since the 1940s there have been classes for 50cc, 80cc, 125cc, 250cc, 350cc, 500cc, Formula One, and Endurance at various times. There are currently three road racing world championship classes — Grand Prix, Superbike, and Endurance — sanctioned by the sport's governing body, the Federation of International Motorcycles (FIM).

The Grand Prix class is now run in four categories and is regarded as the cutting edge of technology. All the bikes are two-strokes and the top, 500cc, class is thought of as the 'Blue Ribbon' of road racing. Grand Prix bikes are hand-

Above: Triple World Grand Prix 500cc champion Wayne Rainey was heading for a fourth title on his Yamaha YZR500 when a cruel accident at Misano circuit, Italy, in 1993, left him paralyzed and ended his racing career.

Right: High-tech bikes gather on the grid for the start of the French 500cc Grand Prix at Le Mans.

ROAD RACING

MOTORCYCLE RACING

Top: Running for the Lucky Strike Suzuki Team, Texan Kevin Schwartz took the 1993 500cc World Grand Prix championship. His performance was one of the big reasons that Suzuki finished second (by only points) in the Constructors Championship that year.

Above: The entire 500cc Grand Prix field sweeps through Craner Curves at Donington Park circuit, England, at the start of the 1993 British Grand Prix. Donington is regarded as one of the safest race circuits in the world.

Right: Australian Michael Doohan pours on the coal on his NSR500 Honda Grand Prix machine. One of the Grand Prix's most consistent performers, Doohan finished fourth in the 1993 season and was second a year earlier.

ROAD RACING

Left: Italian Max Biaggi, on his factory Honda NSR250, takes his first victory of the 1993 Grand Prix season at Catalunya circuit in northern Spain. At some circuits, the 250 GP bikes lap nearly as quickly as the 500s.

Below: Italian Doriano Romboni (NSR250 Honda) was fifth in the closely-contested 1993 250cc world championship. Here, at Hockenheim circuit in Germany, he won by just one tenth of a second.

built using the latest technology (in much the same way as Formula One cars), and without regard to cost. The 500s use specially built two-cycle (two stroke) engines producing around 170 horsepower with a bike weight of only 308 pounds. Some of the technology that is used on these ultra-rapid projectiles (a Honda NSR500 recently broke the 200 mph barrier!) does eventually show up on road bikes.

One step down in World Grand Prix competition is the 250cc class, which has been dominated by Yamaha's TZ250 and Honda's NSR250, though recently Suzuki and Italian manufacturer Aprilia have also proved more than competitive. The current smallest class in Grand Prix racing is for 125cc bikes. These extremely sensitive machines depend on power-to-weight ratio and high cornering speeds to enable them to maintain lap speeds close to those of their bigger brothers. There is also a sidecar class, which is based on a 500cc two-cycle (two stroke) engine. In the old days, a sidecar resembled a motorcycle with an attached platform for the passenger, but now it is more like a three-wheeled Formula One car, with specialized chassis, bodywork, and car racing parts.

Until the 1970s the Grand Prix scene was dominated by Europeans. Between 1966 and 1975, Italian Giacomo Agostini alone won an incredible 15 world titles, in 350cc and 500cc competition. Kenny Roberts initiated the American domination of the sport with 17 race wins and three world

MOTORCYCLE RACING

Previous pages: Italian Loris Capirossi (NSR250 Honda) leads the packed field at the start of the Spanish Grand Prix at Jerez circuit.

Below: German Dirk Raudies (NSR125 Honda) dominated the smallest Grand Prix class in the 1993 season, winning nine races on his way to the championship title.

titles beginning in the late 1970s. Since then, the Americans have set winning trends at the international level, and have won every 500cc world title since 1982.

The Superbike world championship series started in 1988, and since then, American riders have managed five wins. Californian Fred Merkel won the first two titles, in 1988 and 1989. In 1990, the crown went to the gritty Frenchman Raymond Roche, but Texan Doug Polen reclaimed the title for America in 1991 and 1992. In 1993 the successful American reign continued with Georgian Scott Russell.

The series is based on American Superbike racing regulations, but with tighter rules governing changes to the

Left: In 1991, Great Britain's sidecar team won the World Championship. The driver was Steve Webster, while Gaven Simmons fulfilled the all-important passenger role. The team was second in world competition in 1992.

Overleaf: Superbike champ Fred Merkel's left knee scrapes the curbstone at he leads Aaron Slight around the twisty Hungaroring circuit. Merkel (750 RC30 Honda) won the inaugural World Superbike Championship in 1988, and then repeated the feat in 1989.

Page 19: American Scott Russell (ZXR750 Muzzy Kawasaki) gave the Japanese factory its first World Superbike title in 1993.

MULTIPLE GRAND PRIX WORLD CHAMPIONS						
TITLE WINS (ALL CLASSES)	50cc	80cc	125cc	250cc	350cc	500cc
15 Giacomo Agostini (Ita) 1966–75	–	–	–	–	7	8
13 Angel Nieto (Spa) 1969–84*	6	–	–	–	–	–
9 Carlo Ubbiali (Ita) 1951–60*	–	–	–	3	–	–
9 Mike Hailwood (UK) 1961–67	–	–	–	3	2	4
7 John Surtees (UK) 1956–60	–	–	–	–	3	4
7 Phil Read (UK) 1964–74	–	–	1	4	–	2
6 Geoff Duke (UK) 1951–55	–	–	–	–	2	4
6 Jim Redman (SRho) 1962–65	–	–	–	2	4	–
5 Anton Mang (FRG) 1980–87	–	–	–	3	2	–
4 Hugh Anderson (NZ) 1963–65	2	–	2	–	–	–
4 Walter Villa (Ita) 1974–76	–	–	–	3	1	–
4 Kork Ballington (SAf) 1978–79	–	–	–	2	2	–
4 Stefan Dörflinger (Swi) 1982–85	2	2	–	–	–	–
4 Jorge Martinez (Spa) 1986–88	–	3	1	–	–	–
4 Eddie Lawson (USA) 1984–89	–	–	–	–	–	4
3 Bruno Ruffo (Ita) 1949–51	–	–	1	2	–	–
3 Werner Haas (FRG) 1953–54	–	–	1	2	–	–
3 Luigi Taveri (Swi) 1962–66	–	–	3	–	–	–
3 Hans-Georg Anscheidt (FRG) 1966–68	3	–	–	–	–	–
3 Pier Paolo Bianchi (Ita) 1976–80	–	–	3	–	–	–
3 Eugenio Lazzarini (Ita) 1978–80	2	–	1	–	–	–
3 Kenny Roberts (USA) 1978–80	–	–	–	–	–	3
3 Freddie Spencer (USA) 1983–85	–	–	–	1	–	2
2 Umberto Masetti (Ita) 1950–52	–	–	–	–	–	2
2 Fergus Anderson (UK) 1953–54	–	–	–	–	2	–
2 Bill Lomas (UK) 1955–56	–	–	–	–	2	–
2 Cecil Sandford (UK) 1952–57	–	–	1	1	–	–
2 Tarquinio Provini (Ita) 1957–58	–	–	1	1	–	–
2 Gary Hocking (SRho) 1961	–	–	–	–	1	1
2 Dieter Braun (FRG) 1970–73	–	–	1	1	–	–
2 Jan de Vries (Hol) 1971–73	2	–	–	–	–	–
2 Kent Andersson (Swe) 1973–74	–	–	2	–	–	–
2 Rolf Steinhausen (FRG) 1975–76	–	–	–	–	–	–
2 Barry Sheene (UK) 1976–77	–	–	–	–	–	2
2 Carlos Lavado (Ven) 1983–86	–	–	–	2	–	–
2 Fausto Gresini (Ita) 1985–87	–	–	2	–	–	–
2 Sito Pons (Spa) 1988–89	–	–	–	2	–	–
* includes classes no longer competed						

WORLD SUPERBIKE CHAMPIONS			
1988	Fred Merkel	USA	Yamaha
1989	Fred Merkel	USA	Yamaha
1990	Raymond Roche	France	Ducati
1991	Doug Polen	USA	Ducati
1992	Doug Polen	USA	Ducati
1993	Scott Russell	USA	Kawasaki

machines. A Superbike racer looks like a bike anybody can walk into a shop and buy, and to some extent that is true. The chassis, bodywork, and engine size must be the same as the road bike from which it is derived, but a certain amount of tuning is allowed – enough to turn the road bike into a full-blown racer capable of 180 mph. In America, Superbike rules are similar to those for the top class of American stock car racing, the NASCAR Winston Cup series.

The Endurance world championship is for races of 625 miles up to 24 hours. These long distance events have long been popular in Europe, and have been dominated by French riders for many years. However, Britons won in 1992, and a 'privateer,' American Doug Toland, took the world title in 1993. In 1993, four 24 hour races took place, at Le Mans and Paul Ricard (France), Spa (Belgium) and Anderstorp (Sweden). The Suzuka Eight Hours is held annually in Japan.

The Grand Prix, Superbike, and Endurance world championships are truly international, with races taking place all over Europe as well as in Malaysia, Japan, South America, Australia, New Zealand, and the USA. Each year the number of countries wanting to hold races increases, and there is even talk of events to be held in India, Indonesia, and the former Soviet Union in the not too distant future. The FIM restricts each championship to about 14 races a year (less in the case of the Endurance series). Most countries also hold their own national championships, with Superbikes being the most popular class due to lower running costs and availability of machinery.

The 500cc Grand Prix bike is now virtually beyond the reach of private riders – nearly all are factory-run efforts, with big sponsorship to match. In Europe and in other parts of the world, both the Grand Prix and Superbike world championships regularly attract as much publicity as Formula One car races, and are seen as a glorious combination

Left: The French Suzuki Endurance Team at the 1991 Le Mans 24 Hours. The number 1 signifies that this team was the 1990 Endurance World Champion. The riders were Herve Moineau (a five-time World Endurance champion), Patrice Igoa (fifth in the 1992 World Superbike points), and Jean-Michel Mattioli.

Above: The 1993 French Suzuki Endurance Team consisted of a trio of stars: Jehan D'Orgeix was fourth in the 1992 Enduro World Championships while teammate Michel Siméon placed fifth, and Jean-Marc Deletang was the 1992 French Superbike champion.

Left: The Isle of Man Tourist Trophy (TT) races are run on public roads. Here, on the drop down from Cre-N-Ba, the fans are almost close enough to touch Scotsman Jim Moodie as he completes another lap of the 37¾-mile circuit.

Far left: Going up Bray Hill, just after the start in Douglas, the front wheel becomes light and paws the air at speeds in excess of 120 mph.

Above left: Phil McCallen is airborne at Ballaugh Bridge on his way to second place in the 1993 Isle of Man TT Formula One race. Irish riders compete regularly on public roads at home and always seem to do well at the TT.

Above: Beautiful scenery forms a perfect backdrop as the TT competitors speed around the twisting public roads that form the world's best known pure road circuit.

of speed, power, and glamour rarely equalled in any other sport. The Endurance championship is not seen in quite the same context, but the Bol d'Or 24 Hours in Southern France attracted 100,000 fans in 1993, and the Suzuka Eight Hours went even better, with nearly 300,000 spectators over the race weekend.

Not a world championship, but classic in their own right, are the Isle of Man TT races, which have been run since 1911. These races for F1, F2, and F3 classes take place on a gruelling 37¾-mile-long winding mountain road circuit on a small island between England and Ireland. At one time they were part of a world championship, but as bikes got faster and faster the public roads were deemed too fast and dangerous and the event lost its world status. It doesn't seem to have made any difference to the spectators though – thousands upon thousands still make the pilgrimage to the TT year after year from all over the world. Although there are other famous road races in Europe, some on purpose-built tracks and some on public roads, the Isle of Man TT races are still the best known, and are sure to continue as long as there is public demand.

In America, the top class in road racing is Superbikes, and the most popular championship series is sanctioned by the American Motorcyclist Association (AMA). The AMA originally took up road racing as a sideshow to its popular dirt track racing program. Up until the 1960s, there were very few paved tracks for bike racing, so only a few pavement races were shuffled in with the dirt races. Into the 1970s, the number of paved courses in the United States continued to increase, along with fan interest, and the AMA decided to organize a separate series for Superbikes in 1977. The AMA Superbike championship, like the World Superbike championship, has proven to be highly successful and popular, with many events being televised to millions of viewers in dozens of countries.

The AMA Superbike rules state that 'the fairing and bodywork must visually resemble the original parts in design and dimension. No streamlining parts can be used.' The shocks can be relocated, but the same type of unit must be used. But underneath, these are highly tuned machines bristling with high-tech engineering. Superbikes today are using more and more titanium, carbon-fiber and Kevlar throughout. The Japanese manufacturers tend to favor chassis made out of aluminum, whereas the Italian-manufactured Ducati uses state-of-the-art chrome-moly frames. These racers don't come cheap – a crew chief explained that the cost of a factory-sponsored Superbike could run to $50,000, which puts it way beyond the cost of even the most expensive street bike.

Far left top: Jamie James gets his right knee down as he pilots his YZF750 Yamaha in the 1993 AMA Superbike Championship.

Far left bottom: Veteran AMA Superbike racer Dale Quarterly performs some of the pre-race fine tuning on his Team Mirage Kawasaki.

Above left: Carbon-fiber disc brakes are lighter than steel ones, so the Vance & Hines team uses them to improve the power-to-weight ratio of its YZF750 Yamahas.

Above: Air ducts alongside the number direct air to the engine and help keep the Ducati 888cc motor running cool and at the correct temperature.

Left: Doug Polen gave Ducati its first AMA Superbike title in 1993. Here he leads Canadian Miguel Duhamel (ZXR Kawasaki) in a 1993 race.

Two different engine displacements are currently allowed in Superbike racing. Superbikes of up to 750cc displacement can have four cylinders, while the up-to-1000cc engines must have only two cylinders. The two-cylinder bikes have a further advantage in that they are allowed to weigh about 50 pounds less than the four-cylinders. Both types of engines are capable of from 130 to 150 horsepower – a lot to put through the specially designed rear racing tire. In dry weather, racers use 'slicks' – tires without treads or patterns – but in wet weather they use tires with grooves similar to those you find on road bikes. The four-cylinder bikes come from Japanese manufacturers Honda, Kawasaki, Suzuki, and Yamaha, while the twins are made in Italy by companies such as Ducati and Moto Guzzi.

There are some interesting differences in Superbike engines. Ducati, the latest Moto Guzzi, and the new-for-1994 Honda RC45 use fuel injection, whereas Kawasaki, Yamaha, and Suzuki use carburetors. Of the four Japanese-manufactured Superbike engines, Honda employs a V-4 style, while the rest use in-line four-cylinder powerplants. Ducati uses an in-line V-twin, and Moto Guzzi an across-the-frame V-twin.

MOTORCYCLE RACING

AMA SUPERBIKE CHAMPIONS			
YEAR	RIDER	RESIDENCE	BIKE
1977	Reg Pridmore	Goleta, CA	Kawasaki
1978	Reg Pridmore	Goleta, CA	Kawasaki
1979	Wes Cooley	Mission Viejo, CA	Suzuki
1980	Eddie Lawson	Upland, CA	Kawasaki
1981	Eddie Lawson	Upland, CA	Kawasaki
1982	Eddie Lawson	Upland, CA	Kawasaki
1983	Wayne Rainey	Norwalk, CA	Kawasaki
1984	Fred Merkel	Stockton, CA	Honda
1985	Fred Merkel	Carson, CA	Honda
1986	Fred Merkel	Fountain Valley, CA	Honda
1987	Wayne Rainey	Downey, CA	Honda
1988	Bubba Shobert	Lubbock, TX	Honda
1989	Jamie James	Denham Springs, LA	Suzuki
1990	Doug Chandler	Salinas, CA	Kawasaki
1991	Thomas Stevens	Cape Coral, FL	Yamaha
1992	Scott Russell	Monterey, CA	Kawasaki
1993	Doug Polen	Corinth, TX	Ducati

Superbike suspension varies by manufacturer, with air or air-and-oil shocks being the most popular. Some use monitors to feed computers with telemetry data, which in turn can adjust the shocks to their optimum position. As the technology improves, the Superbikes will undoubtedly run some form of 'active suspension' as well in the near future. Absolutely nothing is left to chance on these awesome machines.

Factory involvement is probably the most extensive in road racing, though Motocross also puts heavy demands on the manufacturers. Uniformed crews and well-paid factory riders converge on the tracks in magnificently equipped semi-haulers. It's very similar to the way NASCAR and the car companies work together – only these bikes are much closer to their street bike counterparts. The profile of these teams is high, and manufacturers and teams both benefit from the recognition of the fans as a result.

With the factory teams providing the latest technology to its team riders, it's easy to understand how tough it is for a 'privateer' to compete. But talented teams competing on

Far left: Double World Superbike champion Fred Merkel shows off for the fans by pulling a 'wheelie.'

Left: Bubba Shobert was just one rider who made the successful transition from dirt track racing to road racing, winning the AMA Superbike Championship in 1988.

Below left: Vance & Hines is one of the most professional teams in the United States. In 1993, Jamie James (left) and Colin Edwards were the team's standard bearers in AMA Superbike and SuperSports classes.

Below: Texan Doug Polen wrapped up the AMA Superbike title in 1993 after back-to-back World Superbike titles in 1991 and 1992. All three titles were won on a V-twin Ducati tuned by Eraldo Ferracci.

their own can do well, as Doug Toland proved in the 1993 World Endurance Championship.

Looking at the history of road racing, it's interesting to note that Japanese bikes did not always dominate the scene. British bikes dominated from the 1930s through the 1950s, with the Brough, Triumph, Norton, BSA, and Vincent brands being at the forefront. The 1960s saw Italian bikes become highly successful in competition. Since 1977, though, Japanese engines have powered bikes to all the AMA championships, and it was only in 1993 that Ducati took its first ever AMA title. In the World Superbike championships, Japanese Hondas and Italian Ducatis have shared the limelight, with Kawasaki taking its first title in 1993.

The top rider on the Superbike scene in the 1990s is Texan Doug Polen, who took World Superbike titles in 1991 and 1992, and then followed up by winning the AMA title in 1993. Another top American rider, Scott Russell, using Kawasaki power, won the AMA Superbike championship in 1992 and then moved his skills to the World Superbike

MOTORCYCLE RACING

ROAD RACING

Championship series, where he won the 1993 title.

Most Superbike races are 60 miles long, with starting positions determined in qualifications. The Daytona 200, which opens the American national season, is 200 gruelling miles long, requiring pit stops for re-fuelling and changes of tires. In Superbike pit stops, high technology plays a role in getting the rear tire changed quickly. Honda has developed a single sided swing-arm design which makes it possible to make the change in seconds, rather than in minutes.

The starting sequence for Superbike races is similar to the standing-start technique of Formula One car racing. The bikes leave the pit lane and do one 'sighting' lap, before lining up on the grid. They then do a 'warm-up' lap (to get their tires up to working temperature) and return to the starting line. Then, in a matter of a few seconds (if there are no problems), they get given the start signal and away they go.

The riders try to establish the best 'line' on the track as quickly as possible, and follow each other along it. It is quite beautiful to watch the bikes filter through the turns, leaning to the left and then back to the right in unison.

Everything about the Superbike speaks of speed and streamlining, including the rider who, by laying low over the gas tank, actually becomes part of the machine's aerodynamic shape. The bike and rider are actually acting as one as the rider lifts his body to help slow the bike, and then tucks in low behind the fairing when the bike is at speed on the

Far left above: 1992 AMA and 1993 World Superbike champion Scott Russell heels his Muzzy ZXR 750cc Kawasaki over during the Daytona 200, the highlight at the end of Daytona Speedweek at the world-famous Florida race circuit.

Far left below: The start of a World Superbike Championship race at Misano circuit in Italy. In World Superbikes, a grid normally comprises 36 riders whose positions are determined by qualifying times. For many riders, pole position (fastest in practice) is a big psychological boost to a good race performance.

Left: One of the American road racing superstars of the 1980s was Freddie Spencer, shown here on a Superbike at the 1985 Daytona 200 at Daytona International Speedway. His real accomplishments, though, came in the Grand Prix, where he won three World Championships between 1983 and 1985. Two of his titles were in the 500cc class and one was in the 250cc.

ROAD RACING

Left: A group of Superbike riders, led by Texan Doug Polen on a 888cc Ducati, wind their way through a chicane at the Osterreichring in Austria. In chicanes, riders change direction several times, moving their body weight from one side of the bike to the other as they try to find the best 'line' through the bends.

straightaways. The forces on rider and bike when the bike achieves flat-out speed are truly awesome. In the turns, the rider hangs off one side of the bike and even drags his well-padded knee on the ground for added control.

The shape of the Superbike has evolved over the years, with current fairing design being nearly optimum for its wind-cutting duty. These designs are also available on the showroom floor. Should part of the fairing depart from the bike at speed, however, there are immediate problems for bike and rider in maintaining accurate control. Unlike cars, there is no sheet metal shell, seat belt, or roll-cage to protect the bike rider in the event of a crash.

Road race bikes are built for speed, with handling and braking to match, and for maximum performance the rider has to be at the same high peak of conditioning. The rider's physical conditioning is paramount for optimum performance in this extremely demanding sport. Also important is mental acuity, as the rider has to make split-second decisions constantly while controlling his machine at incredibly high speeds.

The AMA also runs a 250cc Grand Prix class, in which just about every type of powerplant imaginable is allowed: 250cc liquid-cooled twin-cylinder, two-cycle; single-cylinder, four-cycle engines up to 600cc; twin-cylinder, four-cycle engines up to 425cc; and air-cooled, two-cycle, twin-cylinder machines up to 430cc. The Yamaha TZ250 of the last-

Above: Kevin Magee (YZF 750cc Yamaha), Stephane Mertens, and Doug Polen (888cc Ducati) get their right knees down on the curbstones at Phillip Island racetrack, Australia. Curbstones play a vital part in informing the rider of the limit of the track, especially in the corners. On top of his leathers, a motorcycle road racer wears knee pads or sliders which scrape the road surface, letting the rider know exactly where he is when fully leaned over.

Above: Doug Polen (888cc Ducati) shows the seemingly effortless style that took him to two World and one AMA Superbike titles. After years of riding high-revving, four-cylinder Japanese machinery, Polen switched to the torquey, Italian V-twin and adapted right away to the totally different characteristics of the Ducati. Its lightness and excellent power-to-weight ratio allows it to brake, steer, and accelerate better than any of the Japanese 750s with which it competes.

mentioned classification has been the dominant bike in this class of racing.

In the United States there are other classes of racing, no less demanding, that give many riders the chance to race at lesser costs. The SuperTwins class is restricted to twin-cylinder, four cycle (four stroke) bikes up to 1200cc, and features machines predominantly from BMW (Germany), Harley-Davidson (USA), Moto Guzzi and Ducati (Italy) as well as Honda (Japan). With the modifications in this class being practically unlimited, many of these machines are one-of-a-kind prototype vehicles. The SuperTwins class provides flat-out performance in what are usually 40-mile races.

Also in the United States, the SuperSports class uses basically stock engines in two separate categories – 600cc and 750cc. Should a team decide to use four-cylinder versions of either displacement, the engine must be in stock condition. Twin-cylinder bikes up to 750cc are allowed in the 600cc class, and up to 1000cc in the 750cc class. Significant modifications can be made to any twin-cylinder machine having less than four valves. While this class closely resembles the Pro Superbike class, the big difference comes in the tires. While special racing slicks are employed in the Pro class, in SuperSport riders must use street tires. In Europe the SuperSports class is also popular, but the rules do not favor the twins in the same way, so only four-cylinder bikes are raced at present.

In 1990, the AMA introduced the Harley-Davidson Twin-Sport class which uses the Harley-Davidson 883 Sportster, an extremely popular bike in the United States. The class was

Above right: Two riders nearly get their elbows down as they go to extreme angles at Mid-Ohio racetrack, during a 600cc SuperSports race. In recent years, the 600cc class has gone from strength to strength world-wide. In the USA (as in Europe), the Honda CBR600 is the most popular bike and frequently dominates the class. In Europe, racing 'slick' tires are allowed, but in America the 600s must run a 'DOT approved' (i.e. treaded) tire.

Right: Because of the tighter restrictions on technical changes allowed in the AMA 600cc SuperSports class, the racing is invariably much closer than in the Superbike class. The possibility of a privately sponsored rider doing well against the factory teams is therefore much higher.

ROAD RACING

Far left: In America, the 750cc SuperSports class is popular and is contested by all four Japanese manufacturers. The 1993 series was won by Suzuki-mounted Britt Turkington. Compared to the Superbike class, the bikes are relatively standard. The bikes must also run 'DOT approved' tires instead of racing 'slicks.'

Left: Rolling thunder as a grid full of Harley-Davidsons make their earthquaking start at Mid-Ohio racetrack. Harley-Davidsons have proven to be uncompetitive against the high-tech Japanese and Italian bikes in recent years, but the marque is so popular that the AMA gave it its own race series.

Below: The closeness and competitiveness of 600cc SuperSports racing is shown here as racers battle it out wheel-to-wheel. In racing it is not unusual for riders and machines to touch each other as they hurtle around the track.

created in order to provide an economical class for amateurs. The only modifications permitted are removal of the lights and certain changes to the exhaust system. Races in this class are 25 miles in length.

Long-distance racing is also popular in the United States, but the rules are different from those run in other countries. In America, the EBC Endurance Challenge is the marathon of road racing. There is a GTO class for unlimited machines, and a GTU class which allows a number of different engine combinations. Teams of two to four riders accomplish the race, which is a gruelling three hours in duration.

While the AMA is the premier organization in motorcycle racing in the United States, the Western Eastern Roadracers Association (WERA) also sanctions a pro series, as well as mid-Atlantic and Southwest national championship series.

The WERA Pro series is headed by the Formula USA (FUSA) class, which allows unlimited engine displacement (although most are in the 1100cc range) and requires a minimum weight of 300 pounds. These machines are capable of speeds approaching 190 mph on the straightaways. The FUSA bikes are considered to be the 'Superbikes' of the WERA circuit.

The next step down in WERA competition are the Formula II class bikes, which include machines with 250cc water-cooled twin engines, 600cc four-stroke multi-cylinder engines, and unlimited displacement four-stroke engines. The Formula III WERA bikes carry 125cc powerplants. There are also three Superstock classes of 600cc, 750cc, and 1100cc displacements.

WERA also has a National Vintage and Historical Cup Series, in which vintage bikes are brought back to the track

MOTORCYCLE RACING

Above left: Larry Allen (Number 53) and Monti Campion (Number 551) are regular WERA Super Stock competitors. They are shown here during a practice session before the 1993 WERA event at Indianapolis Raceway Park.

Far left below: The 'Superbike' of the WERA series is the Formula USA class. This bike is ridden by Mike Martin, one of the series' top performers. The rules for this class allow unlimited engine displacement, but other than that the rules are similar to those for the AMA and World Superbikes. All of the Superbike-type machines maintain a stock street appearance.

by their often 'vintage' owners. Interest in historical bikes is a trend which is being seen in all aspects of motorcycle racing around the world.

Like its AMA counterparts, WERA bikes are run at a number of prestigious American tracks, including Indianapolis Raceway Park (IN), Pocono International Raceway (PA), and Road Atlanta (GA). As in the AMA series, there are a number of factory-contracted teams in WERA competition. The WERA also offers the Suzuki Riding School, which is run in conjunction with the national events.

A number of organizations in the United States conduct races regionally across the country. In Canada, the Canadian Motorcycle Association (CMA) runs a series of events.

Motorcycle road racing provides some of the most colorful and thrilling competition in motorsports today. From the international world-famous superfast circuits to the smaller regional tracks found in many countries around the world, road racing on two wheels offers an opportunity to fans to witness speed and performance that, in the early days of the sport, would have been thought to be a dream come true. Today, fans and riders both can live the dream.

Left: Braking is a major consideration for the unlimited-displacement WERA Formula USA bikes. Note the size of the front disc brake on this FUSA machine. Also note the many holes that have been drilled in the rotor for weight-saving purposes.

Above: One of WERA's stars is 'Revin' Kevin' Rentzell, whose normal mode of transportation is a 750cc Suzuki. This Pro rider has won many WERA national titles, and finished third at the Daytona 200 Superbike classic in the late 1980s.

DIRT TRACKING

MOTORCYCLE RACING

For many American bike racing fans, dirt track racing is the ultimate in excitement on two wheels. Running on banked or flat mile or half-mile tracks, the riders rocket down the straightaways, then pitch their knobby-tired machines into the turns, throwing the rear ends around and appearing to be on the verge of losing control.

There's never a lack of action in this realm of motorcycle racing as the bikes bunch up in closely-packed groups. Up to ten bikes often run only inches apart at well over 100 miles per hour. Riders in dirt track racing must master a finely-tuned combination of balance, concentration, athletic ability, and mental intensity to pitch a 300-pound, 100 horsepower machine right on the edge through the turns, tires of other bikes rubbing on their legs and handlebars threatening disaster.

American dirt racing began in the 1920s and 1930s, along with oval track racing on wooden board tracks. Both were

Previous pages: Two AMA Pro-Am dirt track racers seem to have blended together as one as they negotiate a turn in this 1993 race action shot.

Above: Chris Carr (Number 1) leads a snarling pack of Harleys at Lima, Ohio, in 1993 AMA Grand National dirt track racing action.

Right, main photo: Dirt bike riders swing through a turn.

Right: Brett Landes demonstrates the use of the left foot to balance the bike in a high-speed turn.

Far right: It's difficult enough to set up for a turn when you're on the track by yourself – add another bike, and the problem is magnified many times over.

DIRT TRACKING

done before huge crowds. Dirt track racing as we know it today, though, began when racing resumed after the war in 1946. The Illinois State Fairgrounds became the premier venue of the dirt sport. The best riders in the country journeyed to the Fairgrounds, where they would compete in a 25-mile race. The winner would be entitled to wear the coveted AMA Number One the following year. That arrangement would last through 1953, when a new national AMA series would be formed.

That 18-race series would be called the Grand National Series, and would feature point races toward a National Championship. It would include competition on both half-mile and mile tracks as well as TT steeplechase events, which feature both right and left turns and jumps over mounds of dirt.

A number of pavement road race events were included with the dirt track events in the early days, but separate classes would evolve as the sport matured. Then, in 1986, the AMA created a separate division for road racing and the two types of racing would go their separate ways.

Joe Leonard, who would later be a superb Indy Car driver, was one of the early dirt track stars and won three of those early championships (1954, 1956, and 1957). Some of the great names of bike racing have scored in this series.

In 1976, Jay Springsteen won his first of three straight Camel Pro (that's what it was called then) titles. In 1985, Team Honda star Bubba Shobert began a run of three

Far left: Scott Parker holds the all-time record in AMA Grand National competition with over 50 wins. He has also won the championship four times.

Above: Track conditions vary from race to race, and each rider must 'customize' his tires for each race, as AMA Pro rider Steve Morehead demonstrates here.

Left center: The twin exhausts of the 750cc AMA Grand National dirt bikes – a view that a successful dirt racer hopes his competitors will see as he pulls away on the track.

Left below: The nature of dirt racing requires that the left side of the tires carries mostly tread and a very small sidewall. This allows the rider to place the bike at extreme angles as he powers his machine through the turns.

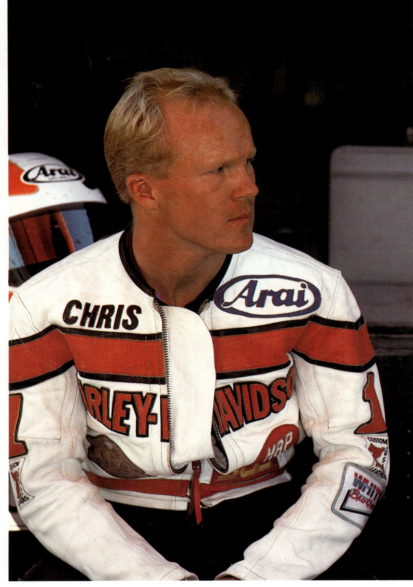

Above left: Ricky Graham, a master on the mile tracks, won the AMA Grand National title in 1982, 1984, and 1993.

Above: Chris Carr captured the 1992 AMA Grand National championship after three consecutive runner-up seasons.

Right: Chris Carr pours on the coal through a turn.

straight Grand National titles. The Scott Parker era began in 1988 with four straight championships before succumbing to teammate Chris Carr in 1992. In 1993, Honda rider Ricky Graham took his third championship.

The popularity of the dirt sport is certainly evident from the national television coverage it receives. Even on TV, the sight of those screaming bikes grouped in a screaming pack is wildly exciting.

This class of racing is characterized by bikes roaring into the turns with the rear ends loose, and the rider's left foot hung out for stability. The bikes, in this process, build up a line of dirt called a 'cushion'. With the engines screaming at up to 8000 RPMs, a tower of dirt is thrown up from the tires. As he crosses the finish line, the winning driver pops a 'wheelie' in a victory gesture.

The tires on these bikes are 'cut' in order to adapt them to the particular type of track being run. One rider explained that on a loose track (where the bike has a tendency to slide), cross-grooves are cut to provide more edges so the tires can grab the track coming off the corners.

It's a touchy balancing act for the riders as the bikes rush into the turns. As the turn approaches, the rear of the bike 'gets loose' and starts to come around in a counterclockwise direction. For balance, the rider's left foot lightly brushes the track. It's a wonder how these machines can maintain traction bent over at such a great angle. It seems that the bike should slide right out from under the rider.

With no sheet metal or roll-cage around the rider for protection, a crash can be extremely dangerous, especially if the bike meets up with the rider after he has departed it. Most of the time, however, these well-conditioned athletes shake off a fall quickly and start worrying about the condition of the bike.

With the short tracks of up to a half-mile in length, aerodynamics are not a major factor. But on the mile-long tracks, the aerodynamic advantage gained by the bikes running in tight groups yields speeds of up to 130 miles per hour. Called drafting, this technique also provides the opportunity for each bike to make a drive to the front. Properly timed, a rider can pull out of the draft and slingshot around the bikes ahead of him. For that reason, it's not always the best position to be in front of the pack near the end of the race.

Although this sport certainly isn't as expensive as car racing, there are still sizable costs involved at the top level. A 750cc bike can cost around $15,000, and that doesn't include any spare or replacement parts. A spare motor alone can cost an additional $6000. Add another couple of thousand dollars for the complete riding uniform and helmet, and

you can see that this sport isn't inexpensive.

A majority of the riders racing in the AMA dirt circuit have to foot most of the bills themselves. Some of the top drivers benefit from factory help, but for the 1993 season, there were only two riders that could be considered pure factory riders: superstars Chris Carr and Scott Parker, who were riding for Harley-Davidson. Many teams operate out of the back of a van or panel truck which also doubles as the hauler which gets the equipment and bikes to the track. A lot of volunteer help from family and friends helps keep these operations running.

Harley-Davidson and Honda are the prime brands in the Grand National Series, with twin-cylinder 750cc powerplants capable of producing up to 100 horsepower. On the short tracks, the single-cylinder engines, like the popular Rotax, are sufficient.

Dirt tracking is a dangerous sport, and there have been some fatalities and serious injuries in this high speed jousting. AMA has provided every safety device any possible through the years, the most visible being hundreds of hay bales strategically located on the turns to help absorb any possible impacts.

The Grand National class gets a majority of the publicity, but two other classes also provide a lot of speed and excitement: the 600cc Support Class and the Harley-Davidson 883 Pro-Class.

The 600cc machines are lighter and simpler than their Grand National brothers. Like the 750s, they are built strictly for racing and carry engines from 361cc to 600cc four-cycle single-cylinder powerplants. The predominant manufacturers are Harley-Davidson, Honda, and Rotax. The 600cc bikes often run on the same tracks as the Grand National bikes. A number of the Grand National drivers also have 600cc bikes.

The 883 class (which has also been added to the road racing circuit) came into being in 1993 and makes use of the tremendous popularity of the Harley-Davidson brand in America. The class uses 1986-and-newer Harley-Davidson 883 Sportster, STD, DLX, and HUGGER models only. Designed from its inception to be an affordable type of racing, only limited modifications are permitted to the engines and bike frames.

In the 883 class, the bikes can be easily converted to the race configuration simply by changing the handlebars, relocating the footpegs, and adding a front brake. Also, the use of stock wheels will be strictly enforced in this fledgling class. The class places the emphasis on the rider's talent and skill rather than the ability to modify the machine.

In all of the three top classes, the condition of the rider is paramount. A pro dirt rider explained, 'You have to be in top shape to ride these bikes. If you're not, you will fade at the end. There's both a physical and mental strain on you. You have to get into this style of racing mentally. If you're not, you'll be drained physically too.'

DIRT TRACKING

Far left: With multiple riders in each event, dirt trackers try to use all of the racetrack to avoid a massive pile-up. But even with skilled professional riders, accidents do happen.

Left: Now in his late thirties, three-time dirt champ Jay Springsteen is still a formidable threat on the track. This Michigan native is looked upon as a cult hero by the thousands of fans who follow the AMA Grand National series.

Left below: Jay Springsteen uses his vast experience to make a pass at a 1993 AMA Grand National event. Springsteen is the oldest former champion still active in the sport.

AMA 750cc GRAND NATIONAL DIRT TRACK CHAMPIONS

YEAR	RIDER	RESIDENCE	BIKE
1946	Chet Dykgraff	Grand Rapids, MI	Norton
1947	Jimmy Chann	Bridgeton, NJ	Harley-Davidson
1948	Jimmy Chann	Bridgeton, NJ	Harley-Davidson
1949	Jimmy Chann	Bridgeton, NJ	Harley-Davidson
1950	Larry Headrick	San Jose, CA	Harley-Davidson
1951	Bobby Hill	Grove City, OH	Indian
1952	Bobby Hill	Grove City, OH	Indian/Norton
1953	Bill Tuman	Rockford, IL	Indian/Norton
1954	Joe Leonard	San Jose, CA	Harley-Davidson
1955	Brad Andres	San Diego, CA	Harley-Davidson
1956	Joe Leonard	San Jose, CA	Harley-Davidson
1957	Joe Leonard	San Jose, CA	Harley-Davidson
1958	Carroll Resweber	Cedarburg, WI	Harley-Davidson
1959	Carroll Resweber	Cedarburg, WI	Harley-Davidson
1960	Carroll Resweber	Cedarburg, WI	Harley-Davidson
1961	Carroll Resweber	Cedarburg, WI	Harley-Davidson
1962	Bart Markel	Flint, MI	Harley-Davidson
1963	Dick Mann	Richmond, CA	BSA/Matchless
1964	Roger Reiman	Kewanee, IL	Harley-Davidson
1965	Bart Markel	Flint, MI	Harley-Davidson
1966	Bart Markel	Flint, MI	Harley-Davidson
1967	Gary Nixon	Cockeysville, MD	Triumph
1968	Gary Nixon	Cockeysville, MD	Triumph
1969	Mert Lawwill	San Francisco, CA	Harley-Davidson
1970	Gene Romero	San Luis Obispo, CA	Triumph
1971	Dick Mann	Richmond, CA	BSA
1972	Mark Briesford	Woodside, CA	Harley-Davidson
1973	Kenny Roberts	Modesto, CA	Yamaha
1974	Kenny Roberts	Modesto, CA	Yamaha
1975	Gary Scott	Springfield, OH	Harley-Davidson
1976	Jay Springsteen	Lapeer, MI	Harley-Davidson
1977	Jay Springsteen	Lapeer, MI	Harley-Davidson
1978	Jay Springsteen	Lapeer, MI	Harley-Davidson
1979	Steve Eklund	San Jose, CA	Harley-Davidson/Yamaha
1980	Randy Goss	Hartland, MI	Harley-Davidson
1981	Mike Kidd	Euless, TX	Harley-Davidson/Yamaha
1982	Ricky Graham	Seaside, CA	Harley-Davidson
1983	Randy Goss	Hartland, MI	Harley-Davidson
1984	Ricky Graham	Seaside, CA	Honda
1985	Bubba Shobert	Carmel Valley, CA	Honda
1986	Bubba Shobert	Carmel Valley, CA	Honda
1987	Bubba Shobert	Carmel Valley, CA	Honda
1988	Scott Parker	Swartz Creek, MI	Harley-Davidson
1989	Scott Parker	Swartz Creek, MI	Harley-Davidson
1990	Scott Parker	Swartz Creek, MI	Harley-Davidson
1991	Scott Parker	Swartz Creek, MI	Harley-Davidson
1992	Chris Carr	Valley Springs, CA	Harley-Davidson
1993	Ricky Graham	Seaside, CA	Honda

MOTORCYCLE RACING

Above: In Europe, oval dirt track racing is similar to AMA Grand National racing, yet it is worlds apart. Called speedway racing, it is run on quarter-mile tracks. The races are extremely short in duration, requiring intense concentration and quick reflexes to make the required move to the front. Speedway bikes are readily recognizable by their extremely narrow tires.

In an effort to bring young riders into the dirt track sport, the AMA also sanctions a Pro-Am Class. Both professionals and amateurs compete together in the class to provide important on-track experience for beginners. There are also many AMA regional events run at fairgrounds tracks all over the country.

Several other organizations besides the AMA carry out flat track racing in the US. The Classic Bike Magazine Dirt Track Series is a popular series that is run primarily in the eastern United States. Because of the great interest in dirt racing that has been done in decades gone by, two vintage bike organizations – the Vintage Dirt Track Races Association and the American Historical Racing Motorcycle Association (AHRMA) – both sanction events. AHRMA's extensive competition has three classes: Modern Vintage (1974 and older), Classic Vintage (1967 and older) and Dinosaur Vintage (pre-1952).

A European version of dirt track racing, speedway racing, involves the use of extremely short, 400-meter tracks. The races are short four-lap sprints. The 500cc bikes use rigid frames, skinny tires, no brakes, and old-style four-valve powerplants. Minor modifications are allowed. The most popular brands are Jawa (Czechoslovakia), Goden and Weslake (Great Britain), and GN (Italy).

Speedway racing is extremely popular in England, where it is treated as a team sport. The more than two dozen leagues enjoy strong fan support. Speedway racing is also competed in other countries, including Germany, Poland, and Sweden. World Championships are held in speedway racing in individual, pairs, team, and long-course events.

Right: Speedway bike riders are among the most colorfully dressed of all those in bike racing motorsports. These no-frills machines have no brakes and minimal suspension. The sport is international in nature, with competition in both Europe and the Far East. The sport is, however, only of minimal interest in the United States.

MOTOCROSS

MOTORCYCLE RACING

Although Motocross might not be the fastest of the motorcycle competition sports, it could well be the one requiring the most skill. The sport tests every aspect of the bike and rider with obstacles, both manmade and natural, of every imaginable description. The sport has achieved huge popularity, with events being held inside arenas (where it's called Supercross) and on larger courses outdoors.

Motocross is a race across rough country involving hills and gullies, sharp right and left turns that bring a bike almost to a complete stop, and straightaways where the bikes can accelerate to high speeds. The bikes also spend much of the time soaring through the air at heights of dozens of feet. Motocross tests the complete athletic capabilities of the riders.

The first Motocross competition was held in Camberley, England, in 1924. The sport was officially formalized in 1947 when the FIM created the Moto-Cross des Nations to determine the World Team Motocross Championship.

Ten years later, an individual World Motocross Championship Series was created. The first competitions were held for 500cc bikes, with Swedish riders monopolizing the early competition. World 250cc competition began five years later, with Americans starting to move into scoring positions in the early 1980s. The 125cc class was first run in 1975, with Belgian riders dominating the early competition. American riders recently showed well in this class, with Trampas Parker and Donny Schmit winning the 1989 and 1990 titles, respectively.

A look at the schedules of the World Motocross Championship Series shows that they really are international in nature. In the 125cc class, the series ventures to San Marino, Brazil, and Guatemala as well as throughout Europe. World 250cc racing is carried out in Italy, Spain, Holland, Switzerland, France, South Africa, Germany, Belgium, England,

Previous pages: Kurt Nicholl (England) flies through the air in the Motocross Grand Prix at Foxhill in England, June 1993.

Above: A Motocross rider doesn't need a pilot's license to fly. International Honda rider Greg Albertyn, the 1993 Individual Motocross World Champion in the 250cc class, shows how it's done.

Left: The top gun international Motocross rider in the 250cc class is Donny Schmit. The Individual Motocross World Champion in 1990 (125cc) and 1992 (250cc) represents Motor-Union Luxembourg (MUL) in European competition.

Right: Donny Schmit (Number 1, at right) is part of a howling horde of 250cc Motocross machines in a World Championship event in 1993.

MOTORCYCLE RACING

MOTO-CROSS DES NATIONS CHAMPIONS (500cc)	
1947	Great Britain
1948	Belgium
1949	Great Britain
1950	Great Britain
1951	Belgium
1952	Great Britain
1953	Great Britain
1954	Great Britain
1955	Sweden
1956	Great Britain
1957	Great Britain
1958	Sweden
1959	Great Britain
1960	Great Britain
1961	Sweden
1962	Sweden
1963	Great Britain
1964	Great Britain
1965	Great Britain
1966	Great Britain
1967	Great Britain
1968	USSR
1969	Belgium
1970	Sweden
1971	Sweden
1972	Belgium
1973	Belgium
1974	Sweden
1975	Czechoslovakia
1976	Belgium
1977	Belgium
1978	(No race)
1979	Belgium
1980	Belgium
1981	USA
1982	USA
1983	USA
1984	USA
1985	USA
1986	USA
1987	USA
1988	USA
1989	USA
1990	USA
1991	USA
1992	USA
1993	USA

TROPHÉE DES NATIONS CHAMPIONS	
1961	Great Britain
1962	Great Britain
1963	Sweden
1964	Sweden
1965	*No result*
1966	Sweden
1967	Sweden
1968	Sweden
1969	Belgium
1970	Belgium
1971	Belgium
1972	Belgium
1973	Belgium
1974	Belgium
1975	Belgium
1976	Belgium
1977	Belgium
1978	Belgium
1979	Soviet Union
1980	Belgium
1981	United States
1982	United States
1983	United States
1984	United States

Merged with the Moto-Cross des Nations in 1985

COUPE DES NATIONS CHAMPIONS	
1981	Italy
1982	Italy
1983	Belgium
1984	Holland

Merged with the Moto-Cross des Nations in 1985

Above right: Showing his championship style, Georges Jobe is seen here on his way to winning the 500cc Belgian Motocross Grand Prix.

Right: Colin Dugmore stands on the gas to negotiate a jump at the British Motocross Grand Prix at Foxhill in June 1993.

France, South Africa, Germany, Belgium, England, Ireland, Venezuela, Sweden, Finland, and the USA.

The Moto-Cross des Nations three-man team competition was dominated by Great Britain until the late 1960s. Belgium then took seven championships from 1969 to 1980. In 1981, the USA moved in and has completely dominated the event since then. Superstar David Bailey was a member of five of those World Championship teams in the early 1980s. In 1993, the USA team won its 13th straight championship.

The Trophée des Nations, a four-man world competition which was competed from 1961 through 1984, was dominated by Sweden during the 1960s, Belgium in the 1970s, and the United States in the early 1980s. The series was merged with the Moto-Cross des Nations in 1985. There was also a short-lived Coupe des Nations series in the early 1980s, with Italy, Belgium, and Holland taking the titles.

In the 1990s, a World Supercross Series, an indoor event, was formed in Europe. The first season was held in 1992.

The Americans were late entries in the World Motocross Championship Series, in 1971. A year later, the AMA would create a National Championship Series of its own, with competition in both the 250cc and 500cc classes. The popularity of the sport instantly skyrocketed, and in 1974 the AMA introduced the 125cc National Championship Series, and the AMA Supercross Series, the latter of which is held in indoor stadiums during the winter months.

Left: Inspired by the popularity of Supercross in the United States, World Supercross competition commenced in 1992. This dramatic high-angle starting line shot was taken at Parc des Princes in France.

Overleaf: This pair of World Supercross riders appears to be jumping out of the stadium at Parc des Princes.

Overleaf inset: Scott Kirkpatrick (Number 628) seems to be headed for a landing right on top of Todd Sheedy (Number 867) during a 250cc qualifying heat at the 1993 AMA Camel Supercross event at the Indianapolis Hoosier Dome.

MOTORCYCLE RACING

		500cc WORLD MOTOCROSS CHAMPIONS					
1957	Bill Nilsson	Sweden	AJS	1976	Roger DeCoster	Belgium	Suzuki
1958	Rene Beeten	Belgium	FN	1977	Heikki Mikkola	Finland	Yamaha
1959	Sten Lundin	Sweden	Monark	1978	Heikki Mikkola	Finland	Yamaha
1960	Bill Nilsson	Sweden	Husqvarna	1979	Graham Noyce	Great Britain	Honda
1961	Sten Lundin	Sweden	Lito	1980	Andre Malherbe	Belgium	Honda
1962	Rolf Tibblin	Sweden	Husqvarna	1981	Andre Malherbe	Belgium	Honda
1963	Rolf Tibblin	Sweden	Husqvarna	1982	Brad Lackey	USA	Suzuki
1964	Jeff Smith	Great Britain	BSA	1983	Hakan Carlqvist	Sweden	Yamaha
1965	Jeff Smith	Great Britain	BSA	1984	Andre Malherbe	Belgium	Honda
1966	Paul Freidrichs	E.Germany	CZ	1985	David Thorpe	Great Britain	Honda
1967	Paul Freidrichs	E.Germany	CZ	1986	David Thorpe	Great Britain	Honda
1968	Paul Freidrichs	E.Germany	CZ	1987	Georges Jobe	Belgium	Honda
1969	Bengt Aberg	Sweden	Husqvarna	1988	Eric Geboers	Belgium	Honda
1970	Bengt Aberg	Sweden	Husqvarna	1989	David Thorpe	Great Britain	Honda
1971	Roger DeCoster	Belgium	Suzuki	1990	Eric Geboers	Belgium	Honda
1972	Roger DeCoster	Belgium	Suzuki	1991	Georges Jobe	Belgium	Honda
1973	Roger DeCoster	Belgium	Suzuki	1992	Georges Jobe	Belgium	Honda
1974	Heikki Mikkola	Finland	Husqvarna	1993	Jacky Martens	Luxembourg	Husqvarna
1975	Roger DeCoster	Belgium	Suzuki				

MOTOCROSS

Far left: Twenty Supercross riders trying to squeeze into a space wide enough for two often results in a pile-up.

Left: The start of an AMA Camel Supercross heat is spectacular and exciting. With only eight laps in a 250cc competition, the riders scramble to get to the front.

Left below: 250cc Supercross riders Steve Lamson (Number 21) and Larry Brooks (Number 17) race for the lead.

Overleaf: High-flying action is what the Camel Supercross fans come to see.

Overleaf, inset left: 1993 250cc Camel Supercross champion Jeremy McGrath lets it all hang out as he nears the finish line.

Overleaf, inset right: Brian Swink crests one of the many humps that are an integral part of the AMA Supercross courses.

250cc WORLD MOTOCROSS CHAMPIONS			
1962	Torsten Hallman	Sweden	Husqvarna
1963	Torsten Hallman	Sweden	Husqvarna
1964	Joel Robert	Belgium	CZ
1965	Viktor Arbekov	USSR	CZ
1966	Torsten Hallman	Sweden	Husqvarna
1967	Torsten Hallman	Sweden	Husqvarna
1968	Joel Robert	Belgium	Suzuki
1969	Joel Robert	Belgium	Suzuki
1970	Joel Robert	Belgium	Suzuki
1971	Joel Robert	Belgium	Suzuki
1972	Joel Robert	Belgium	Suzuki
1973	Hakan Andersson	Sweden	Yamaha
1974	Guenady Mossiev	USSR	KTM
1975	Harry Everts	Belgium	Puch
1976	Heikki Mikkola	Finland	Husqvarna
1977	Guenady Mossiev	USSR	KTM
1978	Guenady Mossiev	USSR	KTM
1979	Hakan Carlqvist	Sweden	Husqvarna
1980	Georges Jobe	Belgium	Suzuki
1981	Neil Hudson	Great Britain	Yamaha
1982	Danny LaPorte	USA	Yamaha
1983	Georges Jobe	Belgium	Suzuki
1984	Heinz Kinigadner	Austria	KTM
1985	Heinz Kinigadner	Austria	KTM
1986	Jacky Vimond	France	Yamaha
1987	Eric Geboers	Belgium	Honda
1988	John Van den Berk	Holland	Yamaha
1989	Jean-Michel Bayle	France	Honda
1990	Alex Puzar	Italy	Suzuki
1991	Trampas Parker	USA	Honda
1992	Donny Schmit	USA	Yamaha
1993	Greg Albertyn	Luxembourg	Honda

The indoor Supercross tracks, most of which are built on football fields, require about 9000 cubic yards of dirt and sand, around 1000 hay bales, some 900 man-hours, and up to $150,000 to construct. Using every available square inch of the floor area, these challenging courses include straightaways, hard left and right turns, bone-jarring bumps (or 'hoops'), and large hills that serve as launching pads for the bikes.

In fact, it's those monstrous jumps which are the trademark of Supercross. Supercross riders achieve heights of up to 30 feet and distances out to 60 or 70 feet. It may look like uncontrolled flight, but the skilled riders in this sport can put their flying machines down exactly where they want – at least most of the time.

Supercross superstar Damon Bradshaw explained that a

125cc WORLD MOTOCROSS CHAMPIONS

1975	Gaston Rahier	Belgium	Suzuki
1976	Gaston Rahier	Belgium	Suzuki
1977	Gaston Rahier	Belgium	Suzuki
1978	Akira Watanabe	Japan	Suzuki
1979	Harry Everts	Belgium	Suzuki
1980	Harry Everts	Belgium	Suzuki
1981	Harry Everts	Belgium	Suzuki
1982	Eric Geboers	Belgium	Suzuki
1983	Eric Geboers	Belgium	Suzuki
1984	Michele Rinaldi	Italy	Suzuki
1985	Pekka Vehkonen	Finland	Cagiva
1986	Dave Strijbos	Holland	Cagiva
1987	John Van den Berk	Holland	Yamaha
1988	Jean-Michel Bayle	France	Honda
1989	Trampas Parker	USA	KTM
1990	Donny Schmit	USA	Suzuki
1991	Stefan Everts	Belgium	Suzuki
1992	Greg Albertyn	South Africa	Honda
1993	Pedro Tracter	Holland	Suzuki

	AMA SUPERCROSS CHAMPIONS	
	500cc	
1974	Gary Semics	Kawasaki
1975	Steve Stackable	Maico
	250cc	
1974	Pierre Karsmakers	Yamaha
1975	Jimmy Ellis	CA
1976	Jim Weinert	Kawasaki
1977	Bob Hannah	Yamaha
1978	Bob Hannah	Yamaha
1979	Bob Hannah	Yamaha
1980	Mike Bell	Yamaha
1981	Mark Barnett	Suzuki
1982	Donnie Hansen	Honda
1983	David Bailey	Honda
1984	Johnny O'Mara	Honda
1985	Jeff Ward	Kawasaki
1986	Rick Johnson	Honda
1987	Jeff Ward	Kawasaki
1988	Rick Johnson	Honda
1989	Jeff Stanton	Honda
1990	Jeff Stanton	Honda
1991	Jean-Michel Bayle	Honda
1992	Jeff Stanton	Honda
1993	Jeremy McGrath	Honda

MOTORCYCLE RACING

tap of the brakes in mid-air will bring the front end of the bike down. He continued, 'You don't want to fly too high, though – straight and low like a dart is best.'

Supercross demands both slow, precise movement through the turns and over the mini-bumps, and flat-out speed on the straights and into the jumps. The rider's mind has to flash ahead to the next situation and prepare every muscle for the next challenge.

The start of a Supercross race is probably the most exciting part of the race. As the engines are brought up to a scream and the starting gate drops, the action is immediate as some 22 bikes dive for that first tight turn. Should a bike go down in that traffic jam, a chain reaction can result. The race goes on regardless, and usually the downed riders are back on their bikes and quickly underway again.

The US fans are wild about Supercross, and crowds of 50,000 and more at an event are not uncommon. Much of the popularity of the sport comes from the pizazz of the riders and the bikes. Each team tries to outdo the other in flashy uniforms and bike paint schemes.

There's huge factory support for Supercross, with Japanese companies Honda, Yamaha, Kawasaki, and Suzuki dominating, along with the Austrian company, KTM. Factory presence is quite evident, with the fancy haulers and uniformed crews. The flashiness of the sport evokes the aura of Indy and Daytona.

AMA Supercross has two classes, the top 250cc and supporting 125cc class. In addition, there are also Eastern and

MOTOCROSS

Far left above: Mike LaRocco finished sixth in the 1992 AMA Supercross Championship and was the 1993 AMA 500cc Motocross champ.

Far left below: Mike Kiedrowski was second in the AMA Supercross points in 1993.

Left center: Cliff Palmer is unique in AMA Supercross competition because of his Austrian-built powerplant. The rest of the field is Japanese-built.

Above: Chad Peterson, riding a Yamaha, powers through a turn in a 125cc race in 1993.

Left: Erik Keyoe (Number 22) challenges Shane Lawson (Number 686) for position in a 125cc heat race during the 1993 AMA Motocross season.

Overleaf: Resembling a motorized stampede, this scene is typical of the start of an AMA Motocross race. Well over two dozen riders can be seen in this 1993 race start.

Far left: Motocross fans have access to most parts of the course. From a spectator's point of view, the most exciting part of the course is the jump and landing area. The crowd roars as their favorite riders negotiate the challenging jumps.

Above: One thing all AMA Motocross riders are careful to do while airborne is to maintain a safe distance from other riders.

Left: In this shot, Brian Swink (Number 19) and Todd DeHoop (Number 38) barely avoid each other in mid-air.

Western Regional Series that bring young riders into the big time. One huge attraction of this series is the fact that the riders race basically stock machines.

When the series first started, the companies built special bikes for racing. But in 1986, that all changed with 'stock' becoming the rule. The factory race bikes are little changed from the showroom floor models, except that they are super-tuned by the skilled factory mechanics. With that kind of technical expertise, it's easy to understand how tough it is for a 'privateer' to compete again those factory assets. Not surprisingly, the bike companies flaunt their success on the track in national advertising campaigns.

Although Supercross is basically an American derivation, there is also a Canadian national Supercross series competed. A number of Canadian riders also regularly come south to compete in the American series.

In the summer months, activity moves outside to Motocross, with AMA national championships held in 125cc, 250cc and 500cc classes. Most of the Supercross participants and teams continue with the outdoor activity, and the points chases start all over again.

Some of the big names in the series in recent years include Kawasaki riders Jeff Ward and Mike Kiedrowski, and Honda rider and three-time 250cc champion Jeff Stanton.

The more challenging outdoor courses and longer races (normally 30 minutes plus two additional laps) put physical conditioning at a high level of importance. Many of the riders ride bicycles and lift weights to maintain the peak conditioning that is required for this sport.

As is the case with Supercross, huge crowds also greet the AMA national Motocross series events. Access to all portions of the courses is usually allowed, and fans can watch the bikes negotiate most parts of the course.

Again, like its Supercross counterpart, the starts in Motocross are the most exciting part of the race. In the outdoor races, even more bikes are trying to negotiate that first turn when there obviously isn't enough room for all to get through.

As is the case with just about every other type of bike racing, numerous local organizations sanction Motocross regionally across the United States.

The nostalgia craze has also hit Motocross in the US, and AHRMA carries out a Vintage Iron National MX Series and a Vintage Iron Northeast MX Series, along with the International Old Timers MX Association Series.

Wherever it is competed, Motocross packs tremendous excitement to rival any other on two or four wheels.

Above right: Expert Motocross riders know that there is an optimum height for maximum speed. A rider who jumps too high takes a chance on landing wrong for the next jump; too low, and he loses speed.

Right: On some hills, it is best to avoid a jump. In this case, a sharp right turn awaits the rider at the bottom of the hill, causing him to keep his bike on the ground so the turn can be negotiated.

Far right: The thrill of victory: 1993 AMA 250cc Motocross champion Mike Kiedrowski crosses the finish line first in a 1993 race. He also won the AMA 500cc Motocross Championship in 1992.

MOTOCROSS

AMA NATIONAL MOTOCROSS CHAMPIONS

	500cc			250cc			125cc	
1971	Mark Blackwell	Hus	1971	Gary Jones	Yam	1974	Marty Smith	Hon
1972	Brad Lackey	CZ	1972	Gary Jones	Yam	1975	Marty Smith	Hon
1973	Pierre Karsmakers	Yam	1973	Gary Jones	Hon	1976	Bob Hannah	Yam
1974	Jim Weinert	Kaw	1974	Gary Jones	CA	1977	Broc Glover	Yam
1975	Jim Weinert	Yam	1975	Tony DiStefano	Suz	1978	Broc Glover	Yam
1976	Kent Howerton	Husky	1976	Tony DiStefano	Suz	1979	Broc Glover	Yam
1977	Marty Smith	Hon	1977	Tony DiStefano	Suz	1980	Mark Barnett	Suz
1978	Rick Burgett	Yam	1978	Bob Hannah	Yam	1981	Mark Barnett	Suz
1979	Danny LaPorte	Suz	1979	Bob Hannah	Yam	1982	Mark Barnett	Suz
1980	Chuck Sun	Hon	1980	Kent Howerton	Suz	1983	Johnny O'Mara	Hon
1981	Broc Glover	Yam	1981	Kent Howerton	Suz	1984	Jeff Ward	Kaw
1982	Darrell Shultz	Hon	1982	Donnie Hansen	Hon	1985	Ron Lechien	Hon
1983	Broc Glover	Yam	1983	David Bailey	Hon	1986	Micky Dymond	Hon
1984	David Bailey	Hon	1984	Rick Johnson	Hon	1987	Micky Dymond	Hon
1985	Broc Glover	Yam	1985	Jeff Ward	Kaw	1988	George Holland	Hon
1986	David Bailey	Hon	1986	Rick Johnson	Hon	1989	Mike Kiedrowski	Hon
1987	Rick Johnson	Hon	1987	Rick Johnson	Hon	1990	Guy Cooper	Suz
1988	Rick Johnson	Hon	1988	Jeff Ward	Kaw	1991	Mike Kiedrowski	Kaw
1989	Jeff Ward	Kaw	1989	Jeff Stanton	Hon	1992	Jeff Emig	Kaw
1990	Jeff Ward	Kaw	1990	Jeff Stanton	Hon	1993	Doug Henry	Hon
1991	Jean-Michel Bayle	Hon	1991	Jean-Michel Bayle	Hon			
1992	Mike Kiedrowski	Kaw	1992	Jeff Stanton	Hon			
1993	Mike LaRocco	Kaw	1993	Mike Kiedrowski	Kaw			

DRAG RACING

MOTORCYCLE RACING

The American-bred sport of drag racing usually brings to mind four-wheeled automotive activity sanctioned by the National Hot Rod Association (NHRA) and International Hot Rod Association (IHRA), but motorcycle drag racing also enjoys a great deal of exposure in America with the NHRA along with a number of other, strictly-bike drag organizations.

Like its car drag racing counterpart, motorcycle drag racing offers a wide variety of classes, from basically stock machines all the way up to the Top Fuel bikes, which are capable of speeds exceeding 200 miles per hour in the quarter-mile. The great performance from these machines makes motorcycle drag racing one of the most exciting aspects of racing on two wheels.

The procedures in motorcycle drag racing are almost identical to those for the four-wheeled version, with bike drag racing carried out in the same facilities. In fact, many of the national bike drag events are competed at the same tracks where the national NHRA and IHRA events are held. It also should be noted that motorcycle drag racing is competed at both one-eighth and one-quarter mile distances, as is also the case with the cars.

Obviously, as the performance increases through the different classes, the greater the modifications on the bikes. In the higher-performance classes, significant modifications to the engines and the use of exotic fuels are allowed. The drag bikes are also quite recognizable from their extremely long 'wheelie bars' which stretch out behind them, in some cases almost doubling the length of the vehicles. The purpose of the bars is to prevent the bikes from rearing up and going over backwards.

The Top Fuel bike is the 'Superbike' of the drag racing

Previous pages: Chuck King prepares for a 1993 race with a smoky burnout.

Above: Drag bikes heat their rear tires before the race to optimize traction.

Below: This Pro Stock rider prepares for a launch at the 1992 NHRA US Nationals.

Right: Riders crouch low to minimize wind resistance and maximize speed.

Far left above: 1993 NHRA Pro Stock champion David Schultz moves to the starting line in preparation for another 180 mph dash to the finish line 1320 feet away. There's no margin for error at these speeds – one slight bobble will quickly put the bike out of control and the rider out of commission.

Far left below: This IDBA Suzuki rider prepares for a run at National Trail Raceway in Columbus, Ohio, in 1993. IDBA is one of several American groups that sanction only motorcycle drag racing.

Left: With four NHRA (1987, 1988, 1991, and 1993) and two IDBA (1986 and 1989) titles to his credit, Dave Schultz is the winningest active motorcycle drag racer at the national level in America.

Overleaf: This futuristic creation from the All-Harley Drag Bike Association could foretell things to come in motorcycle drag racing. The design of the bike allows for an extremely low profile, which should enable great speeds and low aerodynamic drag.

Overleaf, inset: This encounter between a drag tire and the pavement vividly illustrates the principle that friction causes heat. The burnout is one of the most exciting aspects of the bike drag sport for the fans.

sport, and provides performance that is hard to fathom. Just about anything goes with these machines, which can have engine displacements up to 1300cc, use super-powerful nitro-methane fuel, and even employ superchargers. It's hard to believe that a rider can hang on to his horse as it howls down the track.

But no matter how powerful and sophisticated a drag bike is, success depends on the skill of the rider and his (or her) ability to put that power to the track.

A drag racing event begins with the 'burnout,' in which the bike's rear tire is spun up to high speed to heat the rubber, to produce better traction during the race. This is an exciting part of the proceedings for the fans, as the spinning wheels produce towers of thick, white smoke.

The bikes then move up to the starting line, where a Christmas tree lighting system, a tower with a series of yellow, green, and red lights, gets the bikes ready for the start and flashes green to begin the race. Most races are won or lost right there on the starting line. A perfect response to the green light often means victory. But if a driver is just a split-second too quick on the gas, a red light informs the driver that he's left too soon and is disqualified. At the end of the track, the bike's performance is measured by its elapsed time (ET) and top speed.

Most drag bikes carry their front wheel slightly off the ground for the complete length of the run for maximum performance. Professional bike racer Rich Neace explained why: 'Keeping the front tire slightly off the ground allows the

MOTORCYCLE RACING

weight to transfer to the rear tire, where the power is.' But with the front tire not touching the track, there's another situation with which to deal: 'You aren't able to steer the bike in the normal manner,' Neace continued. 'What you have to do is lean left or right on the bike to keep it going straight!' It's hard to imagine how that's even possible at such high speeds!

The greatest national drag bike exposure comes from the Pro Class activities of the NHRA. The Pro Stock Motorcycle Class is run at all the national meets and receives a lot of national television coverage.

These Pro Stock bikes are awesome machines capable of 175 mile-per-hour performance with high seven-second elapsed times. Kawasaki and Suzuki are the prime manufacturers in this class and use four-cycle, four-carbureted 81 cubic centimeter powerplants pounding out around 240 horsepower. The bikes can weigh over 400 pounds without driver, certainly quite a handful to keep running in a straight line. Like their road racing counterparts, these Pro Stock machines (along with many of the other drag bikes) have high-tech aerodynamic fairings to help them slip through the air.

The current kingpin of the NHRA Pro Stock class is David Schultz, who has won the national title four times and finished second once. Throughout his startling career, David has won just about everything possible on his Kawasaki factory machine. Interestingly, David started his drag racing

Top right: This bird's eye view shows a Pro Stock bike just under way at the 1992 NHRA Springnationals at National Trail Dragway.

Above: A good start can mean being first at the finish line, even with a slow top-end speed. Note that the losing bike (on the left) was almost two miles per hour faster, but it took a tenth of a second longer to get to the finish line.

Right: The IDBA Pro Comp Class allows different modifications to the powerplants, such as this turbo arrangement.

career in cars before making the move to bikes. Usually, drivers move from bikes to cars.

There are also a number of NHRA Sportsman classes that run the quarter-mile, which include Top Gas (no faster than 8.20-second capabilities), Super Comp (8.60 seconds), Pro Gas (9.20 seconds), Super Gas (9.90 seconds), and Super Stock (10.50 seconds). Many of the other drag bike organizations have similar classes.

Around the USA, a number of local tracks run bike drag races with the NHRA and other organizations. Most use the 'bracket racing' format, in which two bikes run against each other with a starting line advantage figured on the best previous time each bike has run down the track.

Bike racing is no longer a part of the national IHRA drag organization. During the 1980s, the bikes ran at the large national meets, but that is no longer the case. The AMA was

Top: Drag bikes require extensive maintenance and fine tuning between each run. This IDBA Pro Comp bike receives tender loving care at a 1993 event.

Right: It takes a lot of strength to handle this type of horsepower, especially when it's on only two wheels.

DRAG RACING

Above: The hand grips provide access to the throttle, clutch, and brake. Also note the kill switch cable attached to the rider's left wrist, which will shut down the engine should the rider become separated from his bike.

Left: In addition to a high performance powerplant, striking colors, shiny chrome, and meticulous detail are a part of the drag bike scene in the United States.

not involved in drag racing until it joined forces with PRO-STAR in 1994. A number of purely motorcycle drag organizations, including IDBA and NMRA, are also involved with this enormously popular bike racing activity.

PROSTAR came on the scene in 1990, picking up where the IHRA organization left off, and has become a major force in motorcycle drag racing in the United States. It was the first drag bike organization to have it races televised live on national TV. PROSTAR runs national championships in both quarter- and one-eighth mile distances.

The organization has a number of Professional classes which include the 200+ mile per hour Top Fuel and Top Fuel Harley, Funny Bike, Pro Comp, Pro Stock, and Pro Stock Harley. The PROSTAR amateur classes include Top Gas, Super Comp, Pro Gas, Super Gas, and Super Modified.

The new AMA/PROSTAR series has nine events, in Gainesville, Florida (two events); Commerce, Georgia; Rockingham, North Carolina; Richmond, Virginia; Budds Creek, Maryland; Indianapolis, Indiana; Atco, New Jersey; and Bowling Green, Kentucky.

The International Drag Bike Association (IDBA) also runs both professional and amateur classes. In the Pro Class, IDBA also competes the Top Fuel and Funny Bike classes. Two styles of bikes are allowed: the Top Fuel nitro-methane-burning motorcycles built for all-out competition with few rule limitations, and the stock-appearing bikes burning nitro-methane, alcohol, or gasoline.

Also included in the IDBA Pro classes are Pro Comp and Pro Stock. The Pro Comp bikes can use multiple engines with

DRAG RACING

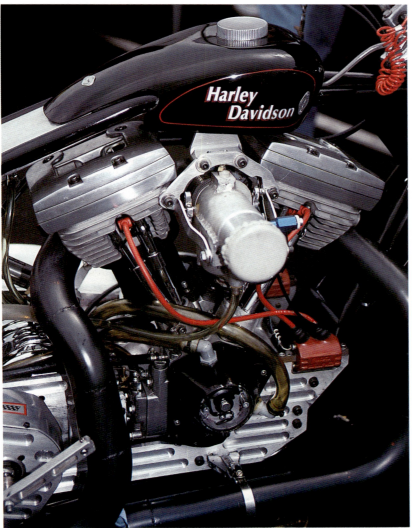

Far left above: IDBA Pro Comp champion Bill Vose lights up his rear tire prior to a qualifying run during the 1993 IDBA season.

Far left below: Bill Vose is one of the top guns in IDBA bike drag racing. As well as having been the Pro Comp champion, he has held both elapsed time and top speed records in his career.

Above: A number of safety features can be noted on this IDBA Pro rider: full leather suit, full-face Snell-approved helmet, leather gloves, and fire-resistant shoes.

Left: Unlike the high-pitched scream of the Japanese bike motors, the Harley-Davidson's deep-throated rumble is music to every Harley owner's ears. The popularity of the American bikes has led several organizations to sanction all-Harley drag events.

nitrous oxide and turbo-superchargers, while the Pro Stock bikes are more conventional machines using gasoline or alcohol for fuel. The amateur category includes Top Gas, Super Comp, Pro Gas, Super Gas, and Super Street classes.

IDBA holds seven national meets a year, at Beach Bend Park, Bowling Green, Kentucky; Bristol Dragway, Tennessee; New York International Raceway Park, Leicester, New York; National Trail Raceway, Columbus, Ohio; Norwalk Raceway Park, Ohio; Texas Motorplex, Ennis, Texas; and Memphis Motorsports Park, Tennessee.

The National Motorcycle Racing Association (NMRA) is a West Coast organization which sponsors bike drag racing in California and Arizona. The organization has eight

MOTORCYCLE RACING

national events each year, culminating with the NMRA Finals held at L.A. County Raceway. There are five professional classes, including Pro Modified (which is unlimited in engine displacement and type of fuel), Top Sportsman (no faster than 7.99-second capabilities), Super Comp (8.60 seconds), and Pro Gas (9.20 seconds).

Because the most popular bike in the United States is – and always has been – the Harley-Davidson, several bike drag organizations hold all-Harley drag meets. The American Motorcycle Racing Association (AMRA) holds national all-Harley races annually in Macon, Georgia; Memphis, Tennessee; Nashville, Tennessee; and Union Grove, Wisconsin. The All-Harley Drag Racing Association (AHDRA) sponsors 15 events across the country. The group runs professional classes including Top Fuel, Pro Fuel, Pro Dragster, Pro Gas, Pro Stock, and Modified, along with eight stock classes. Many local drag strips also carry out their own all-Harley events.

Although motorcycle drag racing is an American born-and-bred activity, interest in the sport is growing in other parts of the world. Bike dragging is carried out on a limited basis in Great Britain, and a number of English riders race in the United States with American organizations. Australia has a number of large drag bike events every year, the biggest being the Grand Nationals. In France, big-money drag events are held annually at the prestigious Le Mans and Paul Ricard circuits. Japan has also seen a growing interest in this exciting aspect of motorcycle racing.

DRAG RACING

Above left: No uniformed crew or fancy hauler here — in bike drag racing, it's usually just the rider himself with maybe a friend, wife, or kids to prepare the bike and get it to the starting line. This kind of do-it-yourself approach results in a real feeling of accomplishment when a race is won.

Left: The staging area is where the riders and crew members make last-minute adjustments to the bikes before moving to the starting grid. Tension is high as the riders prepare themselves for what lies ahead.

Above: Bike drag racing is a popular sport at the grass roots level in the United States. Many of the bikes raced at this level are street legal and are ridden to and from the strip. Obviously, there's a real logistics problem getting the bike home should it go down or blow a motor during competition.

NHRA NATIONAL RECORDS

Pro Stock – John Myers, Suzuki, 10/1991, 7.615 seconds
– David Schultz, Kawasaki, 11/1992, 178.35 miles per hour

PROSTAR NATIONAL RECORDS

Top Fuel – Larry McBride, Suzuki, 10/1991, 6.492 seconds
– Tony Lang, Suzuki, 4/1993, 215.10 miles per hour

Top Fuel Harley – Jim McClure, 9/1990, 7.315 seconds
– Bill Furr, 6/1992, 185.78 miles per hour

Funny Bike – Ralph Smith, Kawasaki, 4/1993, 7.060 seconds
– Ralph Smith, Kawasaki, 4/1993, 192.10 miles per hour

Pro Comp – Scott Kahley, Kawasaki, 8/1992, 7.437 seconds
– Scott Kahley, Kawasaki, 8/1992, 175.16 miles per hour

Pro Stock – David Schultz, Kawasaki, 10/1991, 7.632 seconds
– David Schultz, Kawasaki, 10/1991, 177.75 miles per hour

Pro Stock Harley – Tony Mattioli, 11/1991, 8.800 seconds
– Jim Hausler, 9/1990, 148.30 miles per hour

IDBA NATIONAL RECORDS

Top Fuel – Tony Lang, 10/1991, 7.15 seconds/194.34 miles per hour

Pro Comp – Dennis Strickland, 10/92, 7.09 seconds
– Bill Vose, 10/92, 191.40 miles per hour

Pro Stock – David Schultz, 8/1991, 7.74 seconds/174.38 miles per hour

HILLCLIMBING

HILLCLIMBING

Pages 86-87: Hillclimb bikes are one-of-a-kind hand-crafted creations – and their riders are as unique as their bikes.

Left: The final event each year in the AMA Professional Hillclimb Series takes place at the Devil's Staircase in Oregonia, Ohio. It's one of the toughest and most respected courses on the circuit.

Left below: A combination of speed, balance, power, and luck are the ingredients necessary to go from a standing start to the top of a steep and challenging hill on a specially-made bike. One slight miscue can cause the bike and rider to veer off course, or completely flip over backwards.

Below: Hillclimbing is a great spectator sport. The fans can sense the rider's adrenalin rush as his spiked rear tire claws the hill for traction.

In this wild and crazy segment of motorcycle racing, the rider's task is to propel a powerful modified bike rapidly over the top of a seemingly insurmountable, nearly vertical hill. This is the challenge readily accepted by a tough breed of riders in hillclimbing competitions across the United States and Canada, as well as in parts of Europe.

One bike at a time faces the hill in a race against the clock. The bike's first movement off the starting line breaks a light beam, putting the bike 'on the clock.' The strategy involves flat out speed, full throttle all the way up the hill. This all-weather event can be complicated by rain, as a soggy hill greatly increases the toughness of this endeavor. Breaking a second light beam at the top of the hill provides the rider with his elapsed time (ET). This is then compared with the ETs of the other riders. The rider with the quickest ET is the winner.

Rain or shine, this is a dangerous undertaking. Over the years, a number of riders have suffered broken bones as they departed their bikes on the steep inclines. Body protection is imperative in this sport, and hillclimbers add shoulder pads, flack vests, and high boots to the normal full leathers, helmet, and gloves normally worn in motorcycle competition.

The hillclimbing clan is a closely knit group, with probably less than 100 pro hillclimbers in the United States. A small number of excellent Canadian riders also compete in the national AMA series. Canadians Greg and Wade Williams are top flight contenders every time out. A number of the best hillclimbers are in their 50s and 60s, unusual for such a demanding sport.

Overleaf, main photo: The ultimate goal for a hillclimber is that finish line banner far above the starting line. Many try to reach it, but few succeed. This rider was one of the first to make it to the top in this competition, drawing a thunderous roar from the fans gathered below.

Overleaf, top inset: Every year thousands upon thousands of motorcycle aficionados descend upon a number of sites where the AMA runs its pro hillclimb events. What wouldn't these fans give to put their own bikes at the starting line and give it a shot?

Overleaf, bottom inset: A consistent front runner in the AMA Pro Hillclimb series is Canadian Greg Williams. Hillclimbing is also very popular in Canada, and a number of Canadians go south every year to run in the national events held in the United States.

MOTORCYCLE RACING

Two different classes of bikes comprise the AMA series — 540cc and 800cc machines. For the 540cc class, motorcycle brands used in competition are Honda, BSA, Rotax, Triumph, Yamaha, and Kawasaki. In the 800cc class, Harley-Davidsons are predominant, although Kawasaki, Yamaha, and BSA machines also are run. Engine displacements vary for competition around the world.

All of these bikes are highly modified for this type of racing. At first glance, it is obvious that the bodies of these bikes have been significantly lengthened, sometimes to as long as ten feet, to provide maximum leverage. Locked throttles are also not uncommon with these bikes.

In order to get the power to the ground as thoroughly as possible, chains are placed on the rear tire to increase trac-

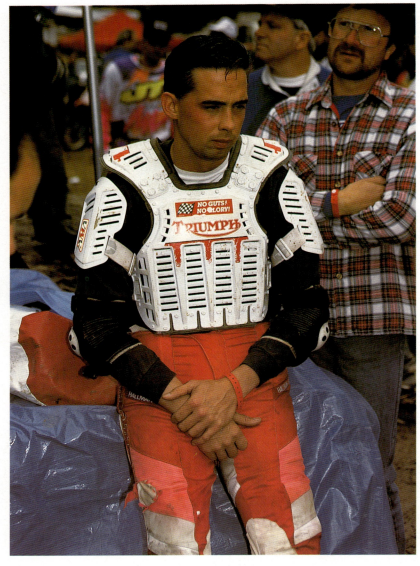

AMA 800cc PRO HILLCLIMB CHAMPIONS		
1947	Clem Murdaugh	Indian
1948	Al Skrelunas	Harley-Davidson
1949	Howard Mitzel	Indian
1950	Willard Bryan	Harley-Davidson
1951	Pete Uebelacher	Indian
1952	Howard Mitzel	Indian
1953	Howard Mitzel	Indian
1954	R. Nealen	Indian
1955	R. Nealen	Indian
1956	Howard Mitzel	Indian
1957	D. Nealen	Indian
1958	Earl Buck	Indian
1959	Joe Hemmis	Triumph
1960	Charles Jacobs	Harley-Davidson
1961	Charles Jacobs	Harley-Davidson
1962	Joe Hemmis	Triumph
1963	Glen Kyle	Vincent
1964	Joe Hemmis	Triumph
1965	Glen Kyle	Vincent
1966	Glen Kyle	Vincent
1967	Joe Hemmis	Triumph
1968	Earl Bowlby	BSA
1969	Bees Wendt	Indian
1970	Carl Wickstrand	Triumph
1971	Doyle Disbennett	BSA
1972	Glen Kyle	Laverda
1973	Carl Wickstrand	Triumph
1974	Doyle Disbennett	BSA
1975	Terry Kinzer	Honda
1976	Earl Bowlby	BSA
1977	Earl Bowlby	BSA
1978	Earl Bowlby	BSA
1979	Earl Bowlby	BSA
1980	Lou Gerencer	Harley-Davidson
1981	Earl Bowlby	BSA
1982	Lou Gerencer	Harley-Davidson
1983	Earl Bowlby	BSA
1984	Earl Bowlby	BSA
1985	Earl Bowlby	BSA
1986	James Clark	BSA
1987	Lou Gerencer	Harley-Davidson
1988	Jeff Yoder	Harley-Davidson
1989	Jeff Yoder	Harley-Davidson
1990	Earl Bowlby	BSA
1991	Lou Gerencer, Jr	Harley-Davidson
1992	Tom Reiser	Harley-Davidson
1993	Tom Reiser	Harley-Davidson

HILLCLIMBING

Above left: Safety equipment is imperative in this sport, in which it is not unusual for the rider to fly over the handlebars or have the bike rear up and fall back down on top of him. This rider displays a suit of armor that provides full protection for the upper torso.

Far left below: These cupped tires are specially designed to provide rear traction in order to maintain momentum on the hills.

Above: For maximum torque to the ground, hillclimb bikes are often built low and long. Although they might look a bit awkward, these elongated machines – often ten feet or more in length – are the best performers on the steep slopes.

Left: Harley-Davidsons are a favorite in the hillclimb sport. Although it might say 'Harley-Davidson' on the fuel tank, the hillclimb versions don't look much like typical Harleys.

MOTORCYCLE RACING

HILLCLIMBING

Above left: A good start is everything in motorcycle hillclimbing. The momentum acquired from a clean start will pay big dividends at the top of the hill.

Above: Normally, straw is not found on a hillclimb course, but in this case, extremely wet conditions caused course officials to lay down straw to help the riders to make it up the hill.

tion. The chains dig deeply into the steep inclines, standing the bikes on their rear tires and spraying out a solid stream of dirt and stones. With the front wheel up on one of these steep slopes, a bike will be standing almost straight up. Going over backwards is not uncommon in this wild style of bike racing.

Many hillclimbers assert that to get the best performance it's best to 'pull a wheelie' all the way up the hill. They explain that it's best to keep the bike perfectly balanced, with all the power being transmitted to the rear wheel. Most riders lean far out over the front of their bikes, enabling them to see exactly what the bike is doing underneath them.

AMA pro hillclimbers will tell you that no two hills are the same, with each presenting its own unique challenge. Each rider's ability to read the hill, and to set the bike up accordingly, can spell victory or defeat.

Track lengths, of course, vary from hill to hill, but all are in the 350-to-500-foot range. Again, depending on the particular hill, the ride usually takes from six to ten seconds. When each rider flashes to the top of the hill, the accomplishment is greeted by enthusiastic applause from the crowd.

Far left below: There's a fine line between achieving maximum traction and spinning the rear tire. It's not unusual to see a rider rev his engine too high and not have enough speed to make it up the first incline.

Above: The width of the hillclimb course is defined here by a pair of parallel chalk lines. Horizontal lines at regular intervals serve as measurements so that, should no rider make it to the top, the rider who gets the furthest up the hill wins.

ICE RACING, DESERT RACING, AND MORE

MOTORCYCLE RACING

While the best known bike racing activities are those that are detailed in previous pages in this book, there are many more interesting and unusual forms of racing that take place. Name almost any kind of motorsport competition, and you'll probably find motorcycles involved in one way or another. Here are just a few of them.

Ice Racing

Using tires studded with spikes to gain traction on ice, ice racing bikes thrill fans with a spray of ice crystals that comes off their rear tires. This predominantly indoor sport is sanctioned by AMA and several other organizations in the United States, and is also quite popular in Europe, where it is referred to as ice speedway.

In American racing, the spikes are created by the use of number 8 screws in the tires. Some 150 screws are used in each tire, with only the screw heads protruding. In outdoor competition, longer screws are used. Needless to say, exposure to a whirling tire with screws protruding can be dangerous to the rider's health. Caution is key as the bikes slash around the track.

Besides AMA, the World Speedway Racing Association (WSRA) sponsors a four-race World Cup Series with races in Phoenix, Arizona, along with a pair of races in Fairbanks and Anchorage, Alaska. The sport is very popular in Sweden, Italy, Norway, Denmark, Germany, and the former Soviet Union.

FIM is in charge of European ice speedway activities, and sanctions both team and individual championships. The Europeans add an extra bit of zest to the sport by using extremely long screws in outdoor competition. The 26mm screws are carried on the left side of the tires as the bikes scream counterclockwise around the track. The bikes literally hang on these screws as they are leaned over up to 65 degrees from vertical. The technique of hanging out the leg in the turns is also used here. Many riders use a piece of tire strapped to the left knee for contacting the ice.

Previous pages: This image from the 1991 World Ice Speedway Semi-Finals demonstrates the cornering technique on ice.

Above: The tire of this bike shows the screws used for traction in ice racing.

Right: Ice racing is not for the timid. A spill could put a rider in the way of the slashing screws on the bike behind him.

Top right: These ice speedway bikes appear to be violating the laws of physics.

ICE RACING, DESERT RACING, AND MORE

Desert Racing

Dodging cacti and diving down arroyos are part of the exciting world of desert bike racing in the United States. These races each cover hundreds of remote miles across hot, dusty desert tracks. It's a sport that attracts many types of motorcycle enthusiast, even the rich and famous — a number of years ago, actor Steve McQueen competed in a desert race under an assumed name.

The motorcycle of choice for this type of racing is the awesome Kawasaki KX500 motocross model. Its light weight, huge power, and super suspension system make it perfect for this dusty competition. In the 1992 Baja 1000, a KX bike averaged over 61 miles per hour.

The top series in desert motorcycle racing is sanctioned by Southern California Off Road Enthusiasts. Three SCORE classes are determined by engine displacement — 125cc, 250cc, and Open — and three are split according to the riders' ages — 30+, 40+, and 50+.

AMA also sanctions 25 amateur races in California, Utah and Idaho. There are also a full 45 desert events a year held in the Mojave Desert in the southwestern United States.

There is also desert racing sanctioned by the American Desert Racing Association (ADRA), which holds six races per year in Arizona and one event in Sonora, Mexico.

Above right: A Baja 1000 pit stop performed by one of the many professional Kawasaki 'Team Green' crews. They place well-stocked box vans every 50 miles to provide any service required during the legendary 600 mile (1000 kilometer) race from Ensenada to Tijuana and back.

Right: A Baja 1000 checkpoint is always the site of near-chaos for the riders and the course workers. The rider must bring the bike to a complete stop, and the course worker deposits a 'check stub' into a can on the handlebars to signify that the rider has made this particular stop.

Far right: Dry, dusty trails winding through junipers characterize much of the gruelling Baja 1000. The race is open to four-wheeled as well as two-wheeled vehicles.

Top left: This twin-engine Harley-Davidson streamliner propelled Dave Campos to a world motorcycle speed record of 322.149 mph at the Bonneville Salt Flats in 1990. Shown here with its body removed, this two-wheeled vehicle looks more like an aircraft fuselage than a motorcycle.

Land Speed Racing

The highest-speed racing in which bikes compete is called land speed racing. This particular type of racing is done against the clock. The bikes have a flying start, and then their speed is clocked through a measured mile.

The most famous venue in the world for land speed racing is the Bonneville Salt Flats in the western United States. The rock-hard, super-smooth, salt-covered surface is the ultimate for super-high speeds. The top speed acquired by a bike at the location was achieved by a highly modified Harley-Davidson machine which set the bike record of over 322 mph.

Main photo: Sam Wheeler's 1052cc Kawasaki-powered machine ran 178.140 mph on this practice run at Bonneville in 1991. The top portion of the body has been removed.

Pikes Peak Hill Climb

This annual race to the summit of 14,109-foot Pikes Peak, 65 miles south of Denver, Colorado, is best known for the performance of four-wheeled machines, but motorcycles of many types have also been involved. The event brings riders from all over the world for this ultimate challenge, in which 12.4 miles of gravel road lead to the top of the famous peak.

In the 1993 event, Clint Vahsholtz on a Rotax won the Pro Open bike division at 12:29.38, while Chuck Lee on a Honda took the Pro 250cc class in 13:19.31.

Main photo: A rider challenges 14,109-foot Pikes Peak in Colorado.

Above: Four riders take the green flag on what will be about a quarter-hour of gut-wrenching, heart-stopping, totally exhausting thrashing to the summit of Pikes Peak.

Right: Although the technique appears similar to that used in AMA flat track racing, these riders are racing against the clock rather than against each other. Other classes of competitors challenge the peak one at a time in this traditional Fourth of July event.

Enduros

The challenge in Enduro competition is in maintaining a strict time schedule while negotiating a lengthy course. An Enduro can take place on a variety of terrain – little-used roads, trails, and even footpaths. Many times, an Enduro course will even cross private property. The events can range in length from 50 miles to 150 miles or more.

There are a number of check points along the course, and the purpose of the sport is to reach each point at exactly the right time. Should a bike arrive too early or too late, points will be taken off the final score.

The bikes used in this sport are of all brands, but they have been extensively lightened to ease their long journeys. There are many different classes of bikes, including 125cc and 250cc, along with an open class and a four-stroke class, and an AA Class for the top riders. The classes are also broken out for different age groups.

Enduro competition has been carried out in Europe for decades. An eight-event World Championship series leads to an individual World title, while the International Six-Day Enduro (ISDE) team championship features three-, four-, and six-man team competition. Enduros are also very popular in the United States, with a number of organizations in addition to the AMA sanctioning events all over the country.

Above: This rider fords a small stream during the 1992 World Enduro Championships. Enduro events can range in length from 50 to 150 miles.

Right: A rocky trail runs perilously close to the edge of a steep drop-off in the 1992 World Enduro Championships.

Top: An Enduro rider is covered in mud after traversing a challenging trail near Athens, Ohio, in an international qualifier event.

MOTORCYCLE RACING

Scrambles

Not all motorcycle competitions are a measure of performance and speed. The motorcycle Scramble tests the rider's ability to control his machine in a number of intricate maneuvers. Much of the time slow precision wins out over flat-out speed.

The Scramble events are held on unpaved courses that are between a quarter-mile and two miles in length. Left and right turns, jumps, hills, and other natural obstacles challenge even the most skilled riders.

AMA sanctions a large national Scramble program, with 11 different classes. Engine displacements range from 86cc in Class 1 to over 501cc in Class 6. There are also two classes for sidecar motorcycles, and two classes for 30-and-over riders. Honda, Kawasaki, Yamaha, and KTM are the predominant manufacturers of bikes in this sport. The AMA also sponsors a Hare Scramble event, which is conducted on a closed course up to 40 miles in length. The Hare Scramble Championship Series runs nine national events. When conditions permit, the bikes can be equipped with ice racing studs on their tires.

As in other types of bike racing, a number of other organizations sanction Scramble competitions regionally in the United States. There is also a Canadian National Championship Hare Scramble Series sanctioned by CAM.

Above: Scramble competition is mostly carried out in the eastern part of the United States, with a heavy concentration of activity along the Eastern seaboard. This particular competition is part of the 1992 Missouri Hare Scrambles Series in Bolivar.

Main photo: Finesse always wins out over brute strength and power in a Scramble competition. This rider attempts to finesse his bike out of the deep mud as part of a Scramble event.

Far right: This colorful sea of bikes and riders is gearing up for the start of the 1991 National Hare Scrambles event at the Loretta Lynn Ranch in Hurricane Mills, Tennessee.

ICE RACING, DESERT RACING, AND MORE

Trials

This type of bike racing emphasizes precise balance and control while negotiating a designated area of difficult terrain. It's really not a race, in that only one rider is 'observed' at a time. It can be slow – so slow that a rider may even stand still or back up, as long as he doesn't put a foot down for balance. Points are gained and lost according to the skill of the rider, who must display control over his machine.

Trials is one of the oldest forms of motorcycle competition, stretching back to the first years of this century. The top event in this activity, the International Six Days Trial, dates back to 1910; the Scottish Six Days Trial was first run in 1909. The first World Trials Championship took place in 1975. It continues in the 1990s with a ten-event World Championship series. The Trial des Nations World Team Championship is carried out annually.

In the United States, Trials competition is popular, with a number of organizations besides the AMA sanctioning series nationwide, including several vintage bike series.

Above: This AMA Trials rider skirts a waterfall at the World Observed Trials in Watkins Glen, New York, in 1992. Precision in negotiating difficult terrain is the nature of Trials competition.

Right: In what appear to be impossible situations, skilled trials riders make the difficult look easy.

INDEX

Page numbers in *italics* indicate illustrations

accidents, 8, 44, 46
Agostini, Giacomo, 13
Albert, Greg, *52*
Allen, Larry, *36*
All-Harley Drag Racing Assoc. (AHDRA), 75, 84
American Desert Racing Assoc. (ADRA), 100
American Historical Racing Motorcycle Assoc. (AHRMA), 48
American Motorcycle Assoc. (AMA), 24, 43, 54, 82, 98, 100, 108
American Motorcycle Racing Assoc. (AMRA), 31, 84
Anderstorp (Sweden), 21
Aprilia, 13

Bailey, David, 54
Baja 1000, 100, *100*, *101*
Belgian Motocross Grand Prix, *1*, 55
Biaggi, Max, *12-13*
BMW, 32
Bol d'Or 24 Hours, 23
Bonneville Salt Flats, *102-03*
Bradshaw, Damon, *59*, 62
brakes, 25, *36*, 48, 62
British bikes, 27
British Grand Prix, *4-5*, 10
Brno (Czechoslovakia), 8
Brooks, Larry, *59*
BSA, 27, 92
burnout, 75, 76

Cadalora, Luca, *4-5*
Campion, Monti, *36*
Campos, Dave, *102*, 103
Canadian Motorcycle Assoc. (CMA), 37
Capirossi, Loris, *14-15*
carburetors, 25
Carr, Chris, *40*, 44, *44*, *45*, 46
chicanes, 31
Classic Bike Magazine Dirt Track series, 48
Constructors Championship, 10
cost of bikes, 24, 44
Coupe des Nations, 54
Criville, Alex, *6-7*
curbstones, *31*

Daytona (USA), 8, 29, 37
DeHoop, Todd, 67
Deletang, Jean-Marc, 21
desert racing, 100
Devil's Staircase, Oregon, *88*, 89
dirt tracking, 24, 40, *40-41*, 43, 44, 46, *46*, 48
Donington Park (Great Britain), 8, 10, *10*
Doohan, Michael, *10-11*
D'Orgeix, Jehan, 21
drafting, 44
drag racing, 72, *72*, *73*, 74, 75, 78, 80, *81*, 82-85, *84-85*
Ducati, 24, 25, *25*, 27, *27*, 30, 31, 32, *32*
Dugmore, Colin, *54*
Duhamel, Miguel, *25*

Eastern Creek (Australia), 8
Eastern Regional Series, 62, 67
EBC Endurance Challenge, 35
Edwards, Colin, *27*
elapsed time (ET), 75, 89
Endurance, 8, *20*, 21, 23
Enduros, 106, *106-07*

Federation of International Motorcycles (FIM), 8, 21, 98
Ferracci, Eraldo, 27
Formula classes (WERA), 35, *36*, 37, *37*
fuels, 72, 75, 84

Funny Bike class, 82

Graham, Ricky, 44, *44*
Grand National Series, 43, 44, 46, 47
Grand Prix, *4-5*, *6-7*, 8, *8-9*, 10, *10-11*, 13, *12-13*, *14-15*, 21

Harley Davidson, 32, *35*, *40*, 46; in drag racing, 76-77; 883 Pro-Class, 46; 883 Sportster, 32, *35*; in hillclimbing, *92*, 93, *93*; land speed record, 103
hillclimbing, *86-87*, 88, 89, *89*, *90-91*, 92, *92*, 95
Hockenheim (Germany), 8
Honda, 25, 27, 32, 46, 104; in hillclimbing, 92; NSR125, *16-17*; NSR250, *12-13*, 13, *14-15*; NSR500, *6-7*, *10-11*, 13; RC45, 25; in scrambles, 108; 750 RC 30, *18-19*; in Supercross, 62; Team, 43; VFR750, *27*
Hoosier Dome (Indianapolis, IN), 55, 59

ice racing, *96-97*, 98, *98-99*
Igoa, Patrick, *20-21*
International Drag Bike Assoc. (IDBA), 82, 83
International Hot Rod Assoc. (IHRA), 72
International Old Timers MX Assoc. Series, 68
International Six-Day Enduro (ISDE), 106
Isle of Man TT, *22-23*, 23

James, Jamie, *24*, 27
Jobe, Georges, *1*, *54*
jumps, 59, 66, 67, *67*, 68, 68

Kawasaki *24*, 25, 27; in hillclimbing, 92; KX500, 100; in scrambles, 108; in speed racing, *102-03*, 103; in Supercross, 62; teams, 63, 100, *100*; ZXR750 Muzzy, *19*, *28*
Keyoe, Erik, *63*, 63
Kiedrowski, Mike, 62, 68, *69*
King, Chuck, *70-71*
Kirkpatrick, Scott, *57*
KTM, 108

Lamson, Steve, *59*
Landes, Brett, *40*
land speed racing, *102*, 103
LaRocco, Mike, 62
Lawson, Shane, *63*, 63
Le Mans (France), 8, *8-9*, 21, 84
Leonard, Joe, 43

McCallen, Phil, 23
McGrath, Jeremy, *60*
Magee, Kevin, *31*
Martin, Mike, *36*
Mattioli, Jean-Michel, *20-21*
Merkel, Fred, *2-3*, 16, *18-19*, *26*
Mertens, Stephane, *31*
Moineau, Herve, *20-21*
Moodie, Jim, *22-23*
Morehead, Steve, *43*
Motocross, *1*, 4, *50-51*, 52, *52*, 53, *54*, 54, 55, 63, *63*, *64-65*, 66, 67, 68, 68
Moto Guzzi, 25, 32
Motor Union Luxembourg (MUL), 52

National Hot Rod Assoc. (NHRA), 72, 78
National Motorcycle Racing Assoc. (NMRA), 83-84
National Trail Dragway (Columbus, OH), 75, 78
Neace, Rich, 75, 78
Nicholl, Kurt, *50-51*
Osterreichring (Austria), *30*

Palmer, Cliff, 62, *63*
Parc des Princes (France), 55, *55*, 56-57
Parker, Scott, 42, 44, 46
Parker, Trampas, 52
Paul Ricard (France), 21, 84
Peterson, Chad, *63*, 63
Phillip Island (Australia), 31
Pikes Peak Hill Climb, 104, *104-05*, 105
Pocono Int. Raceway (PA), 37
Polen, Doug, 16, *25*, 27, *27*, 30, *31*, *32*
pole position, 29
PROSTAR, 82
Pro Stock classes, 72, *72*, 78, *78*, 82, 84

Quarterly, Dale, *24*

Rainey, Wayne, 8
Raudies, Dirk, *16-17*
Rentzell, Kevin, *37*
Road Atlanta (GA), 37
Roberts, Kenny, 13
Roche, Raymond, 16
Romboni, Doriano, 13
Rotax, 46, 92, 104
rules, 16, 24, 27, 32, 37
Russell, Scott, *19*, 27, *28*

safety, 83, *83*, 92, 93
Schmit, Donny, 52, *52*, 53
Schultz, David, 74, 75, *75*, 78, 80
Schwartz, Kevin, *10*
Scottish Six-Day Trial, 110
scrambles, 108, *108-09*
Sheedy, Todd, *57*
Shobert, Bubba, 27
shocks, 24, 26, 48
sidecar class, 13, *16-17*, 17, 108
Simeon, Michel, 21
Simmons, Gavin, *16-17*
Slight, Aaron, *18-19*
Southern California Off Road Enthusiasts (SCORE), 100
Spa (Belgium), 21
speedway racing 48, *48*, *49*
Spencer, Freddie, 29
Springsteen, Jay, 43, *47*
Stanton, Jeff, 68
Superbike, *2-3*, 4, 8, 16, 17, *18-19*, 21, 24, *24*, 25, *25*, 26, *26*, 27, *27*, *28*, 29, *29*, 30, *31*, 31, 32, *32*

Supercross, 52, 54, 55, *55*, 56-57, 59, *59*, *60-61*, 62, *63*, 67
SuperSports class, 32, *33*, 34, *35*
SuperTwins class, 32
Suzuka (Japan), *6-7*, 8, 21, 23
Suzuki, 10, 13, *20-21*, 25, 34, 37, 62, 74, 78
Swink, Brian, 61, 67

tires, 25, 29, 32, 43; chains for, 92, 95; cupped, *92*, 93; dirt tracking, 44; DOT-approved, 33, 34; drag, 75, 76, 82, 83; hillclimbing, 94, 95; 'slicks', 33; speedway, 48; studded, *98*, 98
Toland, Doug, 21, 27
Trials, 110, *110*, 111
Triumph, 27, 92
Troph'ee des Nations, 54
Turkington, Britt, *34*

Vahsholtz, Clint, 104
Vance & Hines team, 25, 27
Vincent, 27
Vintage Dirt Track Races Assoc., 48
Vintage Iron National and Northeast MX Series, 68
Vose, Bill, *82*, 83

Ward, Jeff, 68
Webster, Steve, *16-17*
weight, 13, 78
Western Eastern Roadracers Assoc. (WERA), 35, 37
'wheelie bars', 72
'wheelies', 95
Williams, Greg, 89, *91*
Williams, Wade, 89
world championships: Superbike, 4, 17, 27, 29; Endurance, 21, 23, 27; Enduro, 106; Grand Prix, 21; Motocross, 52, 54, 68; Superbike 16, 21, 24; Supercross, 54; Trials, 110
World Speedway Racing Assoc. (WSRA), 98

Yamaha, *4-5*, 25; in hillclimbing, 92; in scrambles, 108; in Supercross, 62; TZ250, 13; YZF750, *24*, 25, *31*; YZR500, 8

ACKNOWLEDGMENTS

Special thanks to Kel Edge, whose assistance with the writing and captioning of the Road Racing chapter was invaluable.

The author and publisher would like to thank the following individuals and organizations for their assistance in the preparation of this book:

Ruthanne Holder and Mary Fairman; Bill Boyce, AMA Special Projects Manager; Roy Janson, AMA Director of Professional Racing; Duke Finch, AMA Motocross Official; Roger Ansel, AMA Amateur Competition Manager; Bob Moore, AMA Hillclimbing Official; Nina Henderson, IDBA Media Relations; Deanna Longjohn, NMRA; Mark Pétrier, FIM Press Officer; Cheryl Blair and Roger T Young of *American Motorcyclist* magazine; Doug Gonda, WERA; Scott Drake, retired professional dirt track racer; PROSTAR motorcycle drag racing organization; the All-Harley Drag Racing Association; John Ulrich, road racing and motorcycle technology consultant; John Potts, Indianapolis Raceway Park; Michelle Trueman and Joanne Truman-Gajoch, Mid-Ohio Sports Car Course; Barb and Dick Chrysler, Kil-Kare Dragway; Cliff Sherlock, Interrace Motorsports Marketing; Mike Rose, the designer; Jean Martin, the editor; Nicki Giles, the production controller; and Elizabeth A. McCarthy, the indexer.

All photographs are by Bob Fairman except for the following:
Allsport: Howard Boylan 4-5, 6-7, 13, 14-15, 16-17, 22-23(all 4); Simon Bruty 1, 54(top); Phil Cole 50-51, 54(bottom); Mike Hewitt 12-13; Jean-Pierre L'Enfant, Agence Vandystadt 56-57; Bob Martin 96-97, 98-99(all 3); Ben Radford 106(below), 106-07; Pascal Rondeau 20-21; Jean-Paul Thomas, Agence Vandystadt 55.
American Motorcyclist Association: 106(top), 110, 111.
Larry Buche: 104-05(all 3).
Kel Edge: 2-3, 18-19, 19, 26, 28, 28(both), 30, 31, 32.
FIM/Mark Pétrier: 8, 8-9, 10(top), 10-11, 16-17(top), 21, 48, 49, 52(both), 53.
Frank Leivan: 108-09(all 3).
Bert Shepard: 29.
Bill Taylor: 102-03(both).
Anthony Tellier: 100-01(all 3).